Pacer Power

The 1994 Wonder Season of the Indiana Pacers

Steve Mannheimer

Guild Press of Indiana, Inc.

Guild Press of Indiana, Inc.
6000 Sunset Lane
Indianapolis, IN 46208

Printed in the United States of America

Library of Congress
Catalog Card Number
94-77613

ISBN 1-878208-48-9

For Wendy
Emily
and John

Acknowledgments

It should go without saying that no book of this nature is an individual effort. A writer receives immeasurable help from people in obvious and unlikely ways. If this assistance can't be measured, it must nonetheless be acknowledged.

It would have been impossible for me to write this book without relying heavily on accounts of Pacers games written by Dan Dunkin for *The Indianapolis Star*, and by Conrad S. Brunner for *The Indianapolis News*. The reader of this book should join with me to thank them for their diligence and professional skill in covering the Pacers season.

My accounts of the playoff games are based on videotapes supplied by Larry Mago of the Pacers front office. His trust in me is most gratifying. They were the only copies he had of them at the time. Thanks also are due the Pacers media relations office, which provided many of the photos that appear in this book.

I must also thank all of the members of the Pacers organization—the players, management, coaches, and staff—who took the time to share their memories and insights about the season. I must thank LaSalle Thompson for his openness, honesty, and insight. More than any other player, LaSalle helped me understand the players' frame of mind in general and in specific instances. He also taught me a great deal about eating sushi.

Pacers President and General Manager Donnie Walsh was instrumental in providing the overarching view of the season, in helping me understand the slow, often tortuous eight-year process that produced this team and this season, and in offering his deepest thoughts about the nature of the game of basketball.

This book is, in many ways, a tribute to Walsh's commitment to this team, the Simons, and this city, and a testament to his abiding faith that the Indiana Pacers are capable of bringing championship basketball back to Indianapolis. It is also a token of thanks for his friendship with my wife, Wendy Sommers, who began working for the Pacers in 1984, the same year Walsh joined the organization, and of his support of her rise to her current position as Director of Advertising. And, of course, for his agreeing to her two maternity leaves so that we could enjoy our two wonderful children.

I'd also like to thank Wendy. When my wife agreed that I should write a book about her colleagues and employers, it required great faith in my skill to recount the story of the season as I saw it, and, at the same time, to reveal that story as her friends and associates saw it. For me, this was a bit like sailing with both wind and current to consider. I hope the course I charted is ultimately truer than any single perspective.

But more important, I must thank my wife for trusting me to enter her world and take advantage of her friendships. Any marriage is built on some balance of togetherness and independence. This book required my wife to give up some measure of independence, at least momentarily.

Finally, I must thank my daughter Emily for showing me how important Boomer really is and reminding me that even at its most heartbreakingly serious moments, Pacers basketball is still a game—one filled with wonder and delight.

Introduction
A Visit to Nirvana

It was the Zone—and Reggie was in it.

It was that confluence of time and space and sound and vision and anticipation and reflex and movement and...everything. It all flowed together, and Reggie flowed with it.

Somehow he knew how every Knick player would be moving and where he had to be. He knew when he got there he would find the ball waiting for his hands. And when he let it go, he knew the basket would be waiting to catch it.

So Reggie just did it. It was supposed to happen, and he was supposed to be there when it did. So he was.

The Pacers had been down the entire game. The Knicks were back on their home court after two stunning playoff defeats in Indiana. They had come out in the first quarter of Game Five at Madison Square Garden and pounded the ball down the Pacers' throat, dazing them with a 15–2 lead, doubling their score by the end of one, never letting them quite shake off those initial punches.

The Knicks had come out in the second half ready to grind the Pacers even more. They had held them at arms' length, slapping them enough to keep them addled, building their lead slowly but confidently and dragging Indiana into the fourth quarter for what 19,000 screaming New York fans—and millions watching on national television—assumed would be a dull, steady execution, the basketball equivalent of being beaten to death with a five-iron.

Reggie gave no warning. Perhaps he had none himself. The Indiana Pacers knew that New York was next to impossible to beat at the Garden. They knew that if that were to happen something next to impossible would have to occur. A coach does not tell his team, "All right, guys, let's go out there and work a miracle." Larry Brown had spent an entire season talking about less-than-miraculous things: "Playing our game, doing the things we're supposed to do, playing unselfishly."

In a real sense, there was something supremely unselfish about Reggie's fourth quarter. He was beyond himself, out of his mind—and into something larger.

The next day, the New York newspapers would make a big deal out of Reggie's taunting exchanges with filmmaker Spike Lee sitting courtside. As Reggie sprinted back on defense after hitting a shot, he and Spike would be jawing at each other. Reggie wrapped his hands around his own throat to tell Spike something about the fine art of choking. It would be the Knicks, though, who felt his grip.

Soon though, even Spike was silenced. Reggie said later he really couldn't recall the particulars. He wasn't sure that he could recall the basketball.

He just had it in his hand and gave it to the basket: Once. Twice. Then again. And again. And again. It hardly seemed to matter what happened between shots. It was as if Reggie and the net were playing catch and the rest of the game was being played merely as a matter of form.

Other players caught some of the energy flowing off him. LaSalle Thompson, guarding Patrick Ewing down low, suddenly seemed able to see every entry pass before it got there—and almost casually step around Ewing to snare it. He did it once. He did it again. He did it again.

And every time LaSalle found the ball, the ball seemed to find Reggie and Reggie found the basket. After a while it seemed predestined. Standing twenty-eight or thirty feet out—much too far for any real shot—and John Starks almost in his jersey, Reggie just looked through Starks' hand and put the ball up...and down.

At the end, the statisticians would give Reggie twenty-five points for the quarter, a record five three-pointers in a playoff quarter and thirty-nine points for the game. And the Pacers would have a 93–86 victory and a 3–2 lead in the best of seven series with the next game at home.

Pacers President and General Manager Donnie Walsh had seen such things happen before. He talked about the Zone not merely with reverence, but with an acolyte's devotion to what he knew to be the eternal gem at the heart of the game.

Larry Bird had probably lived in the Zone, Donnie said with only half a laugh. It was more than talent—Michael Jordan had that way over other players, but he only got There every so often. Now Reggie had spent a whole quarter, twelve marvelous minutes, in that part of the universe.

Donnie thought that maybe he had visited the Zone briefly back in high school, when he was named MVP of the New York City high school all-star game. But that memory was mixed in with so much run-of-the-mill glory that it was hard to separate the pure white light of the Zone from the glare of the flashbulbs.

In any event, he knew what it was and how hard it was to get there. And he thought he knew what it would take to put his team near enough that they might smell the ozone rolling down from that stratospheric height—near enough that they could just reach out and take the NBA championship. They didn't. Not this time. Walsh's dream fell four points shy of the NBA Finals. But in 1993–94, the NBA Pacers reached farther than ever before, far enough to grab the respect that they—and the fans who follow them—had long yearned for: league respect, national respect, self-respect.

It was—and is—a season to savor.

1
The Years of Preparation

Even before it began, 1993–94 was a season that held the promise of great success. But Pacers fans had heard that promise so many times that they'd *stopped* hearing it. The check was in the mail, but it was coming by pony express.

Certainly the anticipation of success was so great that everyone knew something dramatic was bound to happen. Major changes in team personnel would either prove to be inspired decisions or desperate screw-ups—and perhaps lead to other overwhelming changes.

It was a season that many thought would be the last for the highest-ranking members of the Pacers organization. It was even rumored that it might be the last season for the franchise in Indiana.

Or, maybe nothing would happen. It was the Pacers. You never knew what they'd do next.

As those seven months evolved, it was never quite clear that this season would be worth much more than the pile of stat sheets on the press room floor—not until its end, at least.

The ride certainly wasn't smooth. It was a season to try men's—and women's—souls. To try everyone's patience and then try it again.

Yet it was also a season when the sunshine patriots got an unexpected sunburn and the longtime stalwarts were paid for their patience. And it was a season to take every old hope, and many new ones, higher than anyone had ever imagined they could rise—and finally to leave them there, waiting for next season.

* * *

In Indiana, "in the heart of basketball country" as the Pacers pre-game announcement always put it, June had always been a month devoted to the amateur game. June was when the state's boys and girls all-star teams played their Kentucky rivals. In June, hundreds of Amateur Athletic Union teams throughout Indiana were sweating their way through local tournaments.

But no Pacer team had ever played in June. No screaming crowd of Pacer fans had ever gathered in Market Square arena and heard the thud-thud-thud of a basketball on the hardwood, the trill of the referee's whistle or the wet rip of nothing-but-net.

That's because June is the last playoff month in the NBA. It is the month of conference finals and then league finals. No Pacer team had ever been there. Since joining the NBA in the 1976–77 season, the Pacers had been to the playoffs six times: In 1981, '87, '90, '91, '92 and '93. Each time, the team had been eliminated in the first round. They'd never played past May 6.

As the 1993–94 season began, the team, management and most of the fans were guardedly optimistic that that would change. Other fans were less enthusiastic. They'd been optimistic before.

For most of the last eight years, the team had tantalized the city with its perennial blend of obvious potential and ultimate mediocrity. Its cumulative regular-season record over the last four years was a dead-even 164 wins and 164 losses.

Whatever sweet intoxication the fans might feel after an improbable victory over a strong team—and there had been plenty such victories—would sour to vinegar with the next inexplicable loss to a weak one. It happened time after time. After enough times, even the most devoted Pacers supporters would start to wonder whether it was really worth it, if all their caring would ever be requited.

For many in Indianapolis, the discontent with the Pacers was magnified through the lens of nostalgia. They remembered the hallowed days of the ABA Pacers, when Indiana was thrice crowned champs of the American Basketball Association, the upstart league with its red, white and blue ball, its three-point shot and its experimental can't-foul-out rule—a momentary lapse of sanity that lasted a year.

As far as these folks were concerned, the NBA Pacers were hopelessly mired in a bog of bad management, worse coaching and spiritless players. What this team really needed was…well, take your pick. Every barroom expert had a remedy.

If that weren't enough for the Pacers to contend with, there was also the legion of Hoosier basketball savants convinced that the only way the Pacers could ever win—or even draw consistent crowds to MSA—would be to assemble a team of former players from Indiana University—and maybe even let Bobby Knight call in some plays from Bloomington.

There are some people in Indianapolis who will never forgive Donnie Walsh for not drafting IU star Steve Alford, who, before his eventual release, played back-up point guard for the Dallas Mavericks. The night of the draft, they stood in Market Square Arena and booed as Walsh picked some skinny kid from UCLA instead of Alford. Reggie who?

The Pacers also had to chew on this dry biscuit: For the last few years, Market Square Arena would only sell out for games that featured either Larry Bird or Michael Jordan. And then the Pacers would be forced to listen as a sizable part of their so-called home-court advantage cheered for the opposition.

There had been days over the last eight years, no doubt, when Walsh only drove into MSA because he could park there for free. The city's muttered disgruntlement grew even louder at the end of the 1992–93 season when Walsh fired Head Coach Bob "Bo" Hill, a likable man the fans had embraced after he replaced Dick Versace. Talented but volatile, Versace was a hard man to wholeheartedly like— let alone love. (At his insistence, he and his wife had signed a five-year marriage contract that would be subject to review and/or renewal at the end of its term. Enough said.)

But after two coaches in three years, people were increasingly questioning Walsh's ability to do the job. Many in the city wondered if Hill's dismissal was only an attempt to mask the real reason for the Pacers' achingly average performance.

Rumors flew of all sorts of dramatic changes about to be made at the top of the Pacers organization: Walsh was a few hours or a few days away from the chopping block. He would be replaced by Larry Bird, Rick Pitino, Magic Johnson—the names were tossed out by anyone with an opinion about basketball. Although no one suggested Steve Alford, one respondent to a newspaper poll did think that supermodel Cindy Crawford might have the right stuff to get the Pacers on the right track.

Walsh had never had a contract with Pacers' owners Mel and Herb Simon. When they hired him as general manager, he told them how much money he wanted, and they shook hands. That was it. No legal folderol prevented the Simons from picking up the phone and telling Donnie to clear out of his office by the end of the day.

If they had, Walsh would not have been terribly surprised. He knew the NBA was a world of dramatic hirings and firings. Average performers had as little job security as bad ones—as Bo Hill had learned. And, as Lenny Wilkens had discovered with the Cleveland Cavaliers, even successful performers were disposable in the quest for even greater success.

Walsh had spent seven years laying the foundation of what he hoped would be a successful franchise. He had taken the team from undeniably awful to arguably not-bad-at-all. But the next step up was proving difficult to reach—and a lot of people in Indianapolis were beginning to feel the seven-year itch. Scratching Walsh looked like the answer.

* * *

Joseph Donald Walsh Jr. was born in 1941 on the isle of Manhattan. Sometime around his twelfth or thirteenth year, Donnie found that he liked to play basketball, soon realized that he loved to play it—and that was it.

Donnie has what you might call a sense of commitment learned in the old school of American manners and morals. He married his high-school sweetheart, Judy. They're still married.

She remembers waiting for him as he practiced, practiced, practiced until there was no longer enough daylight to see the rim in the neighborhood schoolyard. As a freshman, he played on the varsity at Fordham Prep. As a senior, he earned all-city first-team accolades—and was named MVP of the high school all-star game at Madison Square Garden, essentially making him Mr. Basketball of New York City. He defers to history: "But that was back in the 1950s when it would have been impossible to elevate a black kid to that position," he said. But such hindsight hasn't dulled the thrill of the memory. "Other than the days my kids were born, that was the greatest day of my life. In some ways I have spent my whole life getting back to that moment."

After high school, Walsh was offered a basketball scholarship at the University of North Carolina. Walsh's father was a friend of Tar Heels' coach Frank McGuire, who had just won a national championship there. Walsh took the scholarship. He had to. "It was a very big honor. At the time, going to North Carolina was like going to UCLA in its heyday or like a kid from Indiana going to Bloomington. If you got a scholarship, you went. You didn't ask questions."

A year later, another guard from New York City made the same decision. He was a kid Walsh had played against in tournaments, a kid named Larry Brown. Besides Brown, Walsh's teammates during the 1958–62 seasons included Doug Moe and Bill Cunningham, both of whom went on to play and coach in the NBA.

Walsh started during his junior and senior years. McGuire had left Chapel Hill to coach Philadelphia in the NBA. However, he took with him sufficiently positive memories of Walsh to draft him in 1961. The six-foot Walsh said no. "I wasn't good enough, and it wasn't the right time. It was the age of the big guards, Jerry West and Oscar Roberston. Maybe if the ABA had been in existence I would have tried. Larry Brown made the ABA, and we basically were the same type of players."

Instead, Walsh decided to go to law school, and figured UNC was the place to go—or stay. He already liked Chapel Hill, it was a very good school, and Dean Smith, who had taken over as head coach in Walsh's senior year, offered him a job as freshman coach and recruiter—a job which entitled him to free tuition.

After graduation from law school, Walsh was offered three jobs. The criminal division of the Justice Department thought he might make a good prosecutor.

The New York law firm of Nixon, Madge, Rose and Alexander—the Nixon of which was the recently, involuntarily retired vice president of the United States—thought he'd fit right in there. Walsh remembered him from the interview. "I thought Nixon was a nice man. It was an honor to get offered that job."

Either legal job would have led to the same point, Walsh said with a grin: "I would have been involved in Watergate, either the prosecution or the defense."

But the trip to New York for the job interview only served to remind Walsh where his heart lay. "When I got back to Chapel Hill I said, 'I don't want to do this.

I'd rather be in basketball.' "

So that's where he stayed. He worked a brief stint as Dean Smith's assistant at North Carolina, then joined Frank McQuire as his associate head coach in cross-border rival South Carolina, where he stayed for twelve years.

With a growing family, Walsh figured it was time to put his legal education to work. He passed the bar exam in 1977 and was about to enter private practice when "out of the blue, I get this call from Larry (Brown). I don't think I'd talked to him in five or ten years. But he called me up and asked me if I wanted to come to work for him in Denver."

Things went well for Walsh as an assistant coach of the NBA's Denver Nuggets. He liked the city, he liked the job. He liked Larry and fellow assistant George Irvine. There were slight problems: Larry liked to jog and thought his assistants should too. Donnie prefered to wait by the car smoking a cigarette.

If the drawbacks were minimal, the promotions were dramatic. Larry left the team in February 1979, as the Nuggets were wading through a 28–25 mid-season record.

"Larry had been talking about it for a while," Donnie remembered. "But nobody thought he'd just quit, like right *then*, right before the game. We were on the road, and he just walked into my hotel room and said. 'I'm leaving. You want to go back to Denver or stay here and coach tonight?' I got on the phone with the president of the club and he just said, 'If you get on that plane with Brown, you're fired.' So I stayed and coached. Hey, I had a family."

Walsh finished the 1979–80 season with a 19–10 record, and was head coach of Denver for two years. His record was 60–82—not good enough to keep him from being fired. So, in 1982, he finally hauled those law books out of his briefcase. Donnie's career in real estate law was financially rewarding, sure, but how much fun can a guy have with a warranty deed?

So, one day in 1984, he called around to his basketball buddies. He talked to Larry and Larry talked to George, who was then head coach of the Pacers. George called Donnie and offered him a job as an assistant coach. Donnie and Judy packed up the kids and headed for Indianapolis. As he explained it, "In this league, you're never going to be too far out of a job as long as you have good friends still in the game. That may sound funny to some people, but the thing is, this system works."

Two years later, in April 1986, Donnie got another call.

Team owners Herb and Mel Simon had decided their team needed a basketball mind at the top. Indianapolis lawyer Bob Salyers had been the general manager, but basketball was just a business to him. The Simons figured that, although legal training was useful—even necessary—to run an NBA franchise, it really wasn't enough. The team might be a business, but it was a very specialized business. It required someone with a deep, almost intuitive grasp of the sport.

They called around for recommendations. They talked to Billy Cunningham, Walsh's former teammate from North Carolina, who told them they need look no farther than their own back yard—or front office, as it were.

With his dual training in basketball and law, Walsh had long felt he was custom-made for a general manager's job. He just didn't know how to go about getting it. He once asked NBA Commissioner David Stern how one became a GM and Stern said, "Easy—you just have to be standing in the right spot at the right time."

Well, he was.

Walsh had no idea he was being considered for the GM job until Herb Simon called him in mid-April and asked him to fly out to Hawaii to look at some players in a post-season college tournament. Oh, and by the way, "We're thinking of putting you in the front office." He meant *the* front office. Walsh went, then came back and interviewed three times with Jay Rosenfeld, then a Simon business associate and member of the club's board of directors.

"In the space of a week I was the general manager. I really don't know how I got the job." Herb Simon knew: "We had someone right under our nose who was very competent. We looked around and felt he was as qualified as anyone we interviewed," he told the press.

Walsh was now at the peak of NBA professions, king of the hill. But he had nowhere to look but up—at the rest of the league. It would be his job to build the Pacers into an elite team. And that required patience—perhaps more patience from the fans than from Walsh, because he knew it was going to be a long, long climb.

"For so long," Donnie explained, "this has been a high-school and college area of fan support for basketball teams. The fans are accustomed to thinking in terms of four-year intervals. Consequently, although their enthusiasm and technical knowledge is as good—I'd say better—then probably anywhere in the country, they can still misunderstand the pro game, mostly because their time sense of the big picture, so to speak, is working at a different rate.

"When I took over the Pacers in 1986, I realized that we had a long way to go to build this team. The only way you can build a better team is through the draft or by trades.

"A team like Chicago or Boston or the Lakers already had a strong group of players, which made it easier for them to find better players—better in the sense of being better for their team—through trades. But in '86 we didn't have the players to trade. Our team wasn't good enough then. So that meant the draft was going to be the main way to improve. And that would take me four years. A successful franchise is made up 50 percent players, 45 percent coaching and 5 percent luck—that's the luck of the ball bouncing this way or that, into your player's hands and not someone else's hands, the luck that your best shooter has only sprained his ankle rather than breaking it.

"And even then, even if you have the talent, it's going to take you three or four years to fine-tune it—and that's only if everything goes perfect. That means no injuries and that your players perform as well as you think they can. So when I took over I realized it was a seven or eight-year process—and that was probably too long for most owners and fans.

"And I said to myself, 'I'm going to be an interim guy here.'"

Nonetheless, Donnie set about trying to do the job. His first big move was to pick Chuck Person in the 1986 draft. "Chuck came in and took the team over with his talent. He was averaging something like 18 points and 8 rebounds a game and won Rookie of the Year.

"We didn't think it would happen that quickly. But it did, and all of a sudden he was the target for every other team's defense—and he didn't know how to cope with that. Neither did we.

"Then Stipo (Steve Stipanovich) got hurt (in the '88–89 season) and that threw everything out of whack. He was a great player, like a Laimbeer only better." Despite Walsh's highest hopes, Stipanovich's injury had ended his career in the NBA. The team Walsh had been slowly constructing was now without one of its main pillars.

"We had built so much of our thinking around his presence that it took us a while to figure out what we were going to have to do. We had drafted Rik (Smits) primarily to be a back-up to Stipo, so when he went down, that put a lot of pressure on Rik to learn to play a lot faster than anyone had expected him to.

"In the '89–90 season, all of a sudden we woke up and realized that we had three Chucks: Chuck, Reggie and Detlef (Schrempf). Someone had to go. We also needed a point guard, and Pooh Richardson looked like the right guy. I would still say that Pooh is one of the six or seven most talented point guards in the league, along with guys like Mark Jackson, Kenny Anderson, Kevin Johnson, John Stockton and Mark Price. He just didn't work out here—probably for one of those personality reasons that are just impossible to calculate.

"Then I got Larry—and I knew there would be some major reworking of the team. I had thought about getting Larry back in 1989 after Jack Ramsay left, but he was committed—and, frankly, I knew we didn't have enough mature talent yet to give Larry the right elements to work with.

"Sure, if I had figured out some way to get Larry Brown to coach the Pacers four or five years ago, we would have been a better team. But it would have frustrated him, probably too much. And he probably would've left and then I couldn't get him back when we were really ready. Hell, Larry leaves good jobs even when he's winning.

"There really aren't any geniuses in NBA basketball. There are certainly what you would call 'master coaches,' guys like Larry and Pat Riley and Lenny Wilkens. But this isn't genius stuff—well, I have to take that back. I don't know what else to call Larry if not a genius. Larry transcends the NBA."

"And I would have to say that Larry is crazy. But he's crazy like Madonna. He's taken 'crazy' to a whole new level."

* * *

Larry Brown played high school basketball in New York City during the same time that Donnie Walsh was making a name for himself. Brown and Walsh occasionally played on opposing teams in post-season play, but they never developed a friendship until the were united in the Tar Heel backcourt in the early 1960s.

He joined the new ABA in 1967 with the New Orleans Buccaneers and earned an asterisk by his stats by becoming the first player in ABA history to be ejected from a game in Indianapolis.

As the story goes, first Larry figured he had just been kicked out of the game, not out of the Coliseum, so he sat down on the bench. The officials told him to leave, so he took a seat in the third row of the stands, until the officials told him a third and final time to hit the showers. The ejection on a double technical cost him fifty dollars.

He came back to Indianapolis one month later to play in the ABA's first All-Star game, held in Butler Fieldhouse. Actually, he wasn't supposed to be there; he was subbing at the last minute for a player who had military obligations that day—it was a strange league. Brown ended up with seventeen points in twenty-two minutes and MVP honors. The votes were counted with five minutes left in the game when it appeared that a late, Brown-led surge would win the game for the West. He aced out Pacer Mel Daniels by one vote for the honor—but Mel's East All-Stars won the game.

Reportedly, the Indiana fans booed the announcement of Brown's award. For his effort, Brown also won a bright red 1968 Chevrolet Chevelle convertible, a color TV and a star sapphire ring that Brown wore until his 1988 Kansas Jayhawks won the NCAA championship—and a bigger ring.

Brown enjoyed a stellar career as an ABA player, winning the league championship with the Oakland Oaks. His last game as a player came in Indianapolis in the opening round of the 1972 ABA playoffs. The Pacers won that Game Seven—and Brown retired from playing.

His subsequent appearances in Indianapolis would be as a coach. As it turned out, he was better at that than playing—better, in fact, then most anyone else in the ABA—and the NBA too, for that matter.

Let the records speak for themselves:

In two seasons with the ABA Carolina Cougars, 1972–74, Brown posted records of 57–27 and 47–37. His first year there earned him Coach of the Year honors. In five years in Denver, two with the ABA Rockets and two-and-a-half with them when they became the NBA Nuggets, Brown went 65–19, 60–24, 50–32, 48–34, 28–25—and split mid-season, leaving his old buddy Donnie to finish up. His first two seasons with the Rockets also garnered him ABA Coach of the Year trophies. Brown was the only ABA coach to win the honor three times.

From 1979–81, he coached the UCLA Bruins and compiled records of 22–10 and 20–7. Then, it was back to the NBA for two years with the New Jersey Nets. In his first year, 1981–82, Coach Brown turned the team around by an NBA record twenty more wins, posting a 44–38 season after a 24–58 tally the year before. The following year, the Nets went on finish even more strongly at 49–33 (with Brown getting credit for 47–29), but Brown—as was his wont—went, too.

He went to the University of Kansas, coaching the Jayhawks in five winning seasons—22–10, 26–8, 35–4, 25–11 and 27–11—culminating in that final year with the 1988 NCAA championship.

Looking for new mountains, Brown again departed, this time to San Antonio, which had suffered a string of losing seasons in the 1980s. Brown's first year was no improvement, posting a 21–61 record in the 1988–89 season. It would be the only losing year in his entire coaching career.

The Spurs went on in 1989–90 to notch a 56–26 record. This 35-win turnaround broke Brown's old record with the Nets—and is unlikely to be challenged until Michael Jordan comes out of retirement to play for the Dallas Mavericks—and they also somehow acquire Glenn Robinson. The following year, the Spurs went 55–27.

And the following year, Brown jumped ship from San Antonio after posting a 21–17 start and took over coaching duties with the L.A. Clippers, who finished with a 23–12 record season under his tutelage. His next full season with the Clippers leveled out to sea-level 41–41—which to Larry was more like C-minus level. So...the rest, as they say, is history.

Pacers history.

It started November 5, 1993, as "Crazy" Larry began the frustrating—but ultimately exhilarating—task of taking the Indiana Pacers to their next level.

2
Off to a Rocky Start

Yes, it was the season that would eventually carve itself in the limestone memory of Indiana and all but obliterate the faint, lingering impressions of the ABA glory years. But it hardly looked that way at the start. The NBA Pacers began 1993–94 fumbling and stumbling, displaying the well-known mix of ineptitude and inconsistency that had been the team's trademark since the early 1980s.

Yet through it all, first-year head coach Larry Brown kept his cool. In those exasperating early games, Brown merely winced at the missteps, overlooked the missed opportunities and donned his post-game smile for the press and the team. Both came to believe him—probably because he believed it himself.

* * *

Game One was played in Atlanta on a Friday night, November 5. It wasn't pretty. The score at the buzzer read 116–110 in favor of the Hawks, but that six-point margin felt more like sixteen—or sixty.

Coach Brown summed it up: "They executed and we weren't very aggressive."

That's executed—as in killed. Veteran forward LaSalle Thompson was more blunt: "Our defense was atrocious."

The Hawks hit their first eight shots, scored on their first twelve possessions and basically plucked the Pacers from the git-go. They penetrated the Pacers' interior the way Sherman marched through Georgia, making twenty-five of their first thirty baskets on dunks or drives.

If that statistic weren't embarrassing enough, consider this: The Hawks needed only five jump shots in the first three quarters to build a 90–79 lead going into the fourth.

Atlanta's Dominique Wilkins, apparently having lost little of his stellar talent to advancing years or to the torn Achilles tendon that almost ended his career the year before, played like a perpetual superstar.

At the only time in the game when the Pacers even vaguely threatened, Wilkins was the ever-dutiful cop on the beat. Trailing by fourteen points in the third quarter, the Pacers fought back to within four, 92–88, three minutes into the fourth quarter.

Wilkins shrugged and scored on the next four possessions, putting the Hawks out of reach. With thirty-three points in thirty-six minutes, Wilkins was only the best of a very good bunch that night. Kevin Willis contributed twenty-five points and eight rebounds. Stacey Augmon chipped in twenty-two, and Mookie Blaylock added fourteen.

The Pacers' starting front line—Rik Smits, Dale Davis and Derrick McKey—were humbled by Wilkins, Willis and Jon Koncak. The Atlanta big men outscored them 65–27.

Atlanta's new coach, Lenny Wilkens, could only be pleased. His team's performance was promising, and the promise was kept in what turned out to be a sensational regular season—one that would see the Hawks compile the best record in the Eastern Conference and earn Wilkens Coach of the Year honors.

Indiana seemed ready for no such accolades, though there were a few glimmers of hope from this first game. Reggie Miller scored nineteen points despite nursing a badly sprained ankle.

Small forward/shooting guard Malik Sealy led the Pacers with twenty-seven points and ten rebounds, hit his only three-point shot and generally started the year looking like a viable alternative to Reggie Miller.

Pooh Richardson handed in a very respectable sixteen points and fifteen assists and started the season looking like the long-lost honest-to-goodness point guard the Pacers have always seemed to need.

So, perhaps it was no great shame losing their first game on the road to the high-flying Hawks. Whatever consolation the Pacers might find in this was quickly erased the next night, November 6, when the Pacers faced the Detroit Pistons at Market Square Arena.

Once bad and mighty, the Pistons were now merely naughty. Even with Isiah Thomas, Joe Dumars and Bill Laimbeer—the redoubtable stars who led them to back-to-back NBA championships in 1989 and 1990—the Pistons were clearly misfiring.

Still, there was enough gas in Detroit to motor past the Pacers 113–107. Reggie Miller kept his personal pedal to the metal, scoring thirty-one points and keeping the team close enough to make the loss that much more frustrating.

Foul problems—a minor rattle in the Pacer engine in Game One, became a cause for major concern in Game Two. In the season opener, the Pacers had played through the third quarter with three key men—Dale Davis, Antonio Davis and Derrick McKey—shackled with four fouls apiece. The Hawks took twice as many free three throws as the Pacers that night.

Even Reggie Miller, who had fouled out only twice in the previous three seasons and only five times in his entire 484-game career, had fouled out in Atlanta.

This Saturday night in Indianapolis, he did it again.

Other fun facts about the Pistons game: In less than half a minute in the game's opening possessions, Dale Davis earned three fouls.

Relegated to the bench because of a sore left hip, center Rik Smits came in to play just three minutes in the first quarter. As it was ending, Smits matched Davis with three fouls of his own in just over a minute.

Brown pulled Smits but reinserted him in the third quarter. Smits drew more whistles than double teams, lasting another three minutes before fouling out. In fact, the game was almost a foul fest, with reserves playing much of the fourth quarter while the starters were sidelined.

Again, though, Brown was restrained in his post-game appraisal: "We lost our poise a little bit."

Brown understood that foul problems were only to be expected for a team slowly coming to grips with a new game—his game. And his game, as the media had consistently told the public, was defense. Past Pacer teams had occasionally sparkled defensively. But Larry Brown wasn't going to be satisfied with occasional sparkle.

"Who's your buddy?" became the slogan on the practice floor—and a self-conscious joke in the locker room. It was Brown's first question to a player every time defensive coverage broke down. The idea was simple: Every player had two men to watch on defense: First, his opponent; second, his buddy, a teammate.

When your buddy left his opponent for any reason—to double-team another player, for example, or because he'd been lost on a pick—you had to cover for your buddy and guard his man. The smooth operation of the "buddy" system is called a rotation. Add to that an aggressive determination not to allow uncontested shots, to get up in an opponent's face, challenge his passes, hound him, and you have a good defense. Sounds simple, almost as if it could be charted and graphed and typed neatly on index cards.

In fact, past Pacer coaches had actually come to practice with index cards filled with notes about who should be doing more of this or less of that. That didn't work, largely because the players soon came to regard such bookkeeping techniques as so much silliness.

If Brown kept files, they were in his head—and in his heart. The immediate and season-long impression he left on the team was that he cared about them. He cared about winning, of course, but the players first. The answer to "Who's your buddy?" soon became obvious: It was Brown.

And because of that, the team responded to his determined focus on defense. At the beginning of the season, the players responded *too* well; they overcompensated for failures and tripped over themselves in an attempt to get it right.

Brown knew what was happening—and remained unfazed. Give it time.

* * *

Three days clearly wasn't enough time to give. The team traveled to Orlando to play the Magic in Game Three on November 9. The good news that night was that the Pacers committed a mere twenty-seven fouls, only one more than the Magic, and only Smits fouled out. They even held Legend-Before-His-Time Shaquille O'Neal to two points under his scoring average.

The bad news: That average was thirty-nine points per game in the Magic's two prior outings and O'Neal had the flu, which would probably shave two points off anyone's game. Worst of all, O'Neal would not be denied when the game was on the line.

With two minutes to go, Indiana was up 91–90. Shaq stepped up and took the game into his larger-than-life hands, scoring the next five points and drawing Smits' fifth and sixth fouls.

The Magic led 95–91 with a minute to play. A pair of Reggie Miller free throws was immediately answered by Anfernee Hardaway's three-pointer as the shot clock was about to expire, giving the Magic a five-point lead with half a minute left. They went on to win 104–98.

Still, it was a solid game for the Pacers. Miller chipped in twenty-five points. McKey added twenty points and seven boards, and Smits looked good with twenty points and eight rebounds. Yet statistics are just that. Down the stretch, the Pacers just couldn't make the crucial defensive stops that win close games.

"It wasn't our offense," Brown said. "Both teams struggled offensively in the fourth quarter. We had two of our best sequences and they hit threes both times. Hardaway's was unfortunate." Still, he concluded with that almost detached confidence, "This was a good basketball game. Both teams played hard and defended well. I thought we had a chance to win."

Miller concurred. "The only good thing is that we've had a chance to win every game. It's frustrating…very tough, very tough."

The loss that night only seemed to confirm the momentum swing in the rivalry between these two teams. The Pacers had seemingly got the best of the Magic at the end of the 1992–93 season when they squeaked by to take the eighth spot in the Eastern Conference playoffs and left Orlando whistling at the draft. The Pacers were bounced in Round One by the New York Knicks, and the Magic snared the Number One pick of 1993.

* * *

On Thursday, November 11, the Pacers traveled to the Meadowlands Arena to play the New Jersey Nets, coming into Game Four as the only winless team in the Eastern Conference. The 0–3 start, their worst in five years, was all the more frustrating because the team had out-rebounded its opponents 124–105.

Somehow, it seemed, the task of learning a defensive system, although at least partially successful, was taking focus off the offense: Fourth-quarter shooting had dropped to a dismal 35.7 percent.

Even with two starters, center Benoit Benjamin and forward Chris Morris, on the injured list, and despite the tragic loss of All-Star guard Drazen Petrovic in an off-season car crash, the Nets could not be taken lightly. Power forward Derrick Coleman, the highest-paid player in the league, dominated the individual statistics with thirty-five points and sixteen rebounds. He and point guard Kenny Anderson provided enough offense to ensure that the Nets would not be outscored in forty-eight minutes of regulation play.

But that night Brown's Pacers were finally given enough time—overtime. The Pacers pulled out their first win of the season with a 108–105 victory in fifty-three minutes of emotional basketball.

During the first quarter, the Nets gave the Pacers a guided tour of the arena and a hands-on demonstration of home-court advantage with a 31–17 lead. The Pacer second unit fought back to trail 50–47 at the half, but the team lost ground in the third and entered the fourth period trailing by seven.

Reggie Miller recovered from a mild first-half shooting slump (two for seven) to score the team's first seven points of the quarter. With 1:22 left in regulation, Miller borrowed a foul from zillionaire Coleman and turned a baseline floater into a three-point play and a 93–92 Pacer lead.

A Derrick McKey post-up gave the Pacers a 95–92 edge, but then Coleman cut the mustard with a drive, a bucket, a foul and a free throw to tie the game; then, following a steal, he drained a seventeen-footer with 7.7 seconds left in the game.

Brown's timely time-out and a deft bit of strategy put the ball into Miller's hands for the Pacers' last possession and—finally—first clutch shot of the season to tie the game at ninety-seven and send it into overtime.

Solid defense stopped Anderson with a minute left in OT. Smits dropped in a fifteen-footer for a one-point lead; McKey swiped the ball; Pooh Richardson hit another jumper for a three-point lead; Coleman lost the ball driving into Dale Davis, who flushed the final points with eight seconds left in the game.

Early in the season, Brown had been particularly hard on Richardson during practice and team talks. In fact, Brown was typically hard on point guards in general, having played that position in high school, college and the ABA. Brown's specific complaint was Richardson's reluctance to shoot.

Richardson was more than relieved to hit that crucial jumper in the final seconds of overtime. And, again, Brown's sense of composed confidence was a contributing factor.

"I was, like, scared," Richardson said, "because I wanted to win the game, to get the monkey off our back." Then, Brown "comes into the locker room cool, like we're 3–0.

"I didn't want to let Coach down. He said, 'We're going to be a good team. Don't worry about it.'"

Speaking for himself, Brown said, "This is probably better than most victories because we've been having problems in the fourth quarter. And we did it defensively."

* * *

The Pacers had barely a day to enjoy their success. Friday night, November 12, the New York Knicks came to Market Square Arena to pick up where they left off in Round One of the 1992–93 playoffs—a relatively easy waltz with the hapless Pacers. The dance continued in Game Five.

The Pacers were humbled 103–84 before a crowd of almost 14,000. If any of them had come to see superstar-Dream Teamer Patrick Ewing, however, they would be sorely disappointed when the Knicks' center left the game with a strained neck after an unintentional elbow from Rik Smits.

Nemesis John Starks was benched about three minutes later with his fourth foul and reappeared only briefly in the last quarter, earning a second technical foul and automatic ejection following a heated exchange with Pooh Richardson.

Even with Ewing and Starks, power and punk, gone for most of the half, the Pacers couldn't earn a victory, and that only made the loss that much more painful.

Knicks coach Pat Riley conducted a kindly post-mortem. The Pacers, he said, "just don't have as many long-range shooters to stretch the defense."

Brown had his own explanation, but offered no excuses. "I don't think it was a matter of our offense," Brown said. "The Knicks were just great defensively. They took us out of everything. They're just much better ... They did all the little things. They got loose balls. They set screens. They hustled back."

Dale Davis could only agree. "Our intensity left us," the Pacer forward said. "A lot of it is attitude. They go after every loose ball and very seldom miss in a help situation."

LaSalle Thompson concurred. "We played too soft."

And Brown bluntly summed it up for the team's medicinal benefit: "To me, the character of their team is what's far and above ours. They're just men and they are committed."

Just men. Ouch.

The season was a week old and already the Indiana Pacers had run—make that crashed headlong—into the three teams they would later meet in the Eastern Conference playoffs. Atlanta over the Pacers, 116–110. Orlando tops the Pacers, 104–98. And then, just when the Pacers thought it might be safe to go back into MSA following their victory in New Jersey, the Knicks trash them by nineteen points.

It looked to most like a painfully long season was in store. Despite Larry Brown's career as a mover of mountains, many fans began to mumble that the Pacers weren't so much a mountain as a slag heap. Build them in one direction and they collapsed somewhere else.

A few vultures circled, albeit distantly, but Brown seemed unflappable. "I ain't even worrying about wins and losses," he said. "I'm worrying about improving. If you lose and you feel you're improving, you can live with it."

At this point in the season, there was plenty of room for improvement. Statistically, the team hovered around the middle of the league (thirteenth) in scoring with 101.4 points per game. Defensively, though, the Pacers ranked a dismal twenty-third, allowing 108.2 points per game. And they were winless in front of a home crowd that was anything but steadfast to begin with.

As much as the team needed to improve statistically, they also needed to improve medically. Miller, their top scorer, was still nagged by his left ankle. Derrick McKey was still bothered by a strained right hamstring.

Bursitis in Smits' right hip and tendinitis in his right knee had the big center tentative at times and occasionally limited his playing time. Dale Davis missed time with a slightly separated right shoulder.

Brown was matter-of-fact, as he knew he had to be. "We just have to keep plugging, get healthy and not get discouraged," he said. In short, give it time.

* * *

Unfortunately, Game Six offered even more cause for discouragement. The Charlotte Hornets came to Indianapolis on Tuesday, November 16 and showed the Pacers just how quickly things can go from dismal to abysmal.

The Hornets won 103–94, but that nine-point margin actually represented a twenty-six-point turnaround; the Pacers had led by seventeen in the third quarter. In the process, Miller reinjured his ankle and left the floor in pain. McKey reinjured his hamstring.

The Hornets, meanwhile, were relishing the end of an embarrassing string. Until that game, they had lost every one of their eleven appearances at Market Square Arena. Later in the season, they would encounter their own injury problems as stars Larry Johnson and Alonzo Mourning went down to the reserved list.

But this game, especially the second half, was Charlotte's. The Pacers repeated the scenario they played out in the Knicks game four days earlier. A strong start to build a lead, then a second-half fizzle to lose the game.

"We had two different teams playing," Brown said after the game. "You expect them to make a run, but we didn't have Reggie or Derrick." He also didn't have Antonio Davis, who left the game to ice down a turned right ankle.

* * *

Game Seven saw one of the NBA's hottest teams get only hotter in Indianapolis, chopping the injury-riddled Pacers as so much firewood. On Thursday, November 18, the Houston Rockets brought their seven-game (i.e., season-long) winning streak to Market Square Arena and came away with Number Eight, a 99–83 victory—to no one's surprise. And virtually no one came to watch; the Pacers could attract barely 9,300 fans for the Rockets' only visit to MSA.

If there was anything surprising about the sixteen-point loss, it may have been that the Pacers got even that close with top scorer Reggie Miller and starting forward Derrick McKey sidelined with injuries. Adding injury to injury, Antonio Davis went down that night with a sprained ankle that began to swell immediately, then Dale Davis pulled his left hamstring.

The insult came late in the game when normally cool Coach Brown committed his second technical foul, earning an automatic ejection. Then Miller was thrown in for good measure, becoming perhaps the first player in civilian clothing ever booted from an NBA game. The statistics on this are not well kept, so it's hard to say with authority.

What *can* be said with painful precision is that this loss matched the dismal 1–6 start in the 1984–85 season—General Manager Donnie Walsh's first year with the franchise, then as an assistant to head coach George Irvine.

On the up side, the team managed a fairly impressive display of heart in the loss. The Rockets came off the opening tip like, well, rockets—zooming to a 14–0 lead as the Pacers missed their first eleven shots.

The Pacers climbed back to actually take the lead 60–59 with just over five minutes to play in the third quarter. Some of that had to do with a hustling defense that forced twenty-one turnovers. Even Smits scrambled out to midcourt for loose balls. But Rik's extra effort took its toll: he fouled out halfway through the second half and the Pacers had no real go-to scorer for the fourth quarter.

Much of Brown's frustration arose from the perceived bias against Smits by the officials. "It's just the worst I've ever seen in my life," Brown said. "It's a joke. They let the other big guys bang each other. With Rik, it's a foul."

In the fourth period, as the Pacers double- and triple-teamed superstar center Hakeem Olajuwon, forward Otis Thorpe took command, hitting all six of his shots and adding four free throws for sixteen of his game-high twenty-four points. The Pacers, meanwhile, shot a sorry 6-for-23 in the quarter.

Brown smiled for the post-game press, telling the media that an exasperated fan had yelled at him to put a shooter into the game. "I'd been trying to do that for forty-eight minutes."

Malik Sealy, who had thirteen points, six boards and three steals in thirty-one minutes, pulled a positive thought out of the loss: "I think in the long run it's going to help us," he said, "because when our big guns come back, the confidence of our younger players will be up a level."

And Brown's final diagnosis showed that his confidence remained constant. "I thought our effort was pretty good," he said. Pretty good wasn't enough, though. "We had to have unbelievable effort" while shooting a measly 39 percent from the floor and a miserable 40 percent from the line.

* * *

Two days later, the misery of the Rockets game seemed a million miles away from Market Square Arena. On Saturday, November 20, the Pacers welcomed the Boston Celtics to town like turkeys to Thanksgiving.

The Celtics had always been more than conference foes to the Pacers. They were a source of embarrassment. Boston's glory years in the 1980s were built on the All-Star play of Indiana-born Larry Bird. Larry Legend he was called, with only half a smirk. It was true; the man was—and is—a legend, and nowhere more legendary than in Indiana.

That meant that every time the Celtics came to play, the Pacers could count on selling those frequently empty seats at MSA. Unfortunately, those once-empty seats were now filled with Bird-Boston fans. And they cheered just as loud as, if not louder than, the Pacer faithful. That hurt.

There was never more painfully obvious than in playoffs. In the 1991 playoffs, Boston beat the Pacers three games to two. The next year, the Celtics swept the Pacers in three games.

But the hurtin' was on Boston this year. The Celtics entered the season without two of their biggest names. Bird had retired, and team captain Reggie Lewis had died over the summer from a congenital heart defect.

One of the bigger names left on the roster, and certainly the most resilient, was forty-year-old Robert Parrish. The normally taciturn "Chief" recounted the game with a backhanded tribute. "A bunch of no-names kicked our butts."

Indeed. And the Pacers did it with twenty–twenty hindsight at all those past embarrassments—not to mention a good deal of foresight, so to speak.

Again playing without their own big names—Miller and McKey—as well as rising star Antonio Davis, the Pacers hitched themselves to power forward Dale Davis. And Dale played like a horse. In fact, that's what team members call him: Horse, or Long Chin Horse, or Mr. Chin—referring to his physical power, his granite jaw or, according to locker room sages, because he looks kind of, well, Chinese. But most of all, he was a man called Horse. "Yo, Dale, how'd ya do in the

Preakness?" Someone actually said that.

That night Dale made the winner's circle, scoring twenty-one points and hauling down twenty-two rebounds in forty-one minutes of very satisfying home-court basketball. His twenty–twenty performance was only the ninth in Pacer history and the sixth since the franchise joined the NBA.

Pooh Richardson was nearly as impressive, contributing twenty-four points and eleven assists in a gut-checking forty-three minutes as the team won 100–94. With the victory, the Pacers improved to 2–6 and 1–4 at home.

The game also saw the first-ever start for shooting guard Gerald Paddio, who had come to the team from Seattle in the Detlef Schrempf trade. Although Paddio's future with the Pacers would be short, he contributed nine pints in the victory. With the win, the team avoided setting a franchise record for worst home start and, more important, gave themselves a much-needed shot of confidence.

The Pacers, who trailed by ten early in the game, regained the lead—and the composure they weren't sure they really had—with a 24–8 run, ending the first half up 50–42.

In the second half, the Pacers never lost their edge despite a few Boston runs. They led by as much as fourteen in the third quarter, but saw that lead whittled to 75–68 as the fourth quarter began. Then, with nearly eight minutes left in the game, the Pacers reasserted themselves—or, rather, Dale Davis asserted himself by blocking a Parrish shot, dashing the length of the court to grab a Smits miss in the middle of three Celtics, and then rise for a dunk to give the team an 85–72 lead.

The Celtics would pull within five at 99–94, but Davis hit one of two free throws with 37.8 seconds remaining, then dove for a loose ball that forced Boston's Sherman Douglas to knock it out of bounds.

"Dale was amazing," Brown would say after the game. Sam Mitchell was more circumspect: "We've got to work with him on his foul shooting."

* * *

In case beating Boston at MSA Indianapolis weren't enough fun for the Pacers, they got more of the same and then some in Game Nine on Monday, November 22, in Hartford, Connecticut.

That night was Larry Bird Night for the Connecticut fans, an evening of tributes and testimonials.

Maybe the Celtics had too much punch and cookies before the game. Maybe the Pacers had just had enough of Larry this and Larry that—as well as their own poor start. Maybe, as Coach Brown noted sympathetically, it was because the Celtics had to take a bus from Boston.

In any event, the Pacers spoiled the party. They sliced and diced the Celtics, waltzing away with a 102–71 victory that sent Celtics fans reeling and sportswriters dusting off the record books to find its equal. The thirty-one-point margin was the largest since the 1955–56 season. It was enough to elicit this from Brown: "I'm kind of shocked."

The Pacers were serenely in command from the outset. Smits had a season-high twenty-seven points. Sealy added seventeen, and Reggie Miller, still tentative on his ankle, scored sixteen. Richardson continued his strong play with fifteen points and eleven assists. Dale Davis had another solid game: thirteen points and fourteen boards.

And the Pacer defense? The Celtics managed only 9-for-44 shooting in the first and fourth quarters combined. The Celtics hit only 5-of-25 in the first and—check this—scored only eight points in the fourth. It was the second-lowest fourth-quarter scoring in NBA history; only Houston, who scored seven fourth-quarter points against the Lakers in a 1991 game, was worse.

* * *

Unfortunately, the warm glow from beating Boston twice didn't last. Back home again in Indiana to meet an inexperienced Philadelphia team on Wednesday, November 24, the Pacers had a tough time swallowing the Seventy-Sixers and their seven-foot six-inch center, Shawn Bradley.

Although not a scoring factor in Philadelphia's 108–97 victory, Bradley was a defensive presence, changing shots and blocking a late Rik Smits shot that might have pulled the Pacers within five with enough time to win it.

Still, Smits had another strong game, playing thirty-eight minutes and contributing twenty-five points and six rebounds. Miller was getting stronger, adding twenty-one points in forty-four minutes. Richardson had sixteen points and ten assists. Dale Davis had eleven points and sixteen boards.

The Pacers looked like real contenders in the first quarter, taking a 39–28 lead on 15-of-22 shooting. But then, Brown admitted, some substitution miscalculations were made.

"I went to the bench, and their bench kicked our butt. The second quarter was the killer. We had control of the game, substituted, and that was the difference" as the Seventy-Sixers began a 23–7 run to take the lead.

Former Indiana University star Greg Graham sparked the run with two fast-break dunks, then a steal. The fickle Pacer fans ate it up.

But fans are generally no more fickle than their team. For longtime Pacer followers, the Philadelphia game seemed a blast from the past. It reminded them that the Pacers were capable of beating the league's best one night, then slipping in their own sweat and losing to cellar-dwellers the next.

Miller acknowledged the irony of the situation. "I'd rather be playing the Knicks," he said.

All in due time, Reggie.

* * *

Game Eleven was no better. On Friday, November 26, the Los Angeles Lakers came to Indianapolis looking for their first road victory in what had begun—and would continue—as a dismal season.

They got it.

The Lakers victory came on an unlikely, last-second, oh-God-I-can't-believe-that-went-in twenty-footer from Vlade Divac, a center who normally shoots from twenty inches. But it did go in and the Pacers did lose 102–100. The game extended their home record to 1–6—and ended an eight-game losing streak that had tied a Lakers record.

In fairness, though, it is hard to say the Lakers stole this one. The Pacers weren't really in the game until the last few minutes. The Lakers led 57–54 at the half and 81–71 at the end of three.

Down eight with four minutes to go, the Pacers got serious and tied the score three times. Reggie hit a three-pointer with just under fourteen seconds in a play that tied the score at 100 and brought the hometown crowd to its feet.

With the ball and a chance to win, the Lakers did just that. They called a play for Sedale Threatt, but a double-team forced a pass outside to Divac. Malik Sealy flew at him. "He actually grabbed his arm," recalled Pooh Richardson in disbelief.

But Divac was too strong. "I forced the shot," Divac remembered. "But as soon as I released it, I knew it was good."

The Pacers got some solid performances: Miller returned to full strength with twenty-five points and a career-high seven rebounds. Sealy had nineteen; Richardson, twenty.

But just as in the Philadelphia game, the bench made the difference: the Laker reserves outscored the Pacers' 36–16. And, just as in that game, the second quarter proved the Pacers' downfall, as the Lakers went on a 16–0 run to establish a lead they would hold until the late-game ties.

* * *

If the Lakers game had been a taste of California, then the Pacers' four-game Western road trip promised to be just awful, however much they might enjoy a break from the chilly November weather. For the last few years, Western swings have been anything but vacations, with front-rank teams such as Utah, Phoenix, and Portland to contend with, not to mention the Lakers and Golden State during their better years.

The Sacramento Kings had never been one of the more potent teams in the West. But with the way the Pacers were playing in the early season, no one was betting the farm on the blue and gold.

On November 29, a sellout crowd at ARCO Arena watched three-quarters of what had to be for them a very satisfying basketball game. For the Pacers it felt like lost luggage and total airsickness.

Down by a seemingly insurmountable twenty-five points in the third quarter, the Pacers again stood on the shoulders of Dale Davis and found themselves tall enough to see an improbable storybook victory.

Davis stepped up big time in the second half with eighteen points and thirteen rebounds, tied the game on a put-back with two minutes to play and generally just pushed the Kings this way and that.

Returning from the injured list for the first time in five games, Derrick McKey had a respectable fifteen points, including a strong late-game stretch that helped give the Pacers their first lead since early in the first quarter. Reggie Miller, despite playing with five fouls, hit key jumpers in the fourth, as well, but finished with only fourteen points.

Improving to 4–8, the Pacers appeared to have figured out the last-quarter dilemmas of November when they had lost a handful of games after strong showings in the three early periods.

* * *

Maybe being back in his hometown was just what Los Angeles native Reggie Miller needed.

Miller was as hot as he had been all season on December 1, pouring in thirty-five points to pace a stunning 120–100 victory over the L.A. Clippers in Game Thirteen. The win improved Indiana's record to 5–8 and, most improbably, gave the Pacers the only winning road record in the Central Division, 4–2.

Initiating a theme he would repeat throughout the 1993–94 season, especially when the playoffs began, Miller attributed the victory and his own superlative performance to the psychology of the disadvantaged:

"We love the underdog role. We've always been comfortable on the road. We like the odds," he said.

His old UCLA teammate Pooh Richardson said Reggie "was being Reggie," then added a small understatement: "His ankle is starting to feel better." Miller agreed, with a bit of overwhelming understating: He estimated that he was operating at only "70 percent."

Well, neither Richardson nor Miller was a math major at UCLA, but they did all the counting they needed to that Wednesday night. They combined for fifty-six points to count the Clippers out, severely disappoint a crowd of 8,737, and cause an untold number of the Indiana TV audience to drop their jaws and channel changers.

The Clippers just wished they could click the whole thing off—especially when Reggie Miller was on. And he was *very* on in the fourth quarter, essentially putting the game away in the first four minutes of the period. With both ankles working— at 70 percent, at least—Miller almost single-handedly took his team from a card-board-thin 83–81 lead to a 96–81 advantage with nine of thirteen unanswered Pacer points. Then he administered the coup de grace—burying a trey despite being fouled by Mark Jackson, then hitting the free throw to complete a four-point play.

Brown could only smile at his team's progress since the start of the season. The Pacer coach was characteristically low-key—and classy—as he watched his born-again team dismantle his dead-again former team. Former University of Kansas pal Danny Manning managed a team-high twenty-two points for the Clippers, but that was hardly enough to deflect the rampaging Pacers. Refusing to offer any comparisons, gloats or told-you-sos, Brown simply referred to the Pacers' improvement: "We haven't played great in the fourth quarter until lately."

* * *

Still savoring their California success, and perhaps still smelling the sweet smell of victory, the Pacers took their winning road show to the cold, high desert of Salt Lake City. There, on Thursday, December 2, they met the Utah Jazz in Game Fourteen and learned a new definition for the term "road kill," losing 103–87.

The Pacers held their own throughout most of the game. They even survived a parching six-minute dry spell at the end of the second quarter, stumbling into the halftime oasis only down 50–48.

Rested, they came back to take a 63–59 lead in the middle of the third quarter. But with about four minutes left in the third, the Jazz put up fifteen unanswered points to take a lead that would never be challenged. That run began when Reggie Miller limped from the court with a gimpy left knee after colliding with center Felton Spencer.

Miller's play that night was relatively quiet—a modest fifteen points in thirty-eight minutes, still a team high. But he was most conspicuous by his absence in the fourth quarter. By the time Miller returned, his opposite two-guard, the Jazz's Jeff Malone, had dropped in nine of his game-high twenty-seven points.

As if they couldn't quite believe that their good road luck would continue, the Pacers helped beat themselves. They surrendered thirteen steals and shot only twelve of twenty-seven in the second half. Their field goal percentage for the game was a dismal 38.7, in contrast to the 56.6 percent they'd shot against the Clippers.

And their crunch-time free throws? Bricks. They made only four of eleven in the fourth quarter, with McKey, Antonio Davis, and LaSalle Thompson combining on seven straight misses.

For the team, it was a disappointing collapse after the exhilaration of the season-high output of the Clippers game and the generally hopeful mood of the road trip. No one was embarrassed to lose to the Jazz, perennially one of the tougher Western Conference teams, especially when Dream Teamers John Stockton and forward Karl Malone started working their tandem game. This time, though, the whole Jazz team had beaten the Pacers and beaten them handily, dropping Indiana to 5–9 while the Jazz were riding high at 10–5.

* * *

Game Fifteen, the last of the road trip, was Saturday, December 4, in Oakland against the Golden State Warriors. The Warriors were playing without Dream Teamer Chris Mullin as well as mini-stars Tim Hardaway and Sarunas Marciulionis, but they were very much enjoying the play of rookie standout Chris Webber.

He looked every inch the future Rookie of the Year that night, pounding in a game-high twenty-six points and grabbing seven rebounds as the Warriors beat the Pacers 99–92.

As much as Coach Brown had preached defense, his team appeared incapable of working against it. After building a 43–29 lead in the second quarter, the Pacers encountered the Warriors' full-court press and unraveled: First a ten-second violation, then two more turnovers. Richardson coughed it up five times, eventually committing a career-high eleven of the team's twenty-five turnovers.

Even while their teammates were slipping and sliding, Miller, Smits, and Dale Davis kept scoring enough to make the game interesting. As a team, the Pacers actually outshot the Warriors 49 percent to 44 percent. If only statistics won basketball games.

3
A Champion Arrives

The Pacers headed back to Indianapolis to regroup and reconsider the lineup. Starting out well enough, their Western road trip had turned into a 2–2 dud. A year or two before, a split series on the road would have been quite acceptable, but now things were somehow different. The difference was one of attitude—and expectations. Larry Brown had been hired because he was a winner. Only once in his twenty-year coaching career had he turned in a losing season. He had come to Indianapolis to turn things around, to take a team basking in lukewarm mediocrity, run it through a cold shower and bring it out tingling with excitement. Everyone—the team, the fans, management and ownership—expected better.

At this point, the Pacers were 5–10. The season was almost a fifth over—only the most diehard fans were saying, "Hey, it's still early." Certainly management was taking the first twenty games seriously. Adjustments had to be made. Something was missing and had to be found.

It was—like a favorite pair of sneakers somehow left in Los Angeles on a road trip, it was identified and shipped immediately to Indianapolis. When he stepped off the plane that Sunday, December 5, Byron Scott wasn't exactly back home in Indiana, but he was definitely among friends.

After ten years with the Los Angeles Lakers, a career that had seen ten playoff appearances and earned him three NBA championship rings, the veteran guard had been released. The Lakers were trying to build for the future, and Scott, despite—perhaps because of—his experience, looked too much like the past.

Moreover, Scott had never been a marquee player. Although he was a starter on those championship teams, as well as the Lakers' all-time shooter from behind the arc (522 three-pointers on 1,407 attempts), Scott had been a relatively low-profile presence through the Lakers' glory years in the 1980s. Then, Magic Johnson's smiling proclamation of "show time" seemed the perfect signature for a razzle-dazzle team from tinsel town.

Even if the spotlight was most often on Johnson and teammates Kareem Abdul-Jabbar and James Worthy, Scott had built a solid reputation with a sixteen-point career scoring average. Even last year, at the ripe-old-NBA age of thirty-two, Scott was scoring 13.7 points per game, hitting nearly 45 percent of his shots. If not a star, he was a solid performer—and he knew what it meant to win. The announcement of his acquisition was greeted with smiles throughout the Pacer office and around the city. When he stepped off the plane that cold Sunday night in December, the Indianapolis photographers were waiting.

So were the fans and the team. The mood in the city was one of quiet delight. Somehow, everyone sensed that the Pacers had picked up a gem that had carelessly slipped through someone else's fingers.

The Lakers had released Scott before the start of the season. It was, Scott would remember, an unnecessarily unpleasant end to what had been a beautiful relationship. "I don't think I was treated the way I should have been," Scott said. "It wasn't so much that I was treated unfairly, but it just left me with a cold feeling.

"Even if you want a young team, you still need players who have been there to lead by example, to show the young players what it takes."

Certainly Donnie Walsh thought so. He had contacted Scott days before, asking two simple questions: First, was he in shape?

Yes, Scott said, definitely yes. After his release from the Lakers, Scott was undeniably a bit disheartened but insisted he was quietly "confident that something would materialize.

"I was working out six times a week—lifting, running, shooting and playing in the gym. I was confident someone was going to call sooner or later."

Walsh's second question: Did Scott want to play for the Pacers?

Yes again. Scott made that even clearer with his first public statements in the Indianapolis airport. There, he expressed confidence that this team had the stuff to go where no NBA Pacer team had gone before—and he was going to make sure they did.

"This team has been to the playoffs a number of times but hasn't won. It's going to be my job to make sure we get there and win."

Such words were all very nice, of course. They were exactly the right words for public consumption, demonstrating just the attitude the Pacers had a right to expect from a new player.

The thing was, Scott believed those words—and in himself and in the team. Seven months later, when the season was over and the excitement had subsided, at a time when Scott might also be expected to confess to a slight exaggeration for PR purposes, he was still talking the good talk.

"I really did believe everything I said when I got off the plane. I thought this team had the ability to be in the Eastern Conference finals. They had the potential. I wasn't trying to blow smoke up anybody's behind."

Confidence and belief. Scott—as well as Walsh and Brown—knew just how important they were. "To be honest," Scott said, "it's attitude that makes a team a winner.

"I've always thought of myself as winner, always thought before every game that the game could be won. When I got to Indianapolis, the guys on the team sensed that—and knew that I wasn't cocky, just confident."

Brown knew a winner when he saw one—fourteen years earlier, in Scott's case. At that time, when Brown was coaching at UCLA, he had tried unsuccessfully to recruit him. Brown finally got him.

"I think he can help us because he's been on winning teams," Brown said when Scott arrived. Using words like "uplifting" to describe his probable effect, Brown predicted that Scott would immediately lend a new note of credibility to the team and a bit more of the league's respect.

Perhaps more important, Scott would command immediate respect from the team, and that should, Brown and others figured, eventually translate into a greater sense of self-respect in the Pacer locker room and on the court. And that meant victory.

Miller concurred. "Hopefully he can put us over the hump," Miller told the press. "We need his leadership and his on-court attitude."

It soon became apparent that all the predictions of Scott's psychological impact were right. The team was quietly awed by him. LaSalle Thompson, who takes pride in his physical strength, calculated that, pound-for-pound, Scott was the strongest player on the team. "We'd be lifting weights and I'd look over and he'd be pressing damn near as much as me—and I outweigh him by fifty pounds."

On a team that specialized in friendly ridicule and humorous nicknames, Scott was not immune. Most of the time, he was "Dryhead," because he never seemed to sweat enough during a game to get his hair wet. On other occasions, Scott was simply "Three Rings"; it was not a reference to the circus.

"He brought in one of his championship rings one day," Thompson remembered, "just to show everyone what it looked like. You could see the effect it had on the younger guys. Hell, it had the same effect on me."

There were also some statistical reasons for bringing Scott aboard. At that point in the season, the Pacers were last in the league in three-point shots made and attempted, 27-of-84—a surprising figure for a team that had once loved the swish of long-range artillery.

Pooh Richardson, who had known and respected Scott since his UCLA days, laced the statistical and psychological reasons in a neat bow, offering a simple bit of praise that would turn out to be prophecy: "He'll be able to help Reggie out a lot with the experience he has at that position. He's made a lot of big shots in a lot of big games."

No kidding.

* * *

In his first game as a Pacer, Byron Scott wasn't spectacular, but he certainly wasn't shy. Shooting ten times in eleven minutes, he made only three of them and ended the game with eight points.

But one of the shots he made had a note of panache to it. It was the jumper that put the Pacers ahead of the Sacramento Kings for good, at 75–74. A small thing, really, in a game that the Pacers really should have won easily anyway. The game was no more or less important than any other, except that for a while it looked like another major embarrassment waiting to happen—and the Pacers had had enough of those to satisfy even the most perverse appetites for upsets.

It was Game Sixteen of the 1993–94 season, played at MSA for a distracted hometown crowd of 9,500. Coming in at 5–10, the Pacers faced the only team in the league still without a road win. Given the Pacers' long-standing propensity to be Sunday-punched almost any night of the week, the scene was set for a surprise attack and subsequent Pacer humiliation. For bad measure, it was December 7— Pearl Harbor Day.

Fortunately, the Kings were oblivious to their historic opportunity. Although they made it a cockfight for the first three periods, in the fourth the Kings offered the Pacers a plucky but ultimately pluckable sitting duck, losing 105–87. But no one knew that when the Kings were up 74–73, and Byron Scott had the ball with a minute left in the third.

After Scott made that shot, the Kings went 8:34 seconds without hitting a shot. Their shooting over that period was inanely inept, They missed thirteen consecutive shots and, for the fourth quarter, hit only 3-of-21 field goals and scored just thirteen points.

Credit the Pacer defense with much of that shutdown. Brown did: "In the second half we defended about as well as we have in a long time."

And credit Kenny Williams with providing an electric jolt. Derrick McKey pulled his left calf muscle early in the first quarter. At that point in the season, Brown would normally have brought Malik Sealy off the bench. But Sealy was down with a sprained right foot.

That left Kenny Williams. "That was kind of scary," Brown recalled. It turned out to be scarier for Sacramento. Williams took a 12–8 lead, injected some of his high-voltage acrobatics and—*shazam*—the lead was 25–10; Williams hit six of those thirteen Pacer points and pulled in six rebounds. He ended the half with twelve points, adding four more in the second.

Williams' incredible jumping ability—a vertical leap of nearly forty inches— had delighted the home-court crowd for three years. But his aerial assault of dunks, alley-oops and improbably blocked shots had failed thus far to impress Coach Brown. The fans and the press felt that Williams' performance that night inched him closer to a regular spot in the rotation—but there was still some way to go.

Oh, one other player besides Scott made his first on-court appearance in a Pacer uniform that night: Haywoode Workman. The Oral Roberts University product played sixteen minutes, contributing eight points, four rebounds and two assists. Again, no one paid a great deal of attention to the performance of a back-up point guard who'd spent the last two seasons as a member of Scavolini Pesaro in an Italian league.

Coach Brown did offer this encouraging assessment: "Haywoode got us going." But it would take some time before the coach and the fans would figure out quite how far they could go with Haywoode. Fortunately, they were willing to give Workman the time he required.

* * *

On Thursday, December 9, Game Seventeen offered the Pacers a Magic rematch at Market Square Arena. Rather, the Pacers and Shaquille O'Neal had a rematch.

The Shaq truly attacked that night, piling up a career-high forty-nine points, and grabbing eleven rebounds. Apparently he was having too much fun—or was just plumb tuckered out—with all that scoring to worry about blocking any shots.

O'Neal provided nearly half of the Magic's total offense (105 points) and one-third of the team's rebounds. It was one heck of a game for a man who apparently has been dubbed to single-handedly save the NBA from the marketing doldrums that have descended with the retirements of Magic Johnson, Larry Bird and Michael Jordan. He looked capable of it this night.

"I think," Shaquille said of his improved performance over their last encounter, "the difference is they weren't double-teaming me." The Pacers also didn't do all that well guarding future All-Star guard Anfernee Hardaway, who had eighteen points.

But that was because the Pacers were guarding everyone else, not to mention playing their own end of what is, after all, a team sport.

Indiana had eight players in double figures. Reggie Miller had twenty-three points and three steals. Pooh Richardson added fifteen points and eight assists but was poked in the eye by former Pacer Scott Skiles. Byron Scott, getting the feel of his new uniform, chipped in ten points, five of them coming as the Pacers went 11-for-15 in the third-quarter and built what proved to be an insurmountable lead. Antonio Davis added twelve points and four boards. Haywoode Workman, spelling a limping, squinting Richardson, contributed thirteen points. "I have something to prove," Workman said.

And Dale Davis out-rebounded Shaq by two.

And when the Pacers stood shoulder to shoulder they managed to add up six more points than Shaq and Associates. Despite O'Neal and Hardaway, the Pacers won 111–105.

The largest MSA crowd of the season, a whopping 15,171 fans (although not necessarily Pacer fans) witnessed the Pacer victory. Among them was former Vice-President Dan Quayle, who dropped in at the last minute to give MSA security conniptions.

If there was any lesson to be learned from this game, it was summed up by newcomer old-timer Byron Scott: "One player can't beat you." That is to say, it educated the Pacers on the importance of being a team, on how one player might step up when another can't. Although it wasn't obvious at the time, the game also gave the Pacers a more particular lesson in playing the Magic—and they graduated with honors, preparing themselves well to take their advanced degree in May.

The Pacer victory might even have converted a few of the Shaq-o-philes in the MSA crowd. There sure weren't any left in town by the end of the season.

* * *

They had just subdued a team with one of the league's premier centers, if not the center himself. Nonetheless, the Pacers came to Madison Square Garden for Game Eighteen hopeful that maybe, just maybe, Patrick Ewing's New York Knicks could be dispatched as well. It was the second meeting of the two teams in the 93–94 season, but if the Pacers were slowly coming together as a team, the Knicks weren't getting any worse.

The Pacers turned in a gutty effort, playing without starting point guard Pooh Richardson as well as his back-up, Vern Fleming. That left Haywoode Workman, who was still getting the feel of the job in his third game after spending the early season on the bench. Workman handled the point for thirty-three minutes; the rest of the time Larry Brown was forced to play Reggie and Byron as a sort of an alternating, all-purpose 1-2-guard—an unfamiliar job for anyone.

That awkward math, multiplied by the home-court advantage, equals no surprise that the Pacers came up short. The surprise was how small the margin of New York victory was: 98–91. If the Pacers still lacked the knack to take the Knicks, they were getting closer—a lot closer, in fact, than the nineteen-point drubbing they absorbed in Indianapolis in early November.

It may be some key to Larry Brown's coaching system that this valiant, improved effort earned only his disappointment. "It's not my responsibility to be excited when we have a chance to win games and don't."

Just as it had in the Pacer win over Orlando, the job of stopping the unstoppable center fell to whoever could handle it. Smits was ineffective, and was benched for the last nine minutes of the game to let Antonio Davis have a crack at Ewing. The

Knick Dream Teamer hardly seemed to notice the change, dropping in thirty-two points, pulling down ten rebounds and blocking five shots. If he couldn't contain Ewing, A.D. at least contributed well—thirteen points and fourteen boards.

At the beginning of the season, the Pacers had struggled to overcome the annoying habit of starting strong and fading in the fourth. That had evened out over the last few games. This game, though, saw the reverse: Over the last three quarters, the Pacers actually outscored the Knicks 78–76—an impressive statistic, but not enough to overcome a 13–22 disadvantage in the first quarter that resulted from nine Pacer turnovers, five by Miller.

The Pacers almost cut the mustard late in the third quarter, pulling within one. A half-dozen Pacer fans in the Garden yelled as mightily as they could to help the team over the edge. But the New York crowd picked up the chant of "Cheryl, Cheryl"—a reference to Reggie Miller's sister, a basketball star in her own right—and drowned them out.

More important, the Knicks knuckled down and buckled the Pacers down, pushing their lead to thirteen in the early minutes of the fourth quarter. Miller accepted some of the blame. "I should have been more aggressive," he said. He was far from humbled. "I think we have as much talent as they do...I just think they play very hard. They know how to win and I don't think we've gotten to that level yet."

No, not quite yet.

At that point in the season, Brown believed that level might never be reached without substantial improvement from his starting center. Rik Smits' performance in this game and the one before it only seemed to confirm Brown's apprehension that the seven-foot four-inch center from the Netherlands was just not up to NBA standards—at least Brown's standards and his emphasis on defense. "We can't win with one block, four rebounds and six fouls," the coach said of Smits.

Brown was certainly aware that General Manager Donnie Walsh had invested a lot of time, money and patience in Smits. Walsh had taken tons of flak from the press and the public for his commitment to Smits despite Smits' inconsistent performance as a pro. Walsh had been impressed with Smits since the Dutchman's college days, when he had been named Player of the Decade at Marist College in New York, where he had averaged more than twenty-seven points per game in his senior year and led his team to the NCAA tournament. In 1988–89, his first year as a Pacer, Smits had demonstrated far more defensive prowess, finishing ninth in the NBA in blocked shots and earning a spot on the all-league rookie team.

Over the past couple of seasons, Smits had shown himself capable of still summoning the occasional brilliant game, at least offensively, and momentarily quieting the criticism. The Monday morning after one such outing, a nationally televised defeat of Boston at MSA, Walsh called a front office staff meeting and spoke emotionally about his faith in Smits, his belief that the big center would someday help the franchise reach the next level of league respect.

Coach Brown was at least nominally obligated to honor and try to redeem Walsh's faith. At this point in the season, though, it looked like a test of Brown's friendship with Walsh as much as a test of Walsh's faith in Smits.

* * *

A year before, the Pacers might have let their New York disappointment disrupt whatever concentration they had been building since the start of the season. The 1992–93 Pacers had done it more than once, losing to better teams and immediately thereafter bungling a game against one of the league's cellar dwellers. A year before, the Pacers had lost a two-point decision at home to Utah, then went out the next day to lose by 10 in Milwaukee. And they had demonstrated almost perfect schizophrenia on a western road trip by beating Phoenix at Phoenix, next losing to Utah, then beating Seattle, then losing to Denver.

Familiar with their Jekyll-and-Hyde team, longtime Pacers fans were holding their breath before Game Nineteen, a home match against the lottery-bound Washington Bullets, losers of seven straight coming into the game. It didn't take long on Tuesday, December 14, before the fans were breathing easy.

The Pacers outscored the misfiring Bullets in every quarter, jumping out to a seven-point lead after one, building it to thirteen at the half, kept it coming to eighteen at the end of the third and finished up nineteen: 106–87.

Smits tried to make up for his recent negligible performances with a game-high twenty-two points on 7-of-12 shooting in twenty-seven minutes—and even got tough enough to commit a flagrant foul. Miller scored twenty-one and Byron Scott connected for sixteen. Haywoode Workman got his second Pacer start, played thirty-five minutes and contributed nine points, eight boards and five assists against his old team. The Bullets had declined to renew Workman's contract after the 1990–91 season.

The fans may have been relieved to see the Bullets missing nearly everything, ending with only 36.4 percent shooting, a season low for Pacers' opponents. Still, they couldn't help but cheer for former IU star and All-America Calbert Cheaney in his first-ever outing against a team calling itself Indiana.

Improving to 8–11 seemed to improve everyone's mood—or maybe it was just the chance to take a little southern swing and escape the Indiana winter for a few hours. In either case, the Pacers seemed relaxed and ready to travel to Atlanta to meet the Hawks for Game Twenty on Thursday, December 16.

The Pacers knew they were still short-handed. They knew they were only 8–11.

They knew they were meeting the hottest team in the league. Going into the game, Atlanta was unbeaten at home. They had risen on a fourteen-game updraft to perch atop the Eastern Conference at 15–4, a height they would still hold at the end of the season. With Coach-of-the-Year-to-be Lenny Wilkens newly arrived from Cleveland to guide them and perennial superstar Dominique Wilkins to lead them, it was common knowledge that the Hawks were headed for the NBA Finals.

A little knowledge, apparently, can be a dangerous thing. And after the game, no one knew who was more surprised—them or us.

Considering the way the game started, it must have come as a very big surprise. Atlanta lead by as much as seventeen early in the second quarter.

Can you spell blowout? Yes, but better to count it: A thirty-three-point turn-around over the next three quarters and—surprise—a 99–81 Pacer victory.

"We knew the streak would end sooner or later," said Dominique Wilkins. He just may not have known that it would be Derrick McKey doing the wing-clipping, holding Wilkins to 7-of-21 shooting.

Then there was Dale Davis. His monster night—nineteen points and eighteen boards—made Kevin Willis' ten-point, twelve-rebound effort look merely adequate. Then there was just about everyone else on the Pacer team. "I'm very proud of this team," Larry Brown said afterward. "It's a big, big win for us."

Before the game, as his team struggled toward a .500 season, Donnie Walsh had told the press that he would have preferred to start the season with a winning streak. "But I think we're improving," he said. "And, as we go on, I'd prefer us to be better later than sooner."

Walsh couldn't know that he would get his wish, both later and sooner, and probably a lot sooner than he—or the Hawks—expected.

Reggie Miller, who waved at the TV cameras and told the audience, "No fifteen here," also advised the Hawks to take their fans out back and shoot them. The attendance figures at Atlanta's Omni were firmly stuck to the bottom of the NBA cage.

As if Reggie really had much room to talk. Market Square Arena was only three notches higher on the attendance charts. MSA fans, of course, had always maintained that when the Pacers started winning, they would start buying tickets. No one in Atlanta had ever made the offer. Even at the end of the season and into the playoffs, the Atlanta fans were curiously unconcerned and unmotivated. One might even say that the Pacers would come to know the Atlanta fans almost as well as the Hawks.

Foreknowledge and hindsight are funny. Looking back on the 1993–94 season and the Pacers' run through the playoffs, it's possible to speculate that things might have been different. What if, for instance, the Pacers had nixed the Knicks in New

York, even in a close game, instead of demolishing the Hawks in Atlanta? Would that have given the team the confidence to take New York in the conference finals?

Maybe, maybe not. Maybe they would have lacked the confidence to beat Atlanta in the second round. Maybe, but probably not.

* * *

Game Twenty-one was held at MSA on Saturday, December 18. The New Jersey Nets had failed against the Pacers in their first meeting. With the new faces in the lineup and new confidence in their hearts, the Pacers again proved the superior team, handling the Nets easily when it counted and finally notching their fourth straight home victory, 108–98, to improve their record to 10–11.

With the score tied at ninety, the Pacers netted New Jersey and hauled in the win with an 18–8 run. Haywoode Workman again made the home crowd wonder "Pooh who?" with a career-high twenty-one points and eight assists. And Rik Smits almost made the fans and Coach Brown wonder why they ever doubted him—twenty-two points, thirteen boards (two coming in the crucial fourth-quarter spurt), four assists and three blocks. Miller was out front with twenty-eight points.

The Pacers couldn't quite contain Derrick Coleman, who kept things interesting with twenty-five points and thirteen boards. But they—and the refs—had to contain Dale Davis after Armon Gilliam pulled (slammed?) him from behind to stop a drive and earn a Flagrant Foul Type II ejection. Davis had bedeviled Gilliam all night long, with two of his career-high six blocked shots. He didn't appreciate Gilliam's revenge. "I definitely wasn't happy," Davis said. Referee Luis Grillo could see that as he wrestled Davis to prevent him from relocating Gilliam's face.

Coming into Game Twenty-two on Monday, December 20 in Phoenix, the Pacers had won five of their last six games and were tantalizingly close to the break-even point with a 10–11 record. Considering the injuries that had strained and restrained the team in 1993, as well as the challenge of adjusting to a new coach and the replacement of Detlef Schrempf, a .500 record would have looked just fine—like the start of a second season.

They were going up against another high-flying and—with Charles Barkley as acting head of the publicity department—high-falutin' team with a seemingly finals-bound 16–4 record, 10–1 at home.

To their credit, the Pacers made a game of it, but couldn't hold on against the Suns. They zoomed out of halftime with eight straight points to take a 61–52 lead, but five turnovers through the middle of the period let the Suns romp past to take a 71–65 edge.

The Pacers pulled even at seventy-six coming into the fourth, but the Suns just kept getting hotter. The Pacers managed to close within four at 96–92 with just over two minutes to play. But then they finally melted, turning it over three straight times leading to six Suns points.

The Pacers gave the ball away twenty-five times in the game, but got no charity in return, losing the free throw contest 11–25. Coach Brown had some reservations about the officiating, which "made it virtually impossible for us to win," he said.

Veteran Scott put a slightly different spin on it: "We let some calls affect us," and chided the team for letting the refs change the Pacer game. Miller could only blame himself for his 4-of-13 shooting: "It was horrible."

And Workman, who had been steadily getting better as he became increasingly comfortable as starting point guard, finally reached a breaking point—or at least the limits of his beginner's luck. "I think I tried to control the game myself. It put a lot of pressure on me. I wasn't aggressive enough. I didn't get into position to make the offense go."

Brown, who has a deserved reputation for riding point guards until they drop, was kinder to Workman than Haywoode was to himself. "He's had to play major minutes against great players. So, he's going to have nights like this."

* * *

Game Twenty-three—the Pacers' first season match-up against the Seattle SuperSonics—promised to be a contest of told-you-sos, pitting recent ex-Pacer Detlef Schrempf against just-as-recent ex-Sonic Derrick McKey.

It was a closer contest than most would have predicted. The Sonics won 91–88, improving to 20–2 and remaining unbeaten in twelve home starts. The outcome was amazingly close considering Reggie Miller produced a measly twelve points and Rik Smits dropped off the map with just two.

For the Sonics, it was just another small step on their way to the league's best season record. Perhaps it was a particularly satisfying win for Schrempf. Although happy with his new team in his old stomping grounds, the University of Washington alumnus had publicly stated that his trade had been handled with little warning and less sensitivity to his family.

Subsequently, he had reminded the media—and anyone anywhere who might be reading, Donnie—that it was nice to finally be in a situation where he could play every bit as hard as he had in Indiana, but now have a very good chance of winning.

Low-key McKey, whose range of emotional expression both on and off the court runs the gamut from A to B, shrugged off any suggestion of the game's special significance. "It's just another game," he told the press.

The Pacers led 47–44 at the half on the strength of 71 percent shooting, but they continued their Phoenix lack of focus, turning the ball over fifteen times. The teams traded leads of one, two and three points for the rest of the game. The Sonics managed one four-point lead, but Kenny Williams zoomed by with three straight buckets in another one of his trademark afterburner bursts of energy.

Detlef won the Schrempf-McKey duel, but it was no blowout: He had fifteen points, eleven boards and three assists to Derrick's eleven points, five boards and three dishes.

The Pacers became real road worriers with a 108–96 loss to Portland in Game Twenty-four on Thursday, December 23. The Trailblazers were having a lackluster season that would end well short of their previous playoff glories. More upsetting, despite playing without injured Dream Teamer Clyde Drexler and ace rebounder Chris Dudley, the Blazers still managed to dispatch the Pacers with relative ease.

Fighting back from a twenty-three-point, second-quarter deficit, the Pacers smelled hope when they cut the Blazer lead to three near the end of the third quarter, the only period in which the Pacers outscored the home team. But Portland outscored Indiana 18–9 in the first minutes of the fourth, and from there the victory was sealed.

In keeping with his personal tradition of personnel decisions, Coach Brown gave the start at center to former Oregon State standout Scott Haskin—but he lasted only six minutes and scored only two points.

* * *

This western swing had cut into the nascent Pacer confidence like an ax. In Game Twenty-five, coming the day after Christmas against Cleveland in Richfield, Ohio, the Pacers again failed to unwrap a win—even though the tag on this package seemed to have Indiana written all over it.

The Pacers were playing a team with the same record—10–14; it was a prime chance to regain a bit of self-respect. But they couldn't win in regulation time and they couldn't win in overtime, despite leading 100–96 with just under three minutes to go. With turnovers and clanked shots, the Pacers let the Cavaliers pull ahead 103–101 with twenty-eight seconds to play.

Reggie Miller had a chance to tie the game—well, almost. As he drove the baseline, he attempted to scoot past Cleveland's Bobby Phills and got whistled for an offensive foul for putting a hand in Phills' face. This was not Reggie's night. He went thirty-two minutes without a field goal.

Nonetheless, as coaches occasionally must, Coach Brown went through the roof after the call. He unleashed a verbal assault on the officials that apparently frightened his assistant coaches—they moved between Brown and the officials. The NBA front office wasn't intimidated. Brown was fined three thousand dollars for his barrage.

The final possessions only confirmed the call. The Cavaliers won 107–103.

With their fourth consecutive road loss, the Pacers fell to 10–15. The loss was also Indiana's tenth consecutive loss to the Cavaliers.

The season went from frustrating to humiliating four days later. Game Twenty-six brought the San Antonio Spurs to Indianapolis and sent the Pacers to the dumps. The Spurs rode all over the Pacers in a twenty-five-point pounding, 107–82, that left Reggie Miller wondering if he had mistakenly boarded the wrong team bus. "Tonight wasn't the Pacers I know."

Unfortunately but predictably, more than a few local fans began to mutter that it sure as heck was the Pacers *they* had come to know over the last few years.

In fact, they did more than mutter. They booed—lustily.

Oh, ye of little faith—including, at least for this night, the team. Fleming and Miller both told the press they deserved whatever razzes, catcalls and hoots they received.

The margin of loss seemed a mystery in view of the fact that the Pacers had out-rebounded Dennis Rodman (who was sporting a vaguely mauve hairdo for his date with the blue and gold), David Robinson, Terry Cummings and the rest of the Spurs.

But the mystery was easily solved. Indiana lost because it couldn't hit the rim with a baseball bat, shooting a horrifying 29 percent in the first half and 35 percent for the night.

Brown and the boys had plenty of time to think things over. Their next game was five days away, when they welcomed their old friends from Cleveland back to MSA after the holiday break. Indiana desperately needed a win—for their fans, for their coach and for themselves.

4
New Year—Same Old Habits

It looked as if the fans had reached the bottom of their optimism. Their honeymoon with Larry Brown was turning out to be less than sweet.

For the first time since Brown had taken over the day-by-day, play-by-play control of the Indiana Pacers, the fans were reduced to boos. To them, the 107–82 loss to San Antonio on December 30 at Market Square Arena was more than the last game of the year, it was the end of their hopes that Brown's magic might work for the Pacers.

More and more it seemed that Brown's much-publicized winning ways were being wasted on a team that would never amount to more than a doormat for the best—and the mediocre, as well. For the Pacers, the 1993–94 season was turning out to be a very long, dark winter.

As the new year began, the team was being dragged behind a five-game losing streak—a streak that included a depressing overtime loss to Cleveland only nine days before. It looked like Santa Claus had just flown right by Indiana.

The upcoming rematch with Cleveland held no particular promise. For the last couple of years the Cavaliers had treated the Pacers like the junior varsity of the Eastern Conference. In fact, the Cavs had beaten them ten straight.

But a belated Christmas present was waiting to be unwrapped on January 4 in Game Twenty-seven: A 104–99 Pacer victory. There *was* a Santa Claus.

Reggie led the way that night, burning the Cavs for a game-high twenty-nine points. Close behind was Derrick McKey, who had his best total effort of the season with eighteen points, seven rebounds, six assists and two blocked shots. Vern Fleming, getting his first start in what seemed eons, added sixteen points and twelve assists. With veteran nerve, Fleming iced the game in the final seconds, sinking four free throws as the Cavs lunged out in desperation. And Dale Davis just kept on being unstoppable: fifteen points, thirteen boards and four blocked shots.

But more important than any statistics was the heart the team showed in overcoming a ten-point halftime deficit, fighting back once, then twice in the third quarter and finally breaking through with five straight points to take a 75–74 lead as the period ended.

Reggie, beginning to emerge from his personal winter blahs, scored a four-point play then immediately scorched another three-pointer to give the Pacers a 92–85 lead. The Cavs were far from finished, reasserting themselves in a 10–2 run to take a 95–94 lead. But McKey drained a jumper with just over two minutes to play, a shot that would prove to provide the stay-ahead points.

After the game, Coach Brown talked about confidence. "Maybe a game like this will restore it a little bit."

Well, a very little bit, anyway. Game Twenty-eight took the Pacers to Washington on Wednesday, January 5. In their first season meeting, the Pacers had almost casually hammered the Bullets flat, 106–87. Since then, the Bullets had gotten no better. In fact, they hadn't won a home game in more than a month.

Santa Claus had missed them, too, this season. So, with that little ray of confident sunshine beaming in their smile, the ever-perplexing Pacers choked big time, blowing a twelve-point fourth-quarter lead to lose 97–95. Fortunately, the game was not televised in Indiana.

Co-Captain Miller fell again into some quagmire of offensive frustration, hitting only five of fourteen shots. McKey matched him at twelve points. Smits had nine. Only Dale Davis looked good in statistical retrospect, contributing twenty-eight points and twelve boards to the embarrassment.

Larry Brown had neither sympathy nor kind words after the game. "That's leadership," he said to anyone who might be listening, Reggie. Then he indirectly chastised even Dale Davis, wondering why Double-D had ignored the defensive strategy plotted in a late-game time out.

There was no ho-ho-hoing in the locker room that night. The inadvertent Santas were red-faced again. "We can't be giving games away," Miller said. "We've got to learn to hold onto a damn lead."

* * *

Up and down, down and up, back and forth, in and out—who could figure the Pacers in January?

Nobody, it turned out.

The team was riding a pogo stick on a roller coaster. It was a miracle they didn't fall out and break their necks. Looking back on all the frenetic failings and flailings, the improbable victories and self-inflicted losses, the best analogy that might be offered would be labor pains—or a cartoon egg with legs running around hoping to finally crack its shell and stretch its wings.

The month at a glance: Beat Cleveland—perhaps unexpectedly but gratifyingly. Lose to Washington—ouch, what an embarrassment. Beat Detroit—satisfying if only for revenge, but hardly a cause for pride this season.

Then, a win in Milwaukee—again, nice, but hardly amazing. Another win at Denver—again, a team running on thin air but, with Dikembe Mutombo never out of the running (as Seattle would discover come playoff time.) Next, an agonizing loss to a dismal team when Philadelphia steals it at the buzzer.

And just when the Pacers needed it most, they came up strong again against Atlanta. Then again versus Miami.

But don't get your hopes up—Chicago takes two back-to-back, the first coming on a real heart-breaker when Toni Kukoc banked in a three-pointer with less than a second—some would say, a second less than a second—to play. The following game the next day might have provided some very sweet revenge, but no dice.

Deflated by Chicago, the Pacers allow Milwaukee to beat them at home. Then they lose to the lottery-bound Lakers in L.A. Teetering on the brink of the slough of despond, the Pacers lean even farther with a loss at Denver. And then, when they appeared shaked, baked and ready for the knife...up they pop to pop the Houston Rockets.

The final record in January was seven wins and seven losses—and the high points and low lights seemed just as evenly distributed:

—Auburn Hills, Michigan, January 8: Byron Scott got his first start in a Pacer uniform. Reggie Miller had the flu, but Scott flew to 21 points, a season high for the veteran, in a 101–92 fly-by of the dismal Pistons. It took a while, though, for Scott to get up to speed. He had shot only 3-of-11, including two lay-ups, until well into the third quarter. He hit four of his next six and finished 5-of-6 from the line.

As a team, though, the Pacers fared poorly in the third, missing eleven of fifteen shots to trail 66–59. Then, with Scott and the Davis men surging back, the Pacers took the game away. The win broke a five-game road slump and increased Detroit's losing streak to nine.

—Milwaukee, January 11: Antonio Davis got his first Pacers start, and just as Byron Scott had done the game before, Davis carried his team to a victory. Standing on Antonio's well-muscled shoulders, the Pacers could almost see the light at the end of their early-season tunnel. Davis, looking like the rookie all-star he would become, scored twenty-six points and hauled in twelve rebounds, replacing Rik Smits (out with a sprained shoulder) as the Pacers beat the Bucks 82–76. Although the victory brought Indiana's record to a less-than-impressive 13–17, it was a game they might have been embarrassed to lose. Milwaukee had the league's third-worst offense and second-worst home record: 3–12 home starts out of a 9–23 record. Despite the win, the Pacers lost Dale Davis to a slight wrist fracture. The fans held their breath to see how bad this loss would be.

—Indianapolis, January 12: The depleted Pacers met Dikembe Mutombo, LaPhonso Ellis and Mahmoud Abdul-Rauf and the rest of the Denver Nuggets at Market Square Arena—and sent them back home. With Vern Fleming, Pooh Richardson and Dale Davis sitting on the sidelines, the Pacers were down three. But they only needed two—two-guard Reggie Miller, who had a game-high twenty-nine points as the Pacers knocked the Nuggets 107–96.

—Philadelphia, January 14: Former high-school quarterback Jeff Hornacek fired a long inbounds pass to a leaping Dana Barros, who caught it in midair, turned and drained a twenty-foot jump shot at the buzzer as the Seventy-Sixers beat the Pacers 104–102 in overtime. As the Pacers would rediscover all too soon, a loss like that hurts like a bowling ball bounced off your foot. Despite the last-half-second dramatics, though, the team pretty much shot itself—or didn't shoot, as the case may be. After coming back from a sixteen-point third-quarter deficit, the Pacers hit just 7-of-15 free throws in the fourth. Haywoode Workman had a chance to win in regulation but missed one of two free throws, tying the game and sending it to OT.

— Indianapolis, January 15: Stunned but hardly demoralized—as they might have been a month before—the Pacers regrouped to battle the high-flying Atlanta Hawks, who were riding a seven-game winning streak. The last time the Hawks and the Pacers had met, the Pacers had snapped a fourteen-game Hawks win streak. Snapping this one should have been twice as easy. It wasn't—the game was on the line with less than a minute to play—but it was an Atlanta loss anyway, 94–91. It came down to "character," Brown said, which may be his way of saying defense. Derrick McKey limited Dominique Wilkins to 7-of-16 shooting.

— Indianapolis, January 19: Game Thirty-four of the season brought the Miami Heat to MSA, but they couldn't even crank their engines in the arctic cold that had enveloped Indianapolis. While the outside thermometer barely rose above zero, the Pacers fired up the arena with a 109–92 scorching of the young Heat, who registered their tenth straight loss in MSA. The Pacers won the game in the first quarter, outscoring Miami 30–13 and holding a sizable lead to the end.

The new year was seeing new energy in Indiana. The Pacers shot nearly 57 percent from the floor, and Reggie Miller extended his successful free-throw streak to fifty-one in the Miami game. With a 1994 record of 6–2, the Pacers seemed to have turned a corner.

If so, they hit a wall.

Indiana lost the next five games.

* * *

If the Philadelphia loss was a stunner, the loss in Chicago on Friday, January 21, was a heartbreaker. Every team in the NBA has some arch-nemesis—if not an arch-rival. The Pacers had always been especially keyed up to beat Boston, mostly because of post-season defeats in 1992 and 1993 and because the Celtics invariably lured a legion of Larry Bird watchers every time they visited MSA. For much the same reason—for the hundreds of anti-Pacers fans they brought to fill the cheap seats—the Chicago Bulls were high on the list of least-favorite opponents. Just the year before, Michael Jordan and Reggie Miller had come to blows—at least Jordan took a punch at Reggie. Even without Jordan, the Bulls were still world champs, and everyone likes to beat the best.

The Pacers almost did—the most excruciating "almost" in years. With eight-tenths of a second in the game, Reggie hit a twenty-two-foot jumper to put the Pacers up by two. On his way downcourt, Miller stopped to take a bow to the unbelieving Chicago Stadium crowd. The game was seemingly sewn up.

With seven-tenths of a second left in the game, Toni Kukoc took an inbounds pass, turned and banked in a three-pointer to win the game 96–95. Fans who had taped the game swore the game clock started only after he had come down from catching the ball and turned to set his feet for the shot. Yeah, maybe.

As the Pacers would later decide, it is pointless to worry about tenths of seconds that depend on some timekeeper's reflex. Some tenths of seconds are longer than others. In the course of a season—and a post-season—the long tenths and the short tenths may eventually even out.

*　*　*

Game Thirty-six brought the Bulls to MSA the next night. When the game was over, Scottie Pippen took his own bow as Chicago walked away with a 90–81 victory. It was the Pacers' ninth straight loss to the Bulls who, despite predictions of gloom in their first Jordan-less season, had accumulated a mid-year record of 27–11, nearly identical to the year before.

In that game, Reggie Miller notched his ten thousandth NBA point, the first Pacer to scale that height. He also broke a club record by extending his free-throw streak to fifty-four. But he only scored seventeen.

Next, as the late-January slump descended even farther, the Pacers dropped a mortifying game to bottom-feeding Milwaukee at MSA. The Bucks were down ten in the fourth quarter. The teams were tied with a minute to play. The Bucks won 96–88. That's almost all that anyone would want to know about this game—except to note that Miller's free-throw streak came to an end at fifty-nine. Failing to compensate, Miller took no shots from the field in the fourth quarter.

The consensus in the press was that Toni Kukoc's game-winner in Chicago had broken some small bone in the Pacers' psyche.

That diagnosis seemed even more accurate after Game Thirty-neight. On Wednesday, January 26, the Pacers flew to Los Angeles where they blew another late-game lead and lost to the Lakers 100–99, their fourth straight loss in this winter of their discontent.

As it had been at the beginning of the season, the fourth quarter proved their undoing. This one witnessed a nineteen-point turnaround before the Pacers reasserted themselves to lose by only four.

After the game, Brown told the press "I don't care about winning or losing, I just care about giving effort and playing unselfishly." LaSalle Thompson remembered thinking, "Damn! What did he mean winning isn't important?"

Any emotional boost to the evening came from the hosts, who showed considerable class by presenting ex-Laker Byron Scott a framed Laker jersey with Number 4—his number as a Laker as well as a Pacer—in a pregame ceremony. Brown also showed class by starting Scott. For his part, Scott poured in nineteen points in the losing cause.

* * *

Game Thirty-nine brought the Pacers to McNichols Sports Arena in Denver. Continuing their unfortunate trend of losing to teams they had recently beaten, the Pacers lost to the Nuggets 113–106 and fell seven games below .500 for the first time all season, at 16–23.

The oddsmakers were betting heavily on 16–24. With the powerful Rockets waiting for them in Houston two days later, the Pacers were looking more and more like road kill awaiting the next semi to spread them even flatter.

Again, as he had following the loss in Los Angeles, Larry Brown closed the locker room to talk with his own lost angels for the better part of a half-hour. Thinking back on those two post-game sessions, Brown could not recall that he'd talked about anything more than the same basics he had emphasized all season: The need to play unselfishly, the need to play with 100 percent of their skills, the need for total effort.

"Generally, I try not to say anything because you might say something that you might regret later," Brown said. "And generally the only times I'll say something is if I'm proud of the way a particular player has performed or how the team did.

"If I think there's been a lack of effort, I have to be careful. You've got to be mindful you've got a long season, and you've got to pick and choose your words carefully," he continued.

"After those two games, I don't think it was anything I said," he said. "It was more a matter of the team saying to themselves that there is a light at the end of the tunnel."

* * *

Larry Brown had come to Indianapolis with a hard-earned reputation as a winner. In twenty seasons as a college and professional coach, Brown had had only one losing season. Three times he'd been named Coach of the Year in the American

Basketball Association. He had an NCAA championship.

He had turned teams around so far and so fast that they were still spinning years after his often brief sojourn. His San Antonio Spurs finished the 1988–89 with a 21–61 record. The next year they finished 56–26, an NBA record for greatest improvement in a single season. The old record was a twenty-game upswing staged by the New Jersey Nets from their 1980–81 season (24–58) to their 1981–82 season (44–38). The Nets' coach? Larry Brown.

The Pacers players knew all of this at the beginning of the season. They were eager to have Brown lead them, eager to build on what they felt had been a constructive season in 1992–93. In fact, they were habitually eager to please—and not just Brown.

This may be difficult for the average fan to swallow, having been fed the highly publicized images of prima-donna players contesting with their coaches for control of the team. As Pacers' radio announcer Mark Boyle put it, "Pro players are not always easy to coach. The NBA is perhaps the only business in America where the employees are more important—and better-paid—than the management."

Yet few pro players are larger-than-life heroes with three-digit hat sizes. The fact is, as longtime front office staffers can attest, many are just as needful of acceptance and approval as any man in his twenties.

Kathy Jordan, the Pacers executive who schedules players' appearances at schools, charity balls, supermarkets and hospitals, will tell you that "most of the guys still have a lot of living and learning to do. They come into the league with such an eagerness for acceptance by the fans, the management and the owners."

Jordan's official title is director of community affairs. But she's really a den mother. She takes care of these young men. She's proud of their accomplishments and feels their hurt. And that's why she stopped attending Pacers' practices. She couldn't take it.

She couldn't handle Larry Brown's focused fury being loosed on her charges like a brickbat out of hell. "I mean it was *intense*," said Jordan. "It wasn't just an occasional flare of temper; it could go on nonstop all practice. I had to leave.

"But I think what this did was force the guys to come together, to support each other. The older guys would tell the younger ones: 'Man, you just take it and hear what the man said. Shake it off and listen to Coach.'

"It even got to the point where the team would start to give it to each other, watching what each other was doing and getting on them if they forgot what Larry had just told them," Jordan said.

"I think a couple of the guys had a harder time adjusting to this, but they would grin and bear it. I'd ask them, 'You doing all right?' and they'd nod and say, 'Sure, just fine,'" Jordan remembered.

The players concurred. Brown could be an emotional Force Ten hurricane. But, as many of them were quick to point out, he was absolutely even-handed. He played no favorites.

LaSalle Thompson explained, "A lot of coaches have double standards, but Larry Brown treated everyone the same. Everyone got his share, whether it was Reggie Miller or a rookie."

And ultimately, despite all of Brown's practice-session invective, the players were impressed with what Reggie Miller called "his overall sense of the game.

"He taught me to be better leader," Miller said, repeating a tribute heard consistently from other Pacers: Brown is a teacher. As Thompson said, he's a coach who "really cares that each of us becomes better."

Veteran Byron Scott credits Brown for being a "disciplinarian—which is basically the same attitude I have. This may have been hard for a lot of guys on our team to take initially, but I've always liked a coach who's been very demanding. There were a lot of times when we thought we were tired and hurt, but he got us through.

"He has a way with players," Scott said. "He talks to you like a person, even though he's The Man and you're a player. Larry doesn't think that his word is golden.

"He's easy to play for, even at the times when he's cussing you out. That doesn't bother me, it just makes me more determined," Scott concluded. "You need somebody who shows he cares."

Perhaps it sounds a bit like a television commercial or a page out of a Hall-of-Fame induction speech: You've got to have the love—of the game, of the team, for the team.

But after you've heard it in so many unrehearsed situations as well, you begin to realize that it's true, at least to this extent: Love may not win games, but it wins over players and teams—and *they* win games. No group of men in such a high-powered profession, in such a long-term test of ability and commitment, can succeed without that depth of emotional bond.

As Brown said, "It can only work if you show them that you care. I do care. I don't always handle every situation right, I have regrets. But it's not because I don't care."

Apparently, Brown handled the situation right at the end of January. Whatever Brown told his team after the Lakers and Nuggets games, it worked.

It convinced them that he cared— and that they could get better. So that's what they did. They got better—and better and better.

Almost best.

5
Fabulous February

Larry Brown and Reggie Miller both remember the point in the season when they knew the team was capable of great things: the last game of January, a Saturday in Houston.

The Rockets, led by eventual league MVP Hakeem Olajuwan, would go on to win the NBA championship that year—and they certainly looked as if they deserved to at this point, having compiled a 31–9 record, second only to Seattle.

The Pacers, on the other hand, had just lost five straight, the last three to weaker teams. After losses that week to the Lakers and Nuggets, Indiana had fallen to 16–23. Most objective observers figured the Houston game would fittingly finish the Pacers' three-city Western tour de farce, and continue their sixteen-game, fifteen-year history of losses at the Summit.

Yes indeed, the stage seemed set for a memorable game, as in, "Fellas, please try not to get too much blood on the uniforms—it's so hard to clean."

Well, if there was any red glare that night, it didn't come from the Rockets blasting through the roof. The red was in Houston's eyes. The Pacers didn't simply steal one from under their noses, they ripped their mustaches off in one, long, painful pull.

It started early and just kept coming as the Pacers pulled away to a seventeen-point lead at 50–33 with four minutes to play in the half. The Rockets regrouped to salvage a more-or-less respectable 57–53 halftime deficit. Houston accelerated into the third, tying the game at fifty-nine then again at sixty-one, but the Pacers threw their game into high gear to race ahead 89–79 as the period ended. From then on, it was all Pacers. Indiana went on a 15–4 run to open the fourth quarter up like a can of sardines. At one point the Pacers were up by twenty-one—that's when the sellout crowd sold out and started to boo.

Reggie Miller, resting as the second unit mopped up, leaned over to tell reporters: "Sounds like Market Square Arena." The game ended 119–108.

It was a team victory. Miller had twenty-one points. Smits had nineteen on 8-of-9 shooting. Derrick McKey had fifteen points and six rebounds. Sam Mitchell contributed 10 points. Vern Fleming added thirteen. Haywoode had nine points and seven assists. Byron was there with ten points and four assists. Kenny Williams had twelve points in sixteen minutes of play. Antonio added nine points and seven boards.

Against Houston, a team that hadn't allowed an opponent better than 50 per-cent shooting on its home court, the Pacers shot 61 percent. The Pacer defense so stymied the Rockets' interior game that Houston was forced to launch thirty three-point shots, the second-highest barrage in league history. They made nine.

After the game, Brown told reporters it had been "our best game of the year—by far." More than that, as Brown realized later, it was the first game of the rest of the season. At the end of the season, Brown looked back with hindsight's accuracy and said, "The Houston game was pivotal."

"We had just had some heartbreaking losses," Brown said. "I told the team, 'Hey, we were in every game.' But this gave us a tremendous boost."

Miller agreed. Months later, he could still feel that win. "I remember it exactly. As far as I'm concerned, it was that one victory that turned the season around.

"It wasn't that I had a particularly great game. We all did it. After losing five or six in a row, we went out and won five or six." (Actually, it was seven wins in a row.) "And in most of those, we didn't just win, we beat the crap out of the other team. After the Houston game, our backs just got a little more erect. I think I started walking with my shoulders just a little more square.

"Then, after one of our practices, Byron brought his rings in to show us, Miller recalled. "It was like he knew right then and there that now was the time to show us what it was all about."

Scott remembered the same time, "It was in the beginning of February, a week or two before the All-Star break. I looked around the locker room and I could see it in everyone's faces. To win in this league, you can't have six guys thinking, 'We can win' and six guys thinking, 'Yeah, right.' But when I looked at everybody I knew we were there. We were all on the same page.

"After that," Scott said, "every win seemed to get our confidence up more and more."

* * *

It seemed the Pacers were feeling a new fire as they came into Game Forty-one on Tuesday night, February 1. And they got a little kindling to feed the flame—the Washington Bullets, who owned the league's fifth-worst record and the worst road record in the Eastern Conference. The Pacers chewed on the Bullets and spat out a very timely and convincing victory, 116–96.

It was a dollop of confidence that couldn't have been better timed. Just that morning, *The Indianapolis Star*'s Dan Dunkin had raised some potentially deflating questions under the headline: "A different band but same old song for Pacers."

Dunkin quoted Reggie Miller's assessment of the city's change in attitude. Things are different now, Miller said. People around the city are much more supportive and positive. A year before "it was tough to go out in the city because people said, 'The same old Pacers.' "

All very nice, but Dunkin made some strong factual points. The team was 17–23, two games behind its record at the same time the previous season. Maybe Larry Brown was on his way to only his second losing season as a head coach.

Dunkin qualified his prediction by admitting that injuries had made the early season difficult. And he credited the Pacers' defense for holding opponents to 98.7 points per game on 45 percent shooting. But, Dunkin observed, the offense was averaging just one point more, and was on its way to the team's first year below 100 points per game.

Dunkin's points were well taken—at that point in the season. Coach Brown knew he was right. "Our team had a hard time scoring all year," Brown remembered.

But not that night, as the team counted seventeen above their season average. It was also the third consecutive game in which they scored above the century mark. Rik and Reggie took them halfway there, combining for fifty points. Both had 25-and-9 games—twenty-five points on Rik's 8-of-12 field goal shooting, another twenty-five on Reggie's 11-of-16. Rik adding nine rebounds; Reggie had nine assists. Derrick scored 16. Byron and Sam Mitchell each had ten points.

For the second game in a row, the Pacers had made better than 60 percent of their shots. In as much as Dunkin was right, that statistic was a significant step in the right direction.

* * *

The Pacers came into Game Forty-two feeling pretty good—in fact, *real* good. So good, in fact, that they played almost the whole first half before realizing that they were supposed to bring the Charlotte Hornets along for the ride. On Wednesday, February 2, the Pacers met the Hornets in their own nest and stung them good, tallying their season-high point total in a game they dominated far more than the 124–112 final might indicate.

Check it out: At the end of the first quarter the Pacers led 33–19. At halftime, the Pacers led by a score of 80 (yes, 80)-to-50. Their forty-seven-point second quarter was a new NBA Pacers record for most points in any period.

The Hornets attempted a comeback in the second half. In fact, it should be admitted that they nearly *did* come back. In the third quarter, they shot a very scary 6-of-8 from three-point land and, about halfway through the fourth quarter, even managed to pull within three points (oh, shades of pre-Christmas past) to send a shudder down the Pacers' spines. But, as was becoming increasingly clear, the Pacers had finally found their backbone and would not collapse—at least on that night. That momentary fourth-quarter symptom would blister forth two months later on a return trip to Charlotte, but that story will come later.

It should also be pointed out that the Hornets were sort of playing without the Hornets. Scott Burrell was gone with a strained Achilles tendon. Commercially famous Larry "Grandmama" Johnson, probably the only NBA player to ever publicly smile while wearing a dress, had been absent without pumps for more than a month. Alonzo Mourning, also in street clothes, demonstrated Reggie Miller-like emotion by getting himself officially booted from the game early in the second half. Maybe he had a date.

The Pacers had some injuries, too, playing without starting forward Dale Davis and starting point guard Pooh Richardson.

Again, the Pacers peppered their opponents with a balanced assault. Reggie led the second-season seasoning with twenty-five points on 9-of-13 shooting. Rik added twenty-three by hitting 10-of-11, obviously taking a cakewalk through the Hornets' depleted front line. Byron had twenty-one on 8-of-9 shooting. McKey added seventeen on 6-of-11. As might be surmised from these brisk numbers, the Pacers had brought their secret radio-controlled ball to Charlotte. The team shot a superlative 5-of-6 from behind the arc and logged their third-consecutive shooting game at or above 60 percent—another NBA Pacers record.

Where had all the offense come from?

An increasing—and increasingly appreciated—amount of it was coming from Rik Smits. Over the last four games (Nuggets, Rockets, Bullets, Hornets) Smits was scoring just the way you'd expect someone seven-feet-four to score.

Against the Nuggets he'd gone 7-of-19 for twenty points. Against Houston, he'd been 8-of-9 for nineteen points. He'd added twenty-five points on 8-of-12 shooting in the Bullets game, then twenty-three points on 10-of-11 shooting against the Hornets. That averaged right around twenty-two points per game, which was up almost 150 percent from the four-game losing streak coming into the Lakers game in late January.

People at Market Square Arena were beginning to wonder who this new center was.

It was the same guy—there was just less of him.

"I lost twenty-five pounds since last season," Smits pointed out. Previous coach Bo Hill had told Smits to beef up, thinking that more muscle would make him a more formidable presence in the low post. Brown took the opposite approach. He asked Rik to lighten up, thinking that twenty-five fewer pounds pounding up and down on his perpetually sore knees might make the difference. Brown appeared to be right.

Brown's and Hill's differing approaches to Smits also indicated a general difference in their view of the game itself. In wishing Smits were a bigger, stronger player, Hill revealed a preference for a more physical game. This approach had been an uncomfortable one for some of the players.

LaSalle Thompson remembered that once Hill had told him to go into a practice and pick a fight with a teammate, believing that a team full of tension would let it out on the opponents. "But with that sort of stuff," LaSalle said, "you end up with a situation like they had in Detroit, where Isiah broke his hand when he punched Laimbeer in practice. Derrick said that he'd seen plenty of tension like that in Seattle, and he would take Larry and the Pacers over that any day."

As far as Rik was concerned, "Larry and the Pacers" meant the coach and the team "finally accepting what you can do and then they just let you do it. It took some time for everybody to get used to each other at the start of the season. But after a while, everybody accepted everybody else."

Acceptance meant something special for a fellow who had been laughed at as a giant teen-ager in the Netherlands. "Being tall was considered a handicap," Smits recalled. "When I was young, I hated going out in a crowd—until I found basketball, until I found a use for my height."

And until Larry Brown found Smits. Now, after the '94 playoffs, Smits said, he is beginning to be well known in his home country, appearing in magazine articles and such. Perhaps more important, he just feels good getting out of bed in the morning. "I used to ache all over. Now, I feel pretty good."

And for that stretch of the season, as Smits went, so went the team. Rik had another strong game on Friday, February 4, going 9-of-16 for a team-high twenty-one points to lead the Pacers to a 114–93 whomping of the Minnesota Timberwolves. It was the fourth-straight victory by ten or more points, and it brought the streak-long shooting percentage to a monster 57.6 percent.

If not exactly neck and neck, the game was at least interesting through the first quarter. In the second period, the Pacers surged ahead 58–40. The T-wolves fought within four points at 66–62, but the Pacers growled back and they tucked their tails between their legs, retreating to a 83–66 deficit. That was essentially the end of the game.

Former Pacer Chuck Person, who returned to Market Square Arena with a few more pounds but only a skeleton of his old offense, contributed seven points on 2-of-6 shooting in nineteen minutes. Rookie star-to-be Isaiah Rider had a team-high twenty-seven points. Former Duke standout Christian Laettner, making no secret of his disgust with the whole state of Minnesota, contributed only five points in nineteen minutes.

Person, who never exactly hid his skepticism of Smits, had nothing but nice things to say about his old teammates. Another ex-Pacer, Micheal Williams, told reporters, "Rik has so much talent and size. I said last year he was worth all that money."

No one could disagree. Not only was Smits simply playing with more confidence—"He's more aggressive demanding the ball," LaSalle said—he was even adding wrinkles to his game that could only make Brown smile. On one possession against Minnesota, Smits had been cut off under the basket by Luc Longley. Instead of retreating, he simply stepped around the bewildered Longley and dunked from the opposite side of the hoop. The coach and the crowd loved it. "He's just playing great," Brown told the press. "He's always been the key," Miller echoed.

Even the most skeptical Pacer-watchers were slowly, perhaps begrudgingly, beginning to admit that Smits seemed to have turned some corner that only he could see—and the team was willing to follow him because he sure seemed to know where he was going.

For almost as long as Smits had been in town, *Indianapolis Star* sports columnist Robin Miller had made no secret of his opinion. "Every time his name comes up, I tell Donnie Walsh that his commitment is going to bury him—and then Rik can be one of his pallbearers."

Ask Miller now, and he'll say, "He was friggin' great half the time. If he plays as well all season next year, and not just for the last three months, the Pacers are going to be right there at the end of the year.

"I think what Larry Brown did was finally coach him. Bringing Bill Walton in for a ten-day clinic just wasn't getting the job done," said Miller, referring to the personal tutor the Pacers hired to enhance Rik's skills a few years back.

Donnie Walsh agrees in general with Miller's assessment, but he adds a more emotional explanation of Rik's emergence. "I think that finally Rik was able to feel like a member of the team for the first time," Walsh said. "Instead of the coach holding practice for everybody else and just sending Rik down to the other basket to go through post-up drills, Larry had Rik practicing along with everyone. And that meant that when the team started winning, Rik was able to share in that joy. And that just made him play better and better."

LaSalle Thompson concurred. "The guys on the team always liked Rik, but it was kind of like he was just in another corner of the world," Thompson said. And after January, when the season began to turn around, the team "really embraced Rik then. You have to give Larry a lot of the credit for that."

Telling proof of Rik's evolution came after one practice when the team was relaxing, trading quips and friendly insults. The informal rules of these exchanges dictated that a player was immune as long as he chose not to participate. Normally removed from the fray, Smits suddenly jumped into the conversation with a barb. "I don't even remember what he said," Thompson recalled, "but it was funny and everybody just kind of stopped and looked at each other and thought, '*Damn*, Rik.'"

* * *

The Pacers' February fever continued into Game Forty-four, as the Pacers welcomed the Charlotte Hornets back to Market Square Arena on Saturday, February 5. Still without Alonzo Mourning and Larry Johnson, the Hornets played like insects for most of the first half, managed a surprisingly exciting comeback in the third quarter but were finally squished under a resilient Pacer attack as Indiana won 111–102. The victory was the Pacers' fifth in a row, balancing the season-high five-game losing streak the team had suffered in late January.

Echoing the locker room consensus, center Rik Smits told the press, "The turnaround was the Houston game. ... We've been on a roll from then on."

Only Dan Dunkin of *The Indianapolis Star*, somehow forgetting the obligatory believe-it-when-I-see-it cynicism of his colleagues, dared look into his crystal computer terminal to suggest that it might be more than that. "There are turnarounds," Dunkin wrote, "and then there are transformations."

The injury-riddled Hornets had suffered through their own team transformation that season. Starless through the winter, they relied this night on veteran Eddie Johnson for twenty-eight points in forty minutes. He was followed by a balanced swarm: Hersey Hawkins had sixteen points, Dell Curry had fifteen, David Wingate had thirteen, Kenny Gattison had eleven, Mugsy Bogues had eight points.

The Pacers were again led by Smits, who poured in twenty-four points and pulled down eight rebounds in thirty-two minutes. Miller was close behind with twenty-one points on 9-of-11 shooting, hit 3-of-4 from behind the arc, but took no free throws. Kenny Williams provided some of his patented electric thrills with stratospheric rebounds and crowd-pleasing slams scattered among his fourteen points.

After the Hornets game, Dunkin's comrade-in-ink Bill Benner publicly revealed that he had bet Pacers' radio announcer Mark Boyle a whopping ten dollars that the Pacers wouldn't win thirty games that season. With twenty-one victories, the Pacers now were nine shy of costing Benner the price of one of his better ties.

* * *

Pacers stalwarts will remember Game Forty-five as the most exciting contest of the winter. It was something of a marquee match as Chris Webber, Latrell Sprewell and their Dream Team buddy Chris Mullin brought their Golden State Warriors and a 25–19 record into MSA to meet the surging Pacers. Together, the teams brought the fair-to-middlin' crowd of 12,000 to their feet to watch the last minutes of a thrilling 104–99 Pacers victory that went down to the last seconds.

In fact, it was exciting from the git-go. The Warriors led by one point at the end of the first quarter. In the second quarter, Golden State looked golden enough to post a fourteen-point lead—before the Pacers made their own statement, fighting back with Smits, Scott and Miller to pull within three points at the half, 54–57.

The third quarter was won on the glass. With aerialist Kenny Williams leading the way with seven rebounds, the Pacers outboarded the Warriors an incredible 20–3, allowing them exactly zero offensive rebounds while the homeboys pulled down eleven of their own.

Credit Brown with a halftime change in defensive strategy that produced these numbers—as well as limiting Rookie-of-the-Year Webber to a meager four points in the second half.

The game was tied at seventy-six going into the fourth quarter—and it was nothing if not a spirited period. The two teams clawed over each other for a lead that skittered back and forth seven times in the last five minutes.

The crucial sequences came in the last three minutes. Leading 93–92, the Pacers intensified their defense to deny Golden State a good look at the hoop, but in a rare second-half rebound, Chris Gatling grabbed an abortive attempt and reinserted the ball for a 94–93 Warrior lead as the shot clock expired. The Pacers reintensified to force three Warriors turnovers in their next four possessions. With a minute-and-a-half left to play, Reggie hit a fifteen-foot jumper from the baseline to give the Pacers a 97–96 lead.

Despite outscoring Miller on the night 26-17, Sprewell could only hit Reggie on the next Warrior possession, drawing a charging foul. When the Pacers came downcourt, Sam Mitchell was fouled but sank only one free throw for a 98–96 lead. Derrick McKey made one of the brilliant defensive plays that the fans would come to recognize, stealing a Golden State pass. The ball ended up in Mitchell's hands on a misguided drive, but Smits found the 'bound and the bottom of the basket for a 100–96 lead with fourteen seconds left.

Those final fourteen seconds proved enough time for one more Warrior stop (bringing the crowd again to its feet), then a Miller breakaway dunk (the crowd jumped), a Chris Mullen three-pointer (the crowd crouched) and two Miller free throws to seal the victory (the crowd exploded).

Rik Smits continued to prove that his personal transformation was for real, with the best all-around performance of the season: twenty-eight points, thirteen rebounds, four assists. Webber admitted, "Smits is hard to guard."

In retrospect, Smits may have sounded prescient when he said, "This is kind of the beginning, the building stage for the playoffs." And he sounded downright funny when he deadpanned, "I think the fans were happy to see a close game for a change."

Damn, Rik.

The Pacers brought home their sixth-straight victory, the first time that had happened in two years, and pulled within one game of .500 at 22–23. As the oh-so-confident club gave the fans something to really cheer about, the uncontrolled crowd would in turn give the Pacers a taste of decibels to come.

"That was the loudest regular-season crowd I've ever heard," Miller said afterward.

Coach Brown told the press, "The crowd was great. They were a big factor down the stretch. I don't think I've ever felt a crowd response like tonight."

Give it time.

* * *

One more win would give the Pacers a .500 record coming into All-Star break. It would also tie the franchise record of seven consecutive victories, which the Pacers accomplished in 1981 and again in '88.

Ironically—or perhaps fittingly—the big win did not come on the backs of the Pacers' top scorers. Rik Smits, who had played the last six games like a house on fire, proved no match for the Heat's Rony Seikaly, fouling out in twenty-five minutes after hitting only one of three shots from the field and one from the line. Reggie Miller managed only sixteen points on 5-of-15 shooting in thirty-five minutes. Vern Fleming, Dale Davis and Antonio Davis were equally ineffective, combining for only five points in a total forty-one minutes.

If anything, this game proved that, as LaSalle Thompson said, "The team didn't just have to depend on Reggie Miller or Rik Smits to win. If someone wasn't playing well, there would always be someone else to step up. We were playing with the confidence that somebody would just get it done."

The somebodies this night were Derrick McKey and Kenny Williams—Mr. Underachiever and Mr. Over-the-Rafters. Since Smits' recent resurgence, the Pacer pundits—professional and barroom variety—had needed an object for the perennial complaint that some player needed to start producing up to his potential. Sleepy-eyed McKey became the natural stand-in at that role. Pacers management and coaches were convinced that McKey was a hugely underrated player who contributed in so many intangible ways—an occasionally brilliant passing game that made McKey the inbounder of choice on crucial dying-shot-clock possessions; tenacious defense with hands quicker than most three-card monte dealers; a solid sense of where to be when the rebound bounced, etc. The fans on the street, however, wanted points.

So McKey gave them points—thirty of them in thirty-nine minutes on 10-of-12 shooting from the field and 10-of-12 from the stripe, probably the first time since the last seven-game streak that a Pacer shot 83 percent from the field and the line.

His supporting cast for that performance was Kenny Williams. It was obvious to most of the team that Kenny was the most athletically gifted Pacer. It was equally obvious that the fans loved his electrifying leaps, his lightning cuts through a crowd of low-flying defenders to spear a high rebound and bring it back down—or flush it for two. This ability to go up and grab what others want may have come from childhood meals shared with fifteen brothers and sisters.

A first-team high school All-America selection, Kenny played only one year of junior college basketball, coming to the Pacers at the unripe age of twenty, which some have blamed for his relative lack of maturity. This night, however, Kenny looked capable of playing every bit as well as two other players who joined the Pacers at even younger ages—Clark Kellogg and George McGinnis.

Despite his popularity with the fans and the team—he was also regarded as the funniest Pacer and quickest with the one-line comeback—and despite the development of a reliable ten to fifteen-foot jump shot, Kenny's playing time had been limited because of some erratic performances and a tendency to foul with no strategic effect.

All was forgiven, at least for this night, when Williams went 9-of-16 from the floor and 7-of-8 from the line for twenty-five points. He also hauled down eight rebounds, three of them at the most opportune moment.

The game had come and gone and come back again over the first forty-six minutes. Indiana led in the first quarter, but fell behind 54–46 at the half. They were still behind 77–73 at the start of the fourth. But in a fast finish that sounded oddly like the end of Golden State game, the Pacers had pulled up by one, 94–93, on Reggie's jumper with three minutes to play. They then stifled the Heat on their next four possessions—and watched in grateful amazement as Glen Rice missed a lay-up with no one within half-a-mile of him.

Bullet? What bullet? I didn't dodge any bullet.

The Pacers had come this far on the strength of Derrick's season-high and Kenny's career-high scoring. On their possession after Rice's missed lay-up, they needed highness in general to pull decisively ahead—and got it as Kenny jumped for a Dale Davis miss, then for his own miss, then for *that* miss, and finally his own put-back.

Rice shook off his embarrassment to make two free throws to pull the Heat within one. Dale was fouled with thirty-eight seconds to play, missed the first freebie and held his breath while the second bounced high in the air—and fell through. Brown would tell the press that, "We got a message from God on that one."

McKey closed out the game with four clutch free throws. Pacers won 102–98, tying their win-streak record and shutting down for the long, All-Star break weekend. Their only regret: It was too bad to go on vacation when they were playing so well.

* * *

Game Forty-seven took the Pacers to San Antonio to visit another of Larry Brown's former coaching homes and to take a forty-eight-minute stroll through Mr. Robinson's neighborhood. David Robinson, perennial contender for this or that league honor—he would win the scoring title this year—was spurring the Spurs along a 36–14 season, second in percentage points to Houston in the Western Conference's Midwest Division.

The game was a clash of winning streaks. The Spurs had won nine in a row; the Pacers, seven. It was also a game of shooting streaks. Three times in the game, the Spurs burst through the Pacers defense to race ahead. First, the Spurs ran off nine points in a tad over two minutes in the first quarter. Second, ahead by nine with a little less than two to play in the half, San Antonio hit for seven points before the buzzer.

And finally, with the Pacers clawing back to within eight points (89–81) with six minutes left in the game, the Spurs extended the lead to fifteen in less than twenty seconds on a three-point shot, a three-point play and a technical foul called on Larry Brown. The streaks had struck. But when the spray had settled, it was Robinson—playing his usual Admiral-ble game with thirty-four points, ten rebounds and nine assists—and the Spurs who extended their streak with a 109–100 victory.

Looking statistically more like the Pacers than the Pacers, the Spurs shot 54 percent and had three players score above twenty. For Indiana, Reggie had a team-high twenty-three points. The totals dropped after that, although production was balanced among McKey, Smits and Scott, each with fourteen points. Antonio grabbed a career-high fifteen rebounds and would have robbed Robinson of game honors— except they both had to stand aside as Dennis Rodman (blond, on this night) skied for nineteen.

The Pacers trailed 58–42 at the half but fought back to outscore the Spurs in the last two periods—but only by seven points.

Despite their fractured win streak, the Pacers would have a hard time feeling terribly shamed by a loss at San Antonio. If, on the other hand, they lost to the Mavericks—in Dallas or Indianapolis or even in their worst nightmares—shame wouldn't begin to cover it.

The Mavs were playing as far from marvelous as might be imagined, sporting a 6–43 record and a 3–22 home tally. This was much the same situation the Pacers had found them in last season when the Mavericks had gone 11–71. They were bad enough to lose to some college teams—but good enough to beat the Pacers 105–104 on February 5, 1993. That was the sort of bad trip that had flashback potential.

There was another reason for concern that night. Larry Brown, complaining of chest pains before the game, put himself on injured reserve and handed the reins to assistant Bill Blair. No one doubted Blair's abilities, but it was a change—and any change can alter a smoothly functioning machine. And, if anyone was really looking for omens, there was always this: Gar Heard, Brown's other assistant, had been interim coach of the Mavericks in 1993, including the period of the Pacers' loss.

The Pacers did manage to play near the level of their competition, conspiring with the conspicuously awful team to tie a Dallas record for lowest combined score: 157 points. Fortunately, they were divided 84–73, with the Pacers on the high end.

The younger Mavs did whatever good work the Dallas team managed that night. Jamal Mashburn had seventeen points and six boards. Jimmy Jackson had fourteen points and six boards—hardly All-Star numbers but as good it got for Dallas. Ex-Pacer Greg Dreiling did, however, shoot 67 percent from the field—as a starter, no less. It was only two for three, but the big center was no doubt happy with the stat.

On the plane ride home from Charlotte on November 28, 1992, the night Reggie Miller scored a phenomenal fifty-seven points—and, incidentally, earned a recurring chant of "Reg-gie, Reg-gie" from the Hornets' crowd—Dreiling told the Pacers TV crew that he was delighted to have contributed to the victory with his one field goal: "I don't think I'll ever forget the night Reggie and I lit 'em up for fifty-nine points," Dreiling quipped.

Dreiling was as decent a fellow who ever wore a Pacers uniform, but he was a journeyman player at best. Perhaps his greatest claim to fame was as the highest-scoring player in Kansas prep history and then as a standout as a Jayhawk. For a while, the university even used an old picture of him at the front of the historical stat section of their programs. Watching U of K play Indiana at the Hoosier Dome two years ago, Pacers President Donnie Walsh flipped through the program, saw Dreiling's picture and moaned, "Don't remind me."

LaSalle said the team remembered Greg as a good guy. But the final book on Dreiling was written in retrospect. "You got to remember," LaSalle said, "that Bo Hill decided to hang on to Dreiling instead of bringing Antonio back from Europe." (In 1990–91 and 1991–92, Antonio toiled in the obscurity of the Greek Basketball Association as a member of Panathinaikos of Athens.)

If the Pacers gave the hometown fans a moment of worry in Dallas, Coach Brown also caused a few furrowed brows. Brown flew back with the team and checked into Methodist Hospital on Friday. After some tests, he was given the green light to resume his coaching duties—and everybody in the city breathed a little easier.

* * *

Although the Pacers had more or less artfully avoided disaster in Dallas, they would have to do considerably better when the Seattle SuperSonics came to Market Square Arena for Game Forty-nine on Sunday, February 20.

If the Pacers should have been unsettled by Seattle's league best-record—36–12 coming into the game—they didn't seem to know it. If Derrick McKey was intimidated at the prospect of playing his old pals on his new home court, he didn't act like it. And if Detlef Schrempf had something special to show his old fans, he couldn't find it.

The Derrick-for-Detlef trade had drawn mixed reviews from most Pacers fans—equally mixed between cries of woe and cries for Walsh's head. But Donnie knew it was a trade in the team's best interest. "We'd been talking about the trade for two years," Walsh remembered. "But we had to wait for a number of reasons, mostly because we didn't like their terms. In the end, though, we had to take the financial deal they dictated because Det was coming to the end of his contract and he would be expecting a pretty big hit in his new contract with us. He pretty much knew he had us—all he had to do was point to his stats over the last year. But he would be asking for that at a point in his career when, simply in terms of his age, his effectiveness would probably be waning. That was one reason to trade him.

"The second reason was to gain an advantage for our team, although that may be difficult for some of the fans to understand," Walsh explained. "Detlef is the kind of player who isn't working well unless he's playing a lot of minutes, and a lot of those minutes would have to be in the low post. But in order to post Det, you have to take Rik out of the post, and Det also replaces Dale at power forward at a point in Dale's career when he needs the experience. So the trade made sense simply from a basketball point of view."

LaSalle remembered something else. "You could see in the pre-season that Larry and Det weren't getting along real well," LaSalle said. "Det gets this kind of scrunched-up look on his face when he listens to you. But if you don't know him, it looks like he's thinking, 'What the hell are you talking about?' He looked at Larry once at practice and Larry just said, 'Take that look off your face.' And, well, that sort of tells you how they were getting along."

All of this was a good four months in the past, in a league where most players are only as good as their last game. But Detlef had been an immensely popular player in Indiana. This, his first trip back to MSA since the trade, had drawn only the third sellout crowd of the season. For many of the fans who came to that Sunday afternoon game, the feelings aroused by the trade were still fresh—and still burned.

They were all but forgotten by dinnertime, after McKey had won the one-on-one game for Indiana's hearts and minds, outscoring Detlef Schrempf 27–6, beating him on the boards 9–5 and handing out five assists to his two. In the process, he lifted his Pacers—now truly *his* Pacers—to a 101–95 victory over the best team in the league.

Although Schrempf had received more than polite cheers when the Sonics were introduced, he may have been unnerved by the direction of those cheers as the game progressed. Sonics coach George Karl called Schrempf's performance "tentative." It may also have had something to do with Derrick McKey, who drew the defensive assignment against Det.

The victory was the Pacers' ninth in ten February games, improving their record to 24–23, above .500 for the first time all season. Things were beginning to click, and the Pacers felt frisky enough to push a little silliness on the promotional end. Dale and Antonio Davis decided to buy tickets for anyone whose last name was Davis. With about 2,000 Davis entries in the Indianapolis phone book, and four free tickets available to anyone who could prove that was their name, the Dynamic Davis Duo ended up buying 1,997 tickets.

Dale later admitted that "it might have been less expensive if our name had been Krystkowiak"—referring to Larry Krystkowiak of the Orlando Magic.

* * *

The fiftieth game of the season brought Dallas to MSA for their only season appearance on Tuesday, February 22. The Mavericks continued to look better than their 7–46 record at that point. Or, if you'd prefer, the Pacers continued to not quite take them seriously enough. Coming off his super performance against the Sonics, McKey told the press that it was "tougher" to get fired up to play a team like Dallas. The Mavs, for that matter, were actually enjoying something of a re-naissance, if you could call it that, having won five of their last twelve games—quite a promising trend for a team that had won only seven games all season.

In any case, the Pacers had a devilishly tricky time with Dallas. Each time the Pacers were able to pull ahead to double-digit leads, the Mavs came back to trail 55–59 at the half and just 76–72 going into the fourth. The game was actually on the line until the final minutes when a 10–2 Pacers run took them from a scary 85–84 lead to a comfortable 95–86 margin that would hold fairly constant until the final: 107–101.

Recovering from a mini slump, Rik Smits had twenty-seven points, eleven re-bounds, a career-high eleven assists and three blocked shots. Perhaps the victory would have been sweeter had the score been more lopsided against this low-volt-age adversary, but a win was a win was a win. The Pacers now enjoyed a 25–23 record on its tenth victory in eleven starts.

* * *

In the fifty-first game of the season, the Pacers traveled to the Magic's kingdom hoping to extend their winning ways. Orlando had other hopes. The Magic would come away with the bigger half of the wishbone on Wednesday, February 23, but only with the help of a much-debatable official's call.

With a minute and a half to play in the first quarter, Reggie Miller and Anthony Bowie were ejected for fighting. However even-handed the double toss may have appeared, it was clearly the Pacers who got the short end of the stick. As the team's all-time leading scorer, Miller's value was obvious. With a five-point-per-game average, Bowie's was too.

This isn't to suggest that their tangle—it's hard to call it a fight—was the result of a deliberate plan. True, Miller had a few words for Bowie after Bowie had checked one of Reggie's patented curls toward an open shot. But Bowie initiated the contact, throwing an arm around Miller's neck and dragging him to the floor where the two thrashed around for almost a minute. No punches were thrown— but the Pacers' offense had been effectively knocked out.

Rik (sixteen points and eleven rebounds), Vern (fifteen points) and Byron (thirteen points) did what they could, aided by Dale's twelve points and eleven boards. But the Miller-light team was ultimately no match for Shaquille O'Neal (twenty-eight points), Nick Anderson (nineteen) and Anfernee "Penny" Hardaway (fifteen points, seven boards and seven assists).

After they stumbled into the half trailing 66–53, the Pacers toughened up in the third, holding the Magic to just fifteen points while they tallied twenty-two. Indiana also outscored Orlando 24–22 in the final period. But in the last minutes, O'Neal was the cop on the beat, dunking the doughnut three times in five possessions—and that provided enough points to lay down the law, 103–99.

* * *

The Pacers were peeved about that Orlando game—so they took it out on the Pistons in Game Fifty-two in Indianapolis on Friday, February 25.

The game was such a lopsided affair that the statistics offer a modest sort of mean-spirited delight. The score at the buzzer was 110–90. The margin was the Pacers' largest over Detroit since November 1989. This tenth victory set a franchise record for most wins in February. Rik tallied twenty-five points and eleven rebounds, his seventh twenty-plus game of the month. The Pacers held an opponent under 100 points for a record-tying twenty-seventh time. OK—you get the picture.

Certainly the Pacers weren't alone this season in taking delight at the Pistons' misfortunes. At their prime in the late eighties and early nineties, the Bad Boys from Motor City had earned a reputation as the nastiest, elbow-throwingest, forearm-shiveringest team in the league. The Pistons were on their well-deserved way to a forward flop to the lottery—and every team who had the chance was all too glad to step on their throats.

Future retiree Isiah Thomas—who always drew some local cheers from fans left-over from his months at IU—still had some spunk in his shot and spring in his legs, hitting for twenty-nine points in twenty-seven minutes. Joe Dumars, the only other Piston left from those championship teams of 1989 and 1990, added nineteen. But they were the only Pistons clicking.

The Pacers took a 59–38 lead into the half and built it as high as thirty-two before dozing through a twelve-point slippage as the Pistons pulled within twenty before the final horn. The glory that was Detroit had passed into Pacers history.

* * *

Game Fifty-three took the Pacers to Chicago Stadium for a rematch with the Bulls, the same team that had broken their hearts a month before—on that Hail-Mary three-pointer by Kukoc—then broken their spirits the next day with a 90–81 beating in Indianapolis. Those had been the first two of a five-game losing streak at the end of an otherwise successful January.

But these weren't the same Pacers. Bolder, braver, more aware of their true potential, the Pacers dominated the game throughout and came away with a 96–86 victory. The win broke a nine-game losing streak to the Bulls that extended back into the 1991–92 season.

True, this was not the same Bulls team that had won three consecutive championships. But even without Michael Jordan the Bulls cruised into that Saturday with a 37–16 record, tied for second in the Eastern Conference. Back in his more gracious days, before he started swinging a bat and certainly before he took that swing at Reggie, Jordan had called Miller the second-best two-guard in the Eastern Conference—behind his truly, of course.

Miller lived up to that praise, scoring a game-high twenty-one points, sixteen in the second half when the Bulls mounted their only serious challenge to Indiana's 47–33 halftime lead. Propelled by a deafening crowd—that only grew louder every time Reggie touched the ball—the Bulls went on a 15–2 sprint to pull within four at 76–72. The Pacers took a deep breath, steadied themselves and pushed their lead back up to ten.

"I think we're just starting to understand what we're capable of," Reggie said after the 96–86 win.

The Pacers advanced to 28–25, the first time they had been three games above .500 since December 1992. It was also their twelfth win in fourteen games and gave them an 11–2 record for February. That record earned Larry Brown accolades as the NBA's Coach of the Month. Many fans also felt that Rik Smits' performance in February deserved something more than runner-up to David Robinson for Player of the Week in the month's first week. Eventually, Smits would get something Robinson may have wanted more—a playoff paycheck enlarged by three rounds. Utah would eliminate Robinson's San Antonio Spurs in the first round.

6
Maddening March

The month of March would prove to be a tough, nearly excruciating exercise in hope and frustration. The Pacers came into the month with a satisfying victory over Portland, but over the twelve-game stretch from March 4 (beating New Jersey) to March 25 (a loss in New York), the Pacers alternated win and loss, win and loss, playing alternately like lions and then like lambs.

A certain schizophrenia might be expected. March was, everyone knew, a very daunting schedule, with back-to-backs against strong teams. But there was also a strong light at the end of the tunnel—a much easier schedule in April with the last eight games played against teams they knew they could beat. The Pacers knew that if they could get through March with their confidence and record reasonably intact, they would have a downhill run to gather momentum for the playoffs.

It would be, of course, much easier to meditate on all of this from the safety of May. In the meantime, March was there to be played.

The first game of March extended the Pacers' march to the post-season with another superb performance in the post. No more Mr. Nice Try, Rik Smits continued to look like seven feet of blond ambition with team highs of twenty-four points and thirteen rebounds as the Pacers knocked off perennial powerhouse Portland.

The Blazers' Cliff Robinson contributed his own team highs of seventeen points and eight rebounds, but got little support from Dream Teamer Clyde Drexler, who managed only nine points on 2-of-12 shooting. Still, Robinson was enough to make it almost a "Cliff hanger" before the Blazers hung it up.

Things looked bleak for the home team halfway through the second quarter with the Blazers leading 41–33. Indiana then commenced a 15–6 run to take a 48–47 lead into the half.

At the start of the third quarter, a brief series of possessions gave the Blazers a 51–50 lead—their last, as it turned out. The Pacers then gave Portland a ten-point demonstration of defensive determination and offensive power. During that unanswered run, which included a technical foul on Cliff Robinson, the only one doing any Trailblazer talking was their radio commentator, Mike Rice. Sitting at courtside, Rice was talking louder and more angrily with every whistle. Somewhere between "bonehead" and "bozo"—or some such words—referee Steve Javie interrupted Rice's broadcast to bring him this official announcement: Yer outta here.

Perhaps more comfortable in the ensuing quiet, Portland blazed to within four at 67–63 before the Pacers punched the lead up to twelve. The Blazers challenged again—sort of—cutting the lead to nine at 81–72. Again the Pacers applied themselves with a 9–0 run. The teams traded spurts before the final score was settled: 106–94. In snapping a six-game Portland winning streak, the Pacers nudged their season record to 29–25—the first time they had been four games over even since February 1990—and their home record to 17–9. If there was any bad news in the drubbing, it was the Pacers' fall from statistical grace: They shot only 46 percent from the field.

* * *

When the Pacers took the floor at Market Square Arena before Game Fifty-five against the New Jersey Nets, the hometown fans gave them their just desserts: A standing ovation for the record-shaking run the team had cooked up to warm the winter. The team, in turn, responded by handing the Nets their fair share of Pacers poundcake.

This time, though, it wasn't Rik Smits serving. After cracking ten eggs over New Jersey's head in the first quarter, Smits' back began to twitch and seize up. Smits sat the rest of the game. All of that emptiness around the rim was quickly filled, however, as the Pacers collectively rose to the occasion. With eleven blocked shots, fourteen dunks, and 56 percent shooting on 46-of-83 field goals, the Pacers occupied most of the available airspace and tied up the Nets, 126–110.

Antonio Davis had a career-high six rejections, Dale added three, and Derrick McKey had twenty-four points. Kenny Williams had fourteen points and eleven rebounds in twenty-six minutes of play. It was the second of four times that year that Kenny would lead the team in rebounds. It always seemed that he should do it more often. The team called him all sorts of things. Hot Breath—don't ask why— Flame Thrower, but most frequently of all, some reference to deer: Bambi, Deerhead. Hey, the guy jumped like a deer.

Although Reggie had a relatively bland fifteen-point night, Nets threat Derrick Coleman was a bowl of cold pudding, choking down his fifth foul in the early minutes of the second half and finishing with eleven points in nineteen minutes.

New Jersey Coach Chuck Daly broke an unwritten rule of the NBA in his postgame comments by complimenting the Pacers as "a nice team." Nice? *Nice?* What exactly does he mean, "nice?"

"Nice" ain't in the league's vocabulary. Daly could have said "tough." Or "determined, energetic, aggressive." Or: "They're a young team playing with a lot of confidence and, of course, Reggie Miller is always going to give you problems"—sure. But "nice?" That's like telling Bill Laimbeer he has pretty eyes.

Perhaps realizing his gaffe, Daly quickly added. "They're probably playing the best basketball of anybody in the East." Well, OK then, that's better.

The crowd certainly wasn't very nice that night. They were, in a word, leonine—roaring with their pride like nothing anyone had ever heard. Vern Fleming said it was the loudest crowd he could remember in MSA. Give it time, Vern.

* * *

The shouting was at least momentarily quieted by the next game, a heart-breaker they lost in Atlanta in the final seven seconds when the Hawks' Danny Manning took a pass from the sidelines and drove up the lane. His lay-up proved to be the final bucket of the evening, giving the Hawks a 90–88 edge that would be threatened, but not dented, by Byron Scott's own last-second drive—which Manning blocked.

Moral victories are not counted in this league—but they can in a team's spirit. Larry Brown could take some solace in the fact that this very narrow loss had come against the league's best home record—26–3—and only after a very close series of possessions in the last two minutes of play. At the beginning of that final span, the Pacers had the lead at 86–83. Kevin Willis hit a hook shot, but Derrick McKey couldn't quite persuade his next shot to go down: It scooped around the rim and scooted away. Then the Hawks' Mookie Blaylock drained a three-pointer to take them up 88–86. On the next Pacer possession, Dale Davis got the ball in the paint but was whistled for walking.

Mookie drove to the cup—but blew the shot. Dale made his amends at the other end by stuffing Workman's missed lay-up and tying the game at eighty-eight with just under eleven seconds to go. From that point, though, it was all Manning, who cut through lanes and seemed to catch the Pacers just watching. A tad more defensive hustle might—just might—have made a difference. Perhaps Larry Brown could take some solace in the thought that his current pupils had been beaten by a player he had coached for four years in college and two years in the pros.

Another bit of salve for the wound: The Pacers had almost beaten the Hawks without Smits, the key that had started their mid-season surge. Rik's back spasms had kept him in Indianapolis while the team flew to Atlanta.

Although Antonio Davis had contributed fourteen points and eight rebounds to the losing cause, he still wasn't catching the coach's eye as consistently as he might be expected to. Smits and Dale had been playing too well for Larry to find many minutes for A.D. It was perhaps still too early for anyone to realize who this other Davis—this big-bodied kid from Oakland, California—really was.

* * *

The team came back to Indianapolis, picked up Rik and headed out again for Game Fifty-seven, played in Milwaukee on Wednesday, March 9. It was a game the Pacers figured to win easily. The Bucks were 17–42, having won just eight home games. They wouldn't get much better as the season progressed and could look forward only to a high pick in the lottery—something they certainly got, using their eventual Number One pick to acquire Purdue's Glenn Robinson.

The Pacers came into the game with a healthy head of steam and an almost healthy Rik Smits. But Rik only played briefly (sixteen minutes) and scored scantily (six points) and was hardly the factor he had been over that recent stretch of season.

If Rik appeared to have forgotten some of his better steps, the rest of the team looked as if they'd forgotten which foot was left and which was right. They turned the ball over an appalling twenty-seven times—one for each foul they committed and eleven more than the Bucks. Such shenanigans couldn't completely cancel another strong shooting performance, 38-of-69, and a decisive 45–28 edge in rebounding.

The pluses and minuses were pretty evenly balanced, though, through the first three quarters. The Pacers led 28–27 after one, took that edge into the half, 51–50, and barely increased it after three periods, 73–71. In the fourth quarter, Pooh Richardson returned to the form he had displayed at the beginning of the season and led the Pacers to a 105–94 victory, contributing eight points and two assists.

With twenty-four minutes of play, it was Pooh's longest game since coming off the injured list. Based on the strength of his performance, Brown announced his intention to return Pooh to the starting lineup in the next game, a road trip to New Jersey.

* * *

For seven-years and an 18.2 million dollar contract, the Pacers were heavily invested in twenty-seven-year-old Pooh Richardson. He had come to the Pacers with Sam Mitchell from Minnesota in the trade for Chuck Person and Micheal Williams, and had been highly recommended by former UCLA teammate Reggie Miller. In his early-season starts, Pooh had seemed able to uphold his end of the deal. He had averaged 14.2 points, 8.4 assists and 3.2 turnovers per game.

The point guard position is generally conceded to be the most important on a team. Even the dominant centers in the NBA—Ewing, O'Neal, Robinson, Olajuwan—understand that someone has to set up the play and pass them the ball. That someone is the one-guard, the on-court glue that holds a team together, the coach's first and most direct representative in the game.

Donnie Walsh laughingly explained how tough Larry Brown could be on point guards: "No coach will ever completely love a point guard, because every coach is always thinking, 'It should be *me* out there.' Because Larry played point guard in college and the pros, it's only worse."

After beginning the season as the Pacers' starting point guard, Pooh had missed thirty-two games with a persistent calf injury. Although he had been eased back into the starting lineup over the course of six games, it was still natural to assume that the team and Pooh would need some time to fully reacquaint themselves after a three-month separation.

Game Fifty-eight in New Jersey would prove that. Richardson played twenty-seven minutes, scored four points and had five assists. His points were hardly the point, though. No one on the team other than Reggie had more than eight. Miller's twenty-six points and the rebounding of the Davis fellows—Dale with thirteen, Antonio with ten—were the only reasons to smile.

Coach Brown told the press that he was especially perplexed by the way Pooh led the team on fast breaks: "Every break was an adventure." Richardson admitted after the game that he'd had difficulty finding his rhythm and controlling his team's tempo. As a result, the Pacers could muster a mere seventy-three points, a season low. Recognizing a bargain win when they saw it, the Nets skated through the game and ended up on top, 87–73.

* * *

In Game Fifty-nine, the Pacers were delighted to see the Milwaukee Bucks back at Market Square Arena—just as a seasick sailor is happy to find a porthole. After botching the New Jersey game, the Pacers weren't exactly looking like—or feeling like—the same team that had run off a record month in February and maintained that momentum in the first two games in March. Now, on Saturday, March 12, they needed a win to keep the month above .500 and their heads above water.

They got it, 104–97—but it was an uneven, sloppy victory. It featured a fourth quarter frighteningly reminiscent of fourth quarters from the season's start, when the Pacers developed a nasty habit of heading to the locker room while the opponents were still playing. Counting this and the previous New Jersey game, Indiana was shooting a miserable 28 percent in the final period. In the Milwaukee game, they were outscored 28–19 in the fourth and were saved only because the Bucks shot barely better at 40 percent, not enough to overcome the 85–69 advantage the Pacers took at the end of the third. The Bucks still closed to within four points with thirty seconds to play. Close doesn't count in the NBA, but it looked very worrisome to the Pacers, who were facing a fourteen-day stretch in which they'd play four pairs of back-to-back games against winning teams.

Although Pooh had a statistically better game with thirteen points, ten assists and no turnovers, the team still expressed some trepidation. Brown told reporters, "He's not in great shape…and he's got to be more of a leader. He's got to earn respect from these guys, because I think Haywoode and Vern gained their respect because of their effort and unselfishness."

Vern, ever the master of the double-entendre when dealing with the press, told reporters, "The bottom line is winning and just waiting your turn." This was a very judicious and only quasi-ironic comment: For the first time in his career, Fleming had drawn a DNP-CD (stat lingo for "did not play—coach's decision").

Others on the team thought Pooh had already had his turn—and perhaps had turned the wrong way. In the 1992–93 season, the Pacers had lost a game in Philadelphia and Coach Bob Hill suspected that some of the team had not played with as much energy as they should have—probably because they'd been out late the night before, gambling in nearby Atlantic City, N.J.

The story goes that Hill approached Pooh after the game and said, in effect, "I know some of the guys were out late, and I want you to tell me who they were." At first, Pooh resisted. But Hill badgered him, saying: "If you were a real team leader like Magic Johnson, you wouldn't put up with that kind of stuff." Pooh finally gave in.

As LaSalle said, "In a sense, Pooh was too nice a guy. He sincerely wanted to be liked and would end up agreeing with whoever he talked to last." Whatever the psychology was behind Pooh's revelation, it ended up costing him. In a team meeting several days later, Hill was chastising the team for their lack of effort and focus. To make his point, he turned his ire on the players who had made the Atlantic City trip. "I know who you are because Pooh told me," Hill said. That was pretty much the end of Pooh's ability to command the team—or his teammates' confidence.

Another version of the same story said that no one actually went to Atlantic City—but that Pooh made up some names just to get Hill off his back. It hardly matters. The effect was the same.

Thompson wouldn't deny or confirm either version, but did say with a smile, "There's no doubt we've got some guys on this team who'd be ideal poster boys for Gamblers Anonymous."

* * *

The scene for Game Sixty—a March 15 meeting with the Knicks at Madison Square Garden—was set by Byron Scott's comment to reporters: "If you want to be the best, you have to beat the best." It was a comment that would be echoed by

Reggie Miller two months later when he said, "I want the Knicks" More than any other team, New York had been the immovable object for the Pacers' all-too-resistible force. So great was the Knicks' reputation, it was easy to forget that the Pacers had beaten them a year ago, on April 16, 1993, 100–94—and then again in the first round of the 1993 playoffs, an awesome 116–93 drubbing in Indianapolis. But winning in the Garden was almost impossible: The Pacers were 2–29 on the Knicks' home court and had lost eight straight coming into this game. New York made it nine straight.

And the Pacers' uncertainties at point guard continued. Richardson started but mustered only four points and four assists. Fleming had eleven points and three assists, reappearing in the rotation as Richardson, complaining of flagging stamina, sat early in the first and third quarters. Workman played only nine minutes, assisted on three baskets but could not score.

On the other side of the scoreboard, Knicks guard Derek Harper had seventeen points and twelve assists—more than the Pacers' quarterbacks combined. And Hubert Davis, replacing the injured John Starks, added fifteen points and four assists.

Ewing had his usual excellent game, as did Miller—roughly a draw on the offense. Unfortunately, Smits wasn't playing with his February fever; he had only ten points.

Yet somehow through all that computation the Pacers were able to make a fine game of it. The teams were tied at the quarter. The Knicks were up only four at the half, 48–44, and only nine at the end of three. The Pacers reached down into recent memories and dragged forth a gutty effort to take the lead 76–74 with five minutes to play. As the national media had noted all year, apparently the Knicks just did that sort of thing because they liked to scare themselves. New York went on to outscore the Pacers 14–6 and win the game handily, 88–82.

* * *

If losing to the Knicks had worn them out or worried their spirit, the Pacers sure didn't show it the next night. Back at Market Square Arena on March 16, the Pacers met the Phoenix Suns and eclipsed them, showing the league and the fans that their honeymoon with victory was far from over.

The shooting star was, no surprise, Reggie Miller, who blazed in thirty-four points on 13-of-19 field goals and 7-for-7 from the line. Richardson and Fleming split the duties at point guard almost evenly, each having an unexceptional outing, scoring in the mid-single digits. Smits, no longer lost in space, chipped in eighteen points and seven rebounds. The unexpected star of the occasion was longtime resident astronaut Kenny Williams, who made good on his first career start as a Pacer:

eighteen points and eleven rebounds.

Phoenix had its way through most of the first half. The Pacers missed eleven of thirteen shots and trailed 54–38 coming into the closing minutes of the half. A 10–0 run fueled their hopes at the half, and the Pacers kept accelerating into the third with a 12–6 run to tie the score at sixty, then pulled ahead at the end of the quarter, 80–74. They would never lose that lead. When the Suns threatened to break through at 96–94, the Pacers just jumped higher: Dale Davis out-rebounded the Suns for his own missed free throw, then found Captain Kenny soaring through the lane on his way to the hoop. Indiana was on its way to a 13–4 run and a 109–98 win—much to the satisfaction of Coach Brown and President Walsh, who told the press, "This was the best."

Walsh's happiness was matched by the fans, who gave the Pacers their fourth sellout of the new year. They may have come to see superstar Charles Barkley, but at the end of the game they were standing up for their Pacers.

Just as he had after the Pacers' 109–108 shocker in Phoenix last season, Sir Charles praised the Pacers and graciously assessed them as a much better team than their record suggested—"definitely a team of the future." Many in Indiana wanted desperately to believe him.

* * *

The Phoenix game put the Pacers on the brink of another franchise record. They welcomed Atlanta to Market Square on Friday, March 18, hoping to extend their home winning streak to a dozen. Earlier in the season, however, the Hawks had learned a lesson about broken win streaks—and were eager to return the favor.

It was close—close enough that a questionable call, or the lack of one, might have turned the game in the last eight seconds. But it went down in the books as just an "L"—no asterisk for Almost, Really Close or even Protested, which is what Larry Brown did.

"That's not fair," Brown said after the game. "That's just not fair. And it's happening to us too much and that's not right."

Maybe the NBA will one day have an instant replay for officials' review…naaaah. Too many calls in too many games.

With the Hawks up 79–78, the Pacers had three chances to take the lead. First, Pooh misfired as the shot clock was about to expire. Then McKey, reappearing in the lineup after missing the Phoenix game with a pulled calf muscle, missed on a dash to the hoop. Dale and Jon Koncak each held a piece of the rebound, but Dale jumped higher on the jump ball. The Pacer possession ended up in Reggie's hands with eight ticks left.

He faked, got Mookie Blaylock into the air and—as the Pacers saw it—down on top of him as he released the shot. The officials figured it had been Miller leaning into the contact and kept their whistles dry. Manning grabbed the rebound, scooted downcourt and jammed the game's last score. Workman got one more desperate look from behind the arc but couldn't connect.

Workman's failure, such as it was, couldn't deflect suspicion that Richardson's reclaimed position in the starting lineup wasn't working out. Although still happy with the developing defense, Brown was anything but pleased with the seventy-eight-point production—a total that will spell L-O-S-S against almost any team. Never shy about critiquing point guards, the coach told the post-game conference, "We had no dribble penetration. We've got to have a point guard to create something for himself or somebody else."

Another culprit in the offensive demise: the whole team's inability to hit free throws. The Pacers shot 13-of-27 that night at MSA, proving that sometimes charity doesn't begin anywhere.

* * *

The Utah Jazz came to Market Square Arena on March 19, dancing happily along their own road to the playoffs. Since the All-Star break in mid-February, the Jazz had won 12-of-16, beating the Rockets twice, the Spurs twice and the Suns twice. Moreover, the Jazz seemed to have the Pacers' number, beating them four straight. In short, it looked like an evening in hell—and another "L"—for the shaky-breaky Pacers. Still, the bookies were smiling at the Pacers. The national betting line for the Pacers' 63rd game of the season had the Pacers by four over the Jazz.

How do they do it?

Pacers, 107; Utah, 103.

The Pacers did it with balanced points and balanced point guards. The offense was well spread to meet the spread. Smits regained his touch for nineteen. Miller hit 67 percent from the field and the line, 6-of-9 and 4-of-6, for seventeen total. Sam Mitchell, Derrick McKey and Kenny Williams had fourteen each.

Richardson and Workman split the duties at one-guard with twenty-seven and twenty-one minutes respectively, but Haywoode turned in slightly more respectable numbers, rolling seven points and seven assists while Pooh had double sixes. Sometimes luck comes down to just a point.

In this case, though, the Pacers made their own luck—good and bad. They came out like gangbusters, pounding out a seemingly bulletproof nineteen-point advantage in the second quarter and holding most of that as they went into the half leading 52–36. They even drew an eighteen-point lead two minutes into the fourth period—then watched the Jazz draw even at 103–103 on two Jeff Hornacek free throws with less than a minute to play.

The Pacers came back with a feed into Smits, who was matched up against Felton Spencer. Spencer drew his sixth joker and cashed out. Smits made both penalty shots.

With thirty-five seconds to make up the 105–103 edge, Tom Chambers saw his short shot knocked out of the lane and eventually into Reggie's hands for two foul shots—made one, missed one. Sam Mitchell, who had pulled the team along this far by sinking five free throws in the final three minutes and shackling Karl Malone in the process, then unnerved Hornacek's final three-point try.

Call it good luck to escape the embarrassment of a loss after such leads. Or say it was about time Rik Smits got back in gear. Or just point to Mitchell. And finally, point to third-year tower of power Dale Davis, who led all rebounders with sixteen—Malone had only eight—as the Pacers outbounded Utah decisively 48–34.

* * *

So, with that gutsy effort behind them, the Pacers continued their own, idiosyncratic version of March Madness by attempting to play the Cleveland Cavaliers with their eyes closed. How else to explain a sixty-one-point effort in Game Sixty-four on Tuesday, March 22? The game was played in Richfield Coliseum—at least the Cavs were there; it was hard to tell exactly where the Pacers were. The Cavaliers may have wondered as well, but kept taking practice shots until they had ninety-three points and figured it was time to go home.

Now, Dale Davis did shoot 60 percent—3-of-5. Haywoode shot 40 percent, 2-of-5, and hit a free throw, which meant that he had more points than Reggie, who contributed just four on 2-of-5 shooting, another whopping 40 percent. Everyone else was shooting thirty-something; but this was no sitcom, or even a drama—it was more like a farce.

Saturday's hero, Sam Mitchell, became Tuesday's color commentator: "Tonight was just the worst thing I've ever been a part of as far as basketball." As far as basketball? Uh, Sam, were you on the Titanic? (No, but he *was* on the Minnesota Timberwolves for three years, during which time they managed to win only sixty-six games.)

Larry Brown opened his post-game press conference with his own version of comedy. "At least we held 'em under a hundred," he said. (It's hard to shoot when you're giggling.)

But seriously, folks, this was one sorry display against a team that was playing without starting center Brad Daugherty, starting power forward Larry Nance and only felt the need to use All-Star point guard Mark Price for fourteen minutes off the bench.

It was the team's most offensively non-offensive game since...well, let's see, where is that box of clippings from the ABA? No, nothing here. Let's just call it the worst night of Pacer basketball since the Civil War.

* * *

Of course, momentum swings, winning streaks and slumps are all part of any sports season. But this was different. For most of March, the Pacers appeared to be two teams in one. The team that beat Utah was not the same team that lost in Ohio.

Some folks were saying, though, that this really wasn't all that different from the same old Pacers of the past four years, the team that was up and down with such metronomic regularity that its four-season record was 164–164.

In past seasons, Pacers fans could take some cold comfort at the thought that such schizophrenia was better than being simply one lousy team waiting for the draft. If nothing else, the old Pacers had offered a certain sort of entertainment quite apart from any athletic display. The fans could amuse themselves wondering who would show up for *this* game, Dr. Jekyll or Mr. R.U. Joking?

But this was a different team, with a different coach and a different spirit. The proof was still two weeks away, but the first shred of evidence came the night after the Cleveland Catastrophe—in a custom-tailored opportunity to reclaim a bit of confidence by playing the same team again. In the infrequent NBA equivalent of schoolyard "do-overs," the Pacers and the Cavaliers met again twenty-four hours later.

Game Sixty-five on March 23 in Indianapolis was another Pacer disaster from a statistical point of view. At least Miller was Mr. Consistency. In his thirty-six minutes of play, the team's all-time leading scorer had a stat-defying four points for the second game in a row. Vern Fleming, who played sixty seconds, had two points.

Team honors that night went to Derrick McKey, who scorched the nets with...twelve. Somewhere in between were Dale, Rik, Haywoode, Pooh and Antonio with ten—all of them with ten points. Byron almost got into the club, too; he had nine.

Looking at the Pacers' quarter-by-quarter score, it's difficult to discern a victory in the making: 18–22–20–18 for a grand total of seventy-eight. Yet victory is what it was, thanks largely to Cleveland's twenty-seven-point first half—that's half, not quarter. They had sixteen in the first quarter, eleven in the second, twenty-eight in the third, twenty-two in the fourth. Total: seventy-seven.

This game was nothing for either team to write home about. The Pacers blew a nineteen-point lead in the third. With eight-tenths of a second to play, Dale won the game on a put-back basket of a Reggie air ball—call it a pass.

Miller had this post-game flash for the press: "We're not playing very well." Brown concurred, again suggesting that bringing Pooh back as the starting point guard had disrupted something. It was hard to say what, but it was easy see the results in the win-loss columns. "I think we need a change."

* * *

On March 25, the Pacers played the season's sixty-sixth game, hoping—if not exactly hopeful, considering their recent play—that they might win just one against the New York Knicks that year. The Knicks had already taken three regular-season contests, and the Pacers wanted to at least equal last year's playoff record against New York: 1–3.

It wouldn't happen this time. Still, the evening was not without its highlights. As Dan Dunkin of the *Star* quipped, "It took a fight for a ballgame to break out Friday night at Market Square Arena."

The pugilists were Haywoode Workman and Greg Anthony, both ejected after officials and teammates pulled them off the floor near the Knicks' bench. It was halfway through the fourth quarter, with the Pacers down by eleven points and reaching new heights of frustration.

Although their tenacious defense had handcuffed New York all night—and would eventually hold the Knicks to just twenty-seven field goals, a record-tying low for a Pacers opponent—Indiana's offense could do nothing against an onslaught of free throws. The Knicks were awarded forty-three penalty shots, twenty-two more than the Pacers.

An exasperated—call him furious—Brown blamed the discrepancy on lopsided officiating. "They spent the whole game on the line," he said of the league's most notoriously rough-and-tumble team. "When we make the play, they're fouls. But when they make the plays, they're clean blocks."

As a result, Smits could muster only 3-of-9 shooting and took only two foul shots in twenty-two minutes of play. Dale Davis was able to put down 6-of-10 shots, and took seven free throws—not exactly a threat given the fact that his season's free-throw percentage hovered around fifty.

Maybe Haywoode was just more frustrated than everyone else. Or maybe he thought that a shot of adrenaline would be the only thing that would pull his team through. It almost did. The team fought back from their eleven-point deficit and with less than a minute to play, Pooh drove the lane and tied the score.

But as they had done so many times in the season, the Knicks just knuckled down and got the win, 85–82. Derek Harper shook the defense and laid it in for the go-ahead bucket with half a minute left. Afterward, Knicks coach Pat Riley told the press, "We just gutted it out. Another possession or two and we probably would have lost." Prophetic words.

* * *

Game Sixty-seven gave the Pacers another chance to test their mettle against the Chicago Bulls on Saturday, March 26. As they had in that last New York game, the Pacers took another longtime Eastern Conference nemesis right to the edge—but couldn't quite push them off the mountain.

Again, it was almost a startling comeback. Down 73–63 late in the third quarter, the Pacers scrapped their way to within one, 89–88, with a minute to play. Their fourth-quarter surge had been the handiwork of bench forward Kenny Williams, who dropped in ten of the next twelve Pacers points, pulling the team within three with most of the fourth left to play. Somebody had to do it that night, because Reggie and Rik had been standing small all evening. Reggie finished the game with only eleven points. Smits was accurate, but not often enough. His 4-of-5 from the field and 6-of-6 from the line only totaled fourteen points. The rest of the Pacers' scoring was well balanced among the Davis duo, Byron, Derrick and Pooh, and the team combined to shoot an impressive 58 percent.

Even the defense looked tough, taking the Bulls by the horns and allowing them to score only one point in the last three minutes—and that was a free throw that boosted Chicago from eighty-nine to ninety. And even then, with sixteen seconds to play, the Pacers couldn't push the rock up that extra few inches to win. It was a deflating loss. But although they couldn't know it for a while, it was one of the last three losses in a season that still had fifteen games to play. If anyone had walked into the locker room and announced that…well, there probably would have been a few laughs in the background. Then again, maybe not.

* * *

In Game Sixty-eight, played on Monday, March 28, in Market Square, the Pacers found all those points they had been looking for against New York and Chicago. As a matter of fact, they almost found more than they had scored all season. Their 126–93 trouncing of the L.A. Clippers tied their season-best output—against New Jersey at the beginning of the month—but the margin of victory was a season high. As a matter of factual pride, the Pacers still use tapes of this game as the telephone background noise when you wait for someone to answer your call. As exhilarating as it may be, after a while it is possible to grow bored with Mark Boyle's voice telling you: "The Clippers are getting blown out of the building and desperately need a time-out."

Still, it was true. Reggie and Rik hit for twenty-two and twenty-seven points, respectively. And after his cast-adrift performance in Chicago, Miller was full-speed ahead going 5-for-6 from behind the arc.

Haywoode, coming back to start after a one-game suspension for his New York fight—and after Larry Brown had reached the conclusion that maybe Pooh was part of the team's recent problems—added sixteen points and nine assists. True, the Clippers weren't exactly title contenders even with the mid-season addition of legendary Dominique Wilkins. But the Pacers seemed to be really enjoying this one—and perhaps having Workman back in the starting lineup had a lot to do with it. The guys genuinely liked Workman and liked the heart he brought to his work. Player of the year in both basketball and football as a high-schooler in Charlotte, N.C., he was among the most well-rounded and athletically gifted players on the team. His locker room nickname was Groucho Marx—because of his bushy eyebrows.

But what he and the Pacers did to the Clippers was no joke. The Pacers were having their way—taking eighteen more shots, out-rebounding the Clippers by nineteen, hitting well over 55 percent while limiting the Clippers to around 42 percent. It felt very good—for the team and the fans—after the two close and disheartening losses in the two previous games.

* * *

Game Sixty-nine, the last game of March, was played Wednesday, the thirtieth, in Boston. It was a gutty performance, but not one for the highlight films in terms of sparkling offense. If anything won it, it was tough-minded defense—that and perhaps a desire to give coach Larry Brown his seven hundredth professional coaching win stretching back to his first season in the ABA.

The Celtics had a three-game winning streak broken by the 103–99 loss. All had been overtime games, so perhaps fatigue was a factor. They didn't seem able to hold a lead, letting the Pacers—who, truth be told, weren't playing too sharply, either—come back from 49–38 deficit to tie the game at fifty-three in the last three minutes of the first half.

The two teams jockeyed back and forth through the second half. Neither could mount any substantial margin. The Pacers took a seven-point lead with half the final period to play, but Boston came back to tie the game with less than a minute left. Haywoode gave the Pacers a 100–98 lead with a drive up the lane. Sherman Douglas could not hit the second of two charity shots. Workman returned the favor by missing two of his own, but Antonio tipped the rebound back to Haywoode who was fouled again and this time did his job.

Boston got impressive performances from Rick Fox (twenty-eight points) and Dino Radja (twenty-three points), both of whom outscored Smits (twenty-one) and Miller (sixteen). So much for stardom and statistics—except of course for the number 700. Brown was awarded the game ball.

There was one casualty of the evening. Pooh Richardson was twice hit with the "X factor." Boston's Xavier McDaniel—"The X Man"—leveled him with a rock-solid back-pick, and subsequent X-rays revealed a sprained shoulder joint that knocked Pooh out of commission. Although dismaying at the time, Richardson's exit turned out to be a blessing in disguise, assuring Workman's starting spot and cementing the chemistry that would eventually carry the team into June. Meanwhile though, there was April.

7
April Awakening

The first day of April—oops.

Game Seventy was played at Miami. This time, after two losses to the Pacers, the Heat turned it up and burned the Pacers 101–91. Coming off a six-game losing streak and playing without starting center Rony Seikaly, the Heat were beatable—if not quite easy pickings. Miami was tough enough to have played to a 37–33 record; the Pacers were only a notch better at 37–32.

This team certainly looked like a playoff contender—and a team to be reckoned with in the future. Atlanta would find that out, in fact, in the relatively near future. And the Pacers would find out that night.

The shadow of the playoffs made the defeat even darker. The Pacers could see the post-season in the distance, but they weren't sure they were getting any closer. This loss took them a step away.

It was a reasonably close game for most of the first thirty-six minutes. In the final period, the Heat boiled over into a 19–6 run to take the game firmly in control. The Pacers committed eleven turnovers in the quarter.

Miller had twelve points, missing seven shots in a row in one late-game stretch. Smits had eleven. Dale Davis and Byron Scott had twenty apiece and Davis pulled down fifteen rebounds—not bad, but not good enough. Davis told the press after the game, "If the season ended today, with the way we're playing right now, if we went up against a Chicago or New York, I don't think we'd stand a chance."

Fortunately, the team got better—a whole lot better.

* * *

The Pacers hadn't particularly liked their last trip to Miami. Vern Fleming hated the whole state after Saturday, May 2, when the Orlando Magic came to Market Square Arena—and knocked his teeth out the window and him off the roster.

Vern must have felt as if he'd been hit by the entire Sunshine State after Shaquille O'Neal came crashing down on him just as Fleming finished a fast break. The 300-pound Orlando center had trailed the Pacers' point guard down the floor in pursuit of the break and, as Vern elevated, Shaq did, too, with unrestrained—some would say, felonious—glee. His mountainous momentum carried him into

Fleming—and gravity did the rest.

The dazed Fleming was left to pick his teeth off the floor. A six-inch gash in his right knee required multiple stitches: "When they got to ten," Pacers trainer David Craig told reporters, "I stopped counting."

Fleming, of course, was in no condition to answer questions immediately after the injury, but he later analyzed the play: "The mother-_____ squashed me. And they didn't even call a foul."

Nonetheless, the Pacers made the best of a painful situation by kicking Orlando's sizable tourist attraction all over the floor, beating the Magic 128–113, a season high for Pacers points scored. In the process, Indiana sent a message to their prospective first-round playoff opponents.

With a record of 42–29, the Magic were solidly in fourth place in the Eastern Conference behind Atlanta, New York and Chicago, who at that point were jockeying for the first three spots. Although the Pacers had a lot of winning left to do before they would know where they would start the playoffs, Orlando looked to be as likely a place as any.

In any event, this night was Indiana's. The first half was a thrilling battle ending in a 61–58 Pacer advantage. The action got even more intense in the third and the Pacers finished strong. Up a dozen as the fourth quarter began, the Pacers fought off an Orlando comeback that cut the lead to only eight—never a safe margin with Shaquille and Anfernee Hardaway in the game. But that lead held solid, and the Magic started to fall apart as the game was closing.

Reggie had a season-high thirty-eight points, including 15-of-15 from the line. The Shaq showed his stuff with thirty-six points and seventeen rebounds. Kenny Williams added ten points in eleven minutes as the Pacers bench outscored the Magic's 31–16. Smits, returning to his February form, popped in twenty-six points—an encouraging sign as the playoff race warmed up. Workman, now the only healthy point guard on the roster, contributed fifteen assists.

With Fleming's injury, the Pacers contacted and shortly thereafter contracted Lester Conner, a thirty-four-year-old veteran point guard who had played for Brown with L.A. Clippers. Conner was playing in the CBA at the time, but earlier in the season had played with Magic Johnson's All-Stars, a team of journeyman players barnstorming through Europe.

Conner, an old friend of LaSalle Thompson, would be almost immediately accepted by the team and eventually become an important emotional fixture in the locker room and on the bench as the Pacers made their playoff run.

* * *

Despite the loss of Fleming, the team was feeling pretty good, especially after beating Orlando so convincingly. Game Seventy-two of the season brought the Detroit Pistons back to Market Square for what was to be Isiah Thomas' last playing appearance in the state that had first applauded him wearing the cream and crimson.

Vern was out and Rik was down with the flu on Tuesday, April 5, but the team didn't need them in their 105–89 mauling of the almost decrepit Pistons.

The Pacers won for the sixteenth time in eighteen games, improved their record to 39–33 and reduced their "magic number" for securing a playoff berth to two victories.

Starting in place of Smits, Antonio Davis looked practically Dutch, scoring eighteen points and bringing down seven rebounds. Dale seldom looked better, putting away nineteen points and getting just about every rebound A.D. couldn't reach—fourteen in all. And Haywoode continued to look like the point guard of choice, with thirteen points, eleven assists and eight rebounds.

The Pistons fell to 20–52 in Thomas' last active season, a sad end to a brilliant career.

* * *

With their playoff seat dangling a tantalizing two wins away, the Pacers traveled to Charlotte hoping to make it three in a row over the Hornets, having beaten them solidly in two February games.

Perhaps the Pacers were feeling a little too good after beating a very good Orlando team then stomping lowly Detroit. More likely, perhaps the Hornets were simply a much stronger team now with Alonzo Mourning and Larry Johnson off the injured list and back on the floor. Moreover, the Hornets were playing with a real mission: Win or die. Though their two headliners had spent most of the midseason in street clothes, the Hornets had climbed to 32–39 and were still in contention for a playoff spot—if they could play almost flawlessly in their last eleven games.

They sure looked pretty good on April 6 in Charlotte. They shot 51-of-79 from the floor, a stellar 64 percent, including 6-of-12 from behind the arc. They also out-rebounded the Pacers 44–37, and stole the ball ten times, twice the Pacers' pilferage.

Still woozy from his flu, Smits played only three minutes and didn't score. Reggie had a mediocre seventeen points on 5-of-11 shooting. Dale Davis (sixteen points) and Kenny Williams (fourteen points) were the only other Pacers in double figures. The team shot a dismal 38 percent. The result: a gosh-awful 129–90 blow-out loss to the Hornets.

But the numbers seemed beside the point. The Pacers' main problem seemed to be lack of intensity. While Charlotte understandably played as if there were no tomorrow, the Pacers inexplicably hummed along on cruise control.

Coach Brown told the press that he was urgently trying to impress upon his team that this last stretch of the season was crucial, a pre-post-season, so to speak. But the team just didn't seem to get it. "These are just like playoff games," Brown said. "And that's the saddest thing"—because, he concluded, if we get there and play like this, our exit is going to be quick.

* * *

Game Seventy-four was played on Friday, April 8 at Market Square Arena against those Bulls. If ever there were a game that the Pacers coulda, shoulda won—but didn't—this was it.

The story is awful, so let's cut it short: The Pacers were down thirteen in the second quarter. They fought back to take a four-point lead, 92–88 with less than two minutes to play.

The Bulls won.

Only Smits looked like a playoff player, hitting for twenty-five points and getting seven rebounds.

Workman, Scott and Miller each had fifteen points, which ranged in quality from very good to respectable to just-another-night-in-Davenport. The Davis duo had five points—not apiece, combined.

"I don't know what the answer is," Larry Brown said to anyone who would listen. "There comes a time in the game when you have to have some discipline and some leadership, and we haven't found that."

Their record now stood at 39–35. Having gone 11–10 since the first of March, their prospects for doing much better than splitting the rest of the season seemed minimal. At their percentage, with eight games left, the Pacers would be middlin' lucky to finish at 43–39, maybe as good as 44–38, but as likely to end up at 42–40. Welcome to 1990, Part V: Recurring Mediocrity.

Or, just suppose, the Pacers might win, say, every game. Each and every one of the eight games left in the regular season. And, say, finish with a record of 47–35—an all-time NBA franchise high.

Sounds pretty darned good. Let's do it.

They did.

* * *

Larry Brown set the tone, first by telling the team exactly what was necessary—and exactly what he thought about their chances of doing it—but then by insisting that it was indeed possible.

He kept the conference standings posted in the locker room: Here's where Cleveland is. Here's where we are. Here's where we'll be if New Jersey wins tonight. Here's where we'll be if we win.

So they did. They won and won and won and won and won and won and won and won—and then they won some more.

It was almost unreal—unlike anything any Pacer team had ever done. Along the way, there were the usual lines in the papers in which coaches and players said how good it felt to finally be playing so well, as well as they knew they could all along. They were gratifying to read, yes. But this is really the only situation where a fact-by-fact run-through is actually more fun:

They won eight in a row, and set a team record for consecutive victories. They won forty-seven regular-season games, setting a record for best record, so to speak.

They beat Boston. Then they beat Philadelphia. They beat Minnesota and Detroit, and then they beat Washington and Cleveland. Then they beat Philadelphia again for good measure—and to pay them back for that last-second shot by Dana Barros back in January.

And then, because they hadn't forgotten that April Fool's surprise and because it would feel so good, they brought Miami home with them and beat them in front of the hometown fans—and beat them silly, 114–81.

In each of these last games, the Pacers scored at least 100 points. They averaged 117 points per game, once scoring 130 points and another time 133. Along the way, they held their opponents to an average of 98 points. If that 114–81 pummeling of Miami looked a tad like a bad boy torturing a frog, then their 133–88 dismantling of the Seventy-Sixers—a forty-five-point margin—was almost a science experiment.

The victories, in order: Monday, April 11, Pacers beat Boston 121–108. Wednesday, April 13, they beat the Seventy-Sixers, 115–87. Friday the fifteenth, they won at Minnesota, 130–112. Sunday the seventeenth they beat Detroit again, 104–99. Tuesday the nineteenth, they beat Washington 111–110—the only close game and the heart-stopper that almost wasn't. But they did it.

On Wednesday, April 20, the Pacers beat Cleveland 109–98 to secure a crucial advantage for the playoffs. By winning the season series against the Cavs three games to two, the Pacers would get the nod over Cleveland if the two teams finished the season with identical won-loss records—which was exactly what happened.

On Friday, April 22, they beat Philadelphia again. And on Saturday the twenty-third, they ended their season by beating Miami 114–81.

During this splendid run, the Pacers passed many milestones. Reggie Miller became the Pacers' leading all-time scorer April 17. Miller scored his 10,786 point that night in Detroit, taking him above Billy Knight's career total of 10,780.

On April 19, the Pacers won their eighteenth road game of the season in Washington, an NBA franchise record. On April 20, the team won its forty-fifth game of the season, breaking its NBA franchise record of 44–38 established in 1980–81— and attracting a record number of fans to MSA.

Then, on April 22, Rik Smits set a personal career record with forty points in the Philadelphia game. The Pacers' official yearbook says Rik's nickname is the Dunking Dutchman. Perhaps that's his official moniker, but it's tough to imagine the guys in the locker room coming up to Rik after the Seventy-Sixers game to say: "Yo, Dunking Dutchman, nice game. You sure earned your nickname tonight, man." Actually, Smits' teammates call him Scooby Doo because of his resemblance to the canine cartoon character.

And if the Pacers were coming up to anyone after that game, they were probably visiting Lester Conner. Conner's ten-day contract had expired, and he was due to head back to the CBA. Pacers management had offered him a new contract. The team liked him and he liked the team. But he knew what was coming and he wasn't sure he was ready for it.

Oh, he was ready physically. And he felt confident that he had the skills to contribute in the playoff run.

No, his concern was for his emotional state. "You have to understand," Conner said, "the NBA is the big time. And the playoffs are even higher. It had been quite an adjustment for me to gear up emotionally and mentally to play with the Pacers for this long, and now, with the playoffs coming...

"Well, I wasn't sure. I knew I could do it, but then I knew I would just have to get myself back down again to that other level—and I wasn't sure I wanted to subject myself to that process. It would hurt. I knew it and I just didn't know if it was worth it.

"I had pretty much decided that I would go when my ten-day contract was up after the Philadelphia game. I sat in the locker room after the game and I looked at all the guys and, well, I just started to cry."

The team talked to Conner. Late that night, Conner knocked on the door of Donnie Walsh's hotel room. Donnie let him in, dressed in his shorts and Pacers sweat shirt. They talked and shook hands and that was that. Conner stayed with the team through the playoff run and received a full share of the playoff profits at the end—more than a month later.

8
Poof! The Magic Disappear

The Pacers powered into Game One of the playoffs with all the momentum of a runaway train—and all the focused direction of a ride on steel rails. They had just set three NBA Pacer records: Most wins in a season—forty-seven. Most road victories—eighteen. Longest winning streak—eight games. Team confidence was as high as it had ever been, and fan support was rolling like a landslide.

By finishing fifth in the Eastern Conference, the Pacers had avoided potential first-round match-ups against the Atlanta Hawks, the New York Knicks or the Chicago Bulls. Instead, they faced the Orlando Magic, in fourth place with a 50–32 season record. The Pacers and Magic had split the season series, each team winning two games on its home court.

As if they needed to be reminded, the Pacers were running headlong into man-mountain Magic center Shaquille O'Neal, last year's Rookie of the Year and this year's runner-up for the NBA scoring title, missing by a whisker to San Antonio's David Robinson. All 300-plus pounds of Shaq had already run into—and fallen on top of—Pacer guard Vern Fleming at MSA on April 2. That night, the Pacers recovered from the shock of the injury to whip the Magic by fifteen. Fleming, sidelined virtually all of April after the injury, would recover weeks later, but well in time to exact his vengeance.

The other Orlando threat was rookie phenomenon Anfernee "Penny" Hardaway, a 6–7 point guard who seemed destined for an All-Star career. Their supporting cast was nothing to sneeze at, either. Fourth-year pro Dennis Scott was second in the league in three-point shooting. Nick Anderson and Donald Royal had explosive potential.

And, of course, the Magic had the home court advantage. The five-year-old franchise had drawn 161 consecutive sellout crowds to the Orena, as the Orlando Arena was called. Now their fans were bristling with excitement over the Magic's first trip to the playoffs—especially against the team that had tied their record the year before but aced them out of the eighth playoff berth with the statistical advantage of more points scored.

Orlando figured that vengeance was soon to be theirs. Of course, with the arrival of O'Neal and Hardaway, the old snickering references to the "Magic Kingdom" and "Mouseketeers" had disappeared. There were still some lingering innuendos that the NBA was very much interested in establishing the Orlando franchise as a power of the future—a size twenty-two foot-in-the-door to the growing Gulf Coast media market. Those whispers said that the league had been very happy that the Magic had somehow managed the statistically improbable trick of drawing the Number One pick in the 1993 draft, despite having the best record of any team in the lottery. And, of course, O'Neal offered all the larger-than-life appeal of the instant superstar. With the retirement of Michael Jordan, there appeared to be a gap in the NBA dream machine that only a player of O'Neal's dimensions might fill.

The Pacers seemed happily oblivious to all of that. The team was, in a word, unintimidated. They led the all-time series 11–8. Their two losses at Orlando had come much earlier in the season. They knew they were a much better team now.

Further, the Pacers felt they had a definite coaching advantage. Orlando was coached by Brian Hill, who had no playoff experience and, frankly, not much of a pro record before O'Neal and Hardaway arrived. Perhaps there was some apprehension that the Pacers were too well known by his chief assistant, Bob "Bo" Hill, who had been the Pacers' head coach for two-and-a-half seasons before Brown and who was still collecting some 300,000 dollars a year from his terminated Indiana contract. But everyone figured this hardly entered into the equation. At a team meeting, the Pacers quietly calculated they would split the two away games and come back to Indianapolis to win the series.

Nonetheless, before Game One, Brown was nervous. "Coaches are always nervous," he said. "They could've just activated a kid from Germany and I'd be nervous about him."

In a pregame television interview, Reggie Miller mouthed the usual game-but-humble platitudes. "I'm just going to try to get my teammates into it." A standard line, certainly, but one that proved delightfully prophetic.

* * *

Orlando controlled the opening tip and Dennis Scott scored the game's first basket. Reggie Miller answered. Then Nick Anderson for Orlando. Then Rik Smits found the stroke over a double team.

Once the opening salvos were fired, the game settled into a less-than-graceful display of basketball skill. The Pacers looked ragged in the first quarter. Smits and Miller were shouldering the scoring load, but the team was bedeviled by blocked shots, poor passes and missed lay-ups.

The Magic were shooting well, however, and led 16–8 less than five minutes into the game. O'Neal was posting up with considerable success, either scoring or kicking the ball out to his perimeter shooters when the Pacers double-teamed him. Even Tree Rollins crept up the basket for a dunk on an O'Neal assist. Brown watched and waited, finally calling his first time-out at the seven-minute mark.

Inheriting a ten-point deficit, back-up point guard Lester Conner began to staunch the bleeding with an awkward, off-balance shot from the wing that went in as the shot clock was running down. Smits hit another clutch bank shot, and the quarter ended with the Pacers down only six. Despite their erratic play, the Pacers never really appeared to be in danger of unraveling. The rhythm would reappear, just give it time.

Between quarters, the television announced the third-quarter score of the other first-round playoff game being played that night: Miami 58, Atlanta 52. The Number Eight seed was beating the top seed by six points, which may have struck the Pacers as a good sign.

The opening exchanges of the second quarter seemed to offer equally positive omens. During the break, Brown had made major lineup changes, all of which seemed to work. Derrick McKey hit the first shot of the period, cutting the Magic lead to four. Then LaSalle Thompson blocked the Magic response and Antonio Davis hauled down an offensive rebound and was fouled. The team looked sharper, more confident.

As the Magic attempted a diving save of a long Pacers' rebound, Haywoode Workman slipped in, stole the pass and found Thompson alone under the basket for a lay-in. The next Pacer possession drew successive fouls from Larry Krystkowiak, Scott Skiles and O'Neal, finally resulting in two Antonio Davis free throws to whittle the Orlando lead to only three.

The tide, however, was far from turned. Two blown transition lay-ups seemed to deflate the Pacers' run. Not even an injection of Byron Scott and his daring, darned-near reckless drives into the paint could restart it. The Magic came alive and proceeded to dismantle the Pacer defense. With one minute and twenty seconds left in the quarter, the Magic had built the lead back up to seventeen, 54–37.

It seemed only Workman was still playing with the intensity of just seven or eight minutes before. He stole the ball, unfortunately blew a lay-up, but doggedly stole the ball right back and finally hit a jumper from the top of the key. Workman would eventually total seven steals and eleven assists. In the meantime, though, the Magic took a twelve-point lead to the locker room at the half.

The Pacers knew what they had to do. First, they had to improve their shooting. The Pacers shot 36 percent in the first half, the Magic, 53 percent. The Magic also blocked seven Pacer shots. Orlando held small edges in rebounding and assists, but not enough to make a coach lose his temper.

Reggie Miller hit the first shot of the second half, but O'Neal dunked his answer. Nick Anderson drilled a three-pointer and Reggie filed his own response. Usually unflappable Rik Smits got into the referee's face on a questionable call and earned at least enough respect to warrant an immediate make-up call at the other end of the court.

Although the Pacers seemed re-energized in these first few minutes of the half, the Magic still played them relatively even. Shaq's presence seemed capable of neutralizing any swing in momentum.

Even when O'Neal began to show signs of fatigue—after a missed lay-up, Shaq just sat on the floor while the Pacers raced downcourt to score—the Magic were far from finished.

As the third quarter wore on, the action became scrappier and more foul-ridden. This worked in Orlando's favor. Their lead, which had shrunk to eight, was stretched on the third-quarter rack out to twelve again.

Brown called time to insert Byron Scott, who had been absent since the first half. Another timely move. Scott got the ball and quickly buried a three-point shot. It was a small spark, but it began to smolder. Vern Fleming, seeing his first action in weeks, joined Scott for the final plays of the third quarter and helped shave the Magic lead to eight.

It carried over into the fourth quarter. A Fleming steal and—presto-change-o—the Magic's lead was six. Another steal by Fleming and the lead was four.

The air had changed, the sea had retreated and suddenly, in just over two minutes of the fourth quarter, any magic on the court was all Indiana. Antonio Davis captured another crucial rebound; Byron Scott punched a pass inside to Antonio who was fouled and sank both free throws. With just under ten minutes to play in the game, the Pacers were suddenly down by only two.

The Magic tightened their resolve and the two teams traded baskets for a couple of minutes. Even though they weren't pulling away, the Pacers looked good in this stretch—playing coolly, with no hint of anxiety. They knew what they had to do and were intent on doing it.

One Pacer in particular knew the territory best. Another shot of Scott would be needed for the final push over the hump.

Asked about the real meaning of Game One in Orlando, Pacers General Manager Donnie Walsh said, "Byron Scott.

"You tell the people of Indiana that the general manager—and the coach—of the Indiana Pacers give the credit to Byron Scott. Just remember, we brought him here for *this*."

"This" was the championship experience, the deep-down knowledge of what it takes to win, and the almost transcendent ability to provide it when needed.

Scott got the ball and drove into the lane. Shut off in front of the basket, he twisted and dished the ball to Antonio Davis waiting on the left baseline. Antonio took the pass, stepped the distance and climbed the mountain, elevating right into and then past the face of O'Neal, flushing the ball to tie the game.

After an empty Orlando possession, the Pacers came back downcourt where Tree Rollins elbowed Reggie Miller and sent him to the line. The NBA's second-best free throw shooter put the Pacers ahead for the first time since the first quarter.

Still, the Magic had a few tricks left. They tightened the screws and climbed back to a six-point lead with four and a half minutes to play.

Brown called a time-out to settle his team. They came out and delivered the ball to Miller, who missed a three-pointer. But the Pacers hung tough. They stopped Orlando and came back down for Miller to try again. This time his long-range delivery was perfect: Pacers down by three.

Shaq got free inside but ran out of steam—and gassed his next two shots. With Scott's magic still in his fingertips, Antonio Davis hit a short buzzer beater and then fouled O'Neal to prevent a dunk. O'Neal converted from the charity stripe—Magic up again by three.

That was the incentive Miller needed. With one minute six seconds to play and with three seconds left on the Pacers' shot clock, Miller drained his second three-pointer to tie the game.

The Magic dug deep on their next possession and Shaq tipped in a jumper to give the Magic a two-point lead with twenty-five seconds left in the game. The Pacers wove an offensive play for Miller, but his shot went wide, and the ball scuttled out of bounds on the baseline—last touched by Orlando with 13.3 seconds in the game.

Brown quickly inserted Scott. The ball went from Scott to Miller, who drove into the paint, drew three defenders and deftly rifled the ball back to Byron waiting behind the arc.

Scott caught the ball with his shoulders already squared to the basket. Without a moment's hesitation he launched a shot that fell through the net and buried itself in Orlando's skull.

Three Orlando time-outs stretched the final two seconds into five minutes. It was as if the Magic hoped that, by waiting long enough, the shock would wear off and that bullet in the brain would suddenly disappear. But they'd run out of tricks.

A final Orlando shot flew past the rim on its way to nowhere, leaving the Magic staring almost in disbelief at the scoreboard: Magic, 88; Pacers, 89. The Pacers and Byron Scott had stolen the lightning in Game One.

There was one casualty, though: Veteran LaSalle Thompson broke his hand in a seemingly casual brush with O'Neal. The contact was so slight that at first Thompson though it might merely be sprained. Still, it felt strange enough that he took himself out of the game and trainer David Craig sent him to the locker room. A mobile X-ray machine was set up in the Orlando locker room, so Thompson and team doctor Sanford Kunkel sat there, watching the last minutes of the game on the Orena's closed-circuit television.

Through the walls, they could hear members of the Magic front-office staff cheering for their team—and the hum of the air-conditioning when Byron Scott nailed the game-winner.

Thompson emerged from of the Orlando locker room for the game's final moments, to share the thrill and study the losers as they left the court. "Bo (Hill) looked like someone just kicked him down the street," Thompson said with only a trace of a smile.

"Gar (assistant coach Garfield Heard) started saying it as soon as the game was over," Thompson recalled. "Everybody was gathering around and hugging each other, and Gar just told them: 'Don't celebrate, not even in the locker room.'

"And then Reggie picked it up. He started saying, 'That's right. We haven't done anything yet.' And that became our slogan—We haven't done anything yet.

"Then Reggie said, 'Let's win two. Let's be greedy. Let's win two.' And we all agreed."

* * *

It's hard to overestimate the emotional impact of this game and Byron Scott's winning three-pointer. Until this night, the Pacers had never won the first game of an NBA playoff series. They'd never walked into their locker room at the end of that first game to find a bunch of winners staring back from the mirror.

That game and that shot were arguably the most significant of the Pacers' NBA history. To his credit, Scott was enough of a veteran to understand that, and enough of a no-nonsense professional to say so matter-of-factly.

"I've hit about five or six shots like that in the pros—buzzer-beaters to win the game. Each shot is different, of course, but I think this was the first in the playoffs.

"Like I said, I knew it was going in when I let it go, and I think we all knew we were going to win this series after that shot. Maybe it was the biggest shot in franchise history," Scott remembered.

Yet, as Scott, Miller, Thompson, and the rest of the team sensed, their victory wasn't really anything—yet. It was a time for restraint. It was time now to bottle the lightning, let it ricochet inside them, quietly electrifying every corner of their psyches. When the time was right, they would let it out again.

* * *

Byron Scott's game-winning three-pointer and Reggie Miller's appeal to team greed set the stage for Game Two, held in Orlando on Saturday afternoon, on the last day of April. The Orlando Magic were stunned but by no means unglued by their last-second defeat in the Game One. After all, no team that had won fifty regular season games could be completely spooked by a one-point loss.

This was the first day of national television coverage of the playoffs, and the network commentators covering the game advised the millions attending via their screens to watch for the Magic to reassert themselves. The most plausible scenario discussed before the game—indeed, throughout forty-seven minutes of play—foresaw Shaq and Hardaway with more than enough up their sleeves to tie the series.

One problem: NBA jerseys are sleeveless.

In the visitors' locker room, the Pacers were talking about their own scenario. Even in the late-spring heat of Orlando, the Pacers remembered the feeling they had first identified at the end of January: They were winners. They could beat anyone in the league. They were all on the same page, awaiting their cues with a kind of calm that only comes from confidence. This locker room wasn't filled with a lot of chest-thumping, adrenaline-pumping cheering and shouts. These guys were discussing game strategy.

LaSalle Thompson, in street clothes after breaking his hand in Game One, an injury that would sideline him for weeks, remembered thinking that something about the team's mood gave him the feeling that he would get a chance to play again. "Somehow—I don't know why—I just never thought I was done for the year." Everyone was quietly reminding himself that, as Miller had said, "We haven't done anything yet."

Yet.

The Pacers came out strong in Game Two. They played well, looking loose and confident, taking a 5–0 lead. There were occasional miscues, of course. But then there would be Reggie, seeming to decide, just as he crossed as the time line, that *now* would be a perfect time for a three-pointer—and draining it. Or, there would be Antonio Davis hauling down rebounds, strong enough to take the ball right from Shaq's hands. Then millions of television viewers could watch Shaq look perturbed, even a little hurt for a moment, as if somebody had handed him a cookie and then taken it away.

The Magic turned the ball over eight times in the first quarter, a disastrous statistic if allowed to continue. Another sign of potential doom: Shaq looked shackled. He exhibited next to no offensive power, committed two quick fouls and was forced to watch much of the quarter from the bench. Hardaway kept his team in the quarter with deft inside moves and three net-ripping three-pointers. He scored five Magic goals in succession and ended with an impressive nineteen points in the quarter.

If the Pacers were concerned by Hardaway's performance, they revealed only a mild exasperation: Now how the heck did the kid make that shot? They'd ask themselves that question several more times that day—and again in Game Three. But for the time being, in the first quarter of Game Two, the Pacers responded with calm, going about their business with a sense of smooth efficiency, a physical match for the mental mood of the locker room. Indiana had built a 32–22 lead with a minute and a half left in the quarter.

But, as they had so many times during the season, the Pacers seemed to lose their edge in the second quarter. With Miller on the bench, the Pacers watched the Magic waltz through an 13–0 scoring run that tied the game at thirty-seven with seven-thirty to play in the half.

Suddenly it seemed that all those little hustle plays the Pacers had made in the first quarter were now going against them. If Antonio Davis dove out of bounds to save a loose ball, his inbound heave went straight into Magic hands. And when Antonio soared to block an O'Neal shot, the rejected shot bounced straight to a Magic player who fed it right back to Shaq for an easy two.

The Pacer offense was equally befuddled, even with Miller back on the floor. A terrific Workman pass to Reggie under the basket led to a seemingly automatic reverse lay-up; it hobbled around the rim for a second, but drifted over and out. Before the Pacers' steam totally dissipated, though, Antonio Davis drew Shaq's third foul with six minutes left in the half. O'Neal again left the game, having contributed a wholly un-Shaq-like 1-for-5 from the field, 2-for-4 from the line, two rebounds and one blocked shot.

After waving bye-bye, the Pacers promptly went on a 9–0 run of their own. Basketball games that swing back and forth like this have an undeniable attraction for fans. Either your team is looking very good, in which case you're ecstatic, or your team looks like a blend of Silly Putty and Swiss cheese, in which case you're mad, sad and ready to throw popcorn at someone. In either case, emotions run high and you are reminded that you care intensely about something. It is, in a word, fun.

What happened next on the court wasn't fun. It was ugly. Over the last few minutes of the second quarter, every possession seemed to end badly—for both teams. Fouls piled up; turnovers mounted. Each team made bad decisions or failed to execute their good ones.

Only Hardaway and second-unit Magic forward Anthony Avent appeared to be consistently in the game. Hardaway ended the half with twenty-one points. Avent did much of his work slogging through this second quarter bog. He was there for put-backs and rebounds, eventually coming away with thirteen points— after scoring in double digits only twice in forty-one games with the Magic.

It is possible to attribute this end-of-the-half malaise to stepped-up defensive pressure from both sides. As NBA veterans will tell you: Defense wins championships. But for the average fan, defense can be tough to watch—especially when its your team that's getting the worst of it. The Pacers trailed at the half 55–51.

For the first six or seven minutes, the third quarter looked a lot like the end of the second. Then Reggie Miller seemed to remember why he was Pacers co-captain.

In an Indiana minute, Miller scored three baskets to give the Pacers a six-point lead. He then hit on two more Pacer possessions, scoring 11 points. When Miller starts to feel it, the results can be beautiful. After a long spell of awkward and abortive basketball, Miller's graceful run changed the tone and rhythm of the game. And as such things can go when good teams meet, the Magic picked up the tune.

Hardaway responded with a three-pointer of his own. Even O'Neal chimed in with an almost ballet-like spin move to score two in the lane. As much as he might admire the beauty of the game played well, Larry Brown had seen enough of this. When the Magic had pulled back within five with just under two minutes to play in the third, Brown called time.

After the grace of the preceding minutes, Brown figured the Magic might be caught unawares by a quick punch in the gut—and the guy to deliver it was Haywoode Workman. If Miller was the rapier in the Pacer offense, Workman was the chisel. He drove right down the lane to draw O'Neal's fifth foul with forty-five seconds left in the quarter. A shudder went through the Orlando team—maybe through the whole city.

Smits connected on the first possession of the fourth quarter as the Pacers regained and maintained their composure through the early minutes of the last period. Wholesale substitutions on both sides with just over eight minutes to play altered the flow again—and not entirely to the Pacers' advantage.

Let's just say the Magic finally realized they'd better get busy. Dennis Scott stepped up to show why he was second in the league in three-point scoring. He sank a three-pointer and the Pacers responded with a shot-clock violation. When Hardaway dunked, the sellout Orlando crowd roared into the game. Suddenly it was a puny three-point lead for the Pacers, 95–92.

Emotions were welling up on both sides now. But the blue and gold dug deeper and pushed it to five, then to seven. With 3:20 to play the game looked as if it was in the Pacers' pocket.

Then Nick Anderson hit a three. Antonio Davis answered with a circus drive that sent the ball scooping, arching, falling and *in*. The Pacers were up 103–98 with 33.2 seconds to play. But then Dennis Scott pulled the three-point trigger yet again—the last of what would be a record-setting 11 three-pointers by a team in the playoffs.

Here it is. The Pacers have the ball, half a minute to play, up by two. They dribble. They pass. Workman looks for an entry to the post. Finally he realizes the shot clock is about to expire. He drives to the right baseline and forces up an ugly shot that is deflected into O'Neal's hands as the shot-clock hangs at one second.

The buzzer sounds and Smits slaps O'Neal in the face even while Shaq releases a long pass downcourt to a sprinting Hardaway—all of that is sandwiched into a second of play that will be dissected and argued about for some time to come.

In any event, the referees whistled the ball back just as Hardaway, running unopposed, flushed the tying basket. The Magic called time to regroup and chart what they desperately hoped would be the play to officially tie—or win—the game. But it didn't work. Catching the midcourt in-bounds pass, Hardaway drove to his left at the top of the arc, turned right for the basket, started to slip but managed to launch a shot that bounced high off the back of the rim...just as the final buzzer sounded.

All of the force of Shaq's put-back slam couldn't reverse even a tenth of a click from that unforgiving clock.

The Pacers had taken two. Larry Brown could not contain himself as his team ran out of the arena. He punched the air and smiled through clenched teeth like a fighter who sees blood on his glove.

The Orlando team walked away slowly, scarcely glancing up at the final count: Magic 101, Pacers 103.

* * *

Neither of the first two playoff games against Orlando was what you could call a ritual of basketball beauty. The teams seemed a perfectly balanced mismatch. Compare leading scorers? You can't. Shaquille O'Neal versus Reggie Miller? What's to compare?

How to weigh the toughness of the Davis duo against the perimeter accuracy of Dennis Scott and Nick Anderson? Perhaps the only obvious comparison would be between the finesse of Anfernee Hardaway and the lunch-bucket delivery of Haywoode Workman. And even then, after admitting that Hardaway is the more gifted player in an abstract sense, you would be forced to conclude that Workman was the right player at the right time for the right team.

No wonder sports fans turn to statistics. In such matters of the heart, any fact is seized upon to prove the point.

Example: Shaquille O'Neal scored an average of 37.5 points against the Pacers during the regular season, 8.2 points higher than his average versus the rest of the league.

But the Pacers held Shaq to a season-low fifteen points in Game Two.

Yeah, but the Magic only lost three games in a row just once in the season. And the Pacers have never made it past the first round of the playoffs. No NBA franchise ever won fifty games in only its fifth year. No team before the Magic had ever made eleven three-point shots in a playoff game.

Statistics and second-by-second analyses can show you the way the game looked, and perhaps suggest some of the reasons why it might have gone this way or that. But if basketball were just an exercise in number-crunching, accountants would be superstars.

When it got down to it, Larry Brown and the Indiana Pacers knew that the tick-by-tick dissection of the shot clock is only the abstract count of young men's heart-beats. And all the percentages of percentages are just dry measures of sweat.

* * *

Game Three of the Pacers-Magic playoff series was played before a sellout crowd at Market Square Arena on Monday, May 2.

The sellout was something of a relief. During last year's first-round playoff series against the New York Knicks, the Pacers had been unable to fill MSA, even after they'd won Game Three.

After the Pacer victory in Game Two in Orlando, Pacers co-owner Mel Simon had come to the team's locker room—a rare event for an owner who freely admitted that he was no basketball expert and normally limited his input to screaming at the officials. (Simon once got so vociferous from his midcourt seat that one referee almost had him ejected—until someone discreetly pointed out that this particular screaming man had a long-term lease on the building.)

Never one to pal it up with the players, Simon quickly congratulated the victors but told them: "If Market Square Arena isn't sold out on Monday, I'm selling the team."

Simon may have been kidding—maybe not. No one will ever know.

The crowd that gathered at MSA that night wasn't just a sellout; it was a buy-in—an investment.

"And for once," recalled LaSalle Thompson, "we knew they weren't there to see Shaquille, Jordan or anyone else. They were there for us."

The city of Indianapolis—and everyone watching on television and anyone else who cared at all—was there that night to claim the Pacers as their own. A couple thousand had already embraced them at the airport in the small hours of Sunday morning, waving brooms at them to suggest a three-game sweep of Or-lando—as if any hints were necessary.

Monday night, although MSA had officially prohibited brooms and were con-fiscating them at the door, more had snuck in—along with signs urging the team to "Sweep the Shaq." The brooms would be useful later that night.

Another prohibition of sorts was also being taken rather casually by the fans that night. After Reggie Miller appeared in a nationally televised interview wear-ing a kerchief tied over his head, someone in the NBA offices in New York had contacted the Pacers to caution that such apparel was suggestive of street gang dress and should be avoided for fear that its use by such a notable NBA figure as Mr. Miller might be misconstrued.

Right.

The Pacers handed out some 17,000 kerchiefs to the fans entering the arena that evening. Local game announcers were careful to inform everyone in the arena and on television that these were not kerchiefs.

They were "rally rags."

People of all ages, races and economic circumstances stood in the MSA corridors, asking each other how to tie a rally rag over the head to look just like Reggie.

The stage was set for something special, something larger than life. The teams knew it. They were ready to do it, to get down to it. In other playoff games around the league this year, an ominous note of violence had crept in at the corners, like organized crime taking over a legitimate industry, and the NBA wanted it stopped. Now.

No need to worry about the Pacers and the Magic. Emotions were as high in this series as anywhere else in the NBA, but these two teams had come to play.

Together, they produced a game that had all the fire and guts of a boxing slugfest. Just as important, it displayed all the finesse and cinematic delight of a choreographed karate fight.

From a basketball purist's point of view, it was by far the most gratifying game of the series. From the Pacers' perspective, it was the greatest game of their eighteen-year NBA history—so far.

* * *

It started slowly.

The first three shots came up empty. Reggie Miller was primed, making two steals of early Orlando possessions. But neither team was able to move the scoreboard off zeros until a Magic foul sent Miller to the line for two successful free throws.

With the ice broken, Miller kept going with a three-pointer, then a two. Smits drew Shaquille's first foul. Workman then forced Hardaway to commit his second and, thumping a fist over his heart before shooting, drained two free throws. The Pacer hometown crowd needed no jumpstart. Their hearts were in their throats and the decibel level started climbing. No one had ever heard this much noise in MSA before.

To their credit, the Magic rose to the occasion and gave the crowd something to really cheer against. The early minutes of the game saw both teams performing at playoff capacity. The Pacers hit four of their first seven shots; Orlando was 5-for-10.

When the Magic weren't capitalizing on Shaq's inside strength, they took his passes back to the perimeter, dashed the ball around the arc and found the open man. This strategy worked well enough to give the Magic a 17–16 lead well into the first quarter.

When the game is played at this level of balanced intensity, the slightest change can tip the psychological scales. Commentators can describe it—they call it a shift in momentum—but no one can really explain it.

Sometimes the shift starts with a moment of beauty. Derrick McKey provided such a moment in the middle of the quarter.

Cut off by defenders on the left baseline with his back to the basket ten feet away and no shot to manufacture, McKey somehow blindly propelled the ball around his right side, past the defense and into the paint for a Dale Davis dunk.

It was one of those plays that immediately grabs everyone's attention—and is burned into fans' minds for years.

And it worked. Suddenly the Pacers could do no wrong. Even a fumbled, fast-break pass bounced off Reggie's foot and into Dale's arms for another dunk. Indiana was on top 22–17 with two minutes left in the quarter.

Orlando certainly wasn't about to fold. They created their own brand of beauty, the long-range kind that ignites a team with the sheer physical thrill of shooting hoops. And Hardaway was certainly not going gently into any long summer night. He was making some incredible plays, the stuff of highlight tapes and post-season memories of what might have been. On one play he would hit from the perimeter. On the next he would drive and score.

At this point, essentially a two-man offense was keeping Orlando in the game—not counting the referees. Reviewing the game tapes may lead some observers to the conclusion that O'Neal was receiving the benefit of the officials' doubt on more than one occasion—or getting away with murder, as the case may be. One no-call after Shaq body-blocked Byron Scott on a drive to the hoop was particularly blatant. So much so that Pacer assistant coach Bill Blair even checked with the TV announcers. Either everyone had seen it and chosen to ignore it—and it was there on tape—or it had been an incredible fluke of angle of vision.

In any case, no call.

If the Pacers were upset by any perceived favoritism, they hardly showed it. In fact, they hardly missed a beat. Their defense continued to swarm all over Orlando. Reggie swiped the ball again, pushing it up court where Smits, who had been running the floor like a rampaging giraffe, took the pass at the free throw line and one-stepped to flush it through the hoop.

In every way this was a faster, more elegant game. Both teams appeared so pumped up that they had no patience for a grind-it-out game.

While the game ebbed and flowed through four- and six-point leads, the Pacers tried to shake the game loose and couldn't.

Inexperience and overeagerness took its toll: A driving reverse lay-up by Workman—a play that should've, could've, would've looked so sweet—fell off the rim. So Workman immediately fouled Nick Anderson in an attempt to steal the ball back. Trying to compensate for a blown defense of Shaq in the post, Antonio committed a blocking foul while trying to set a screen.

Orlando took the game into the half leading 52–46. A six-point lead, of course, is just two sneezes and a double-dribble in the NBA.

The second half started like the first. Smits missed his first shot, but Hardaway walked bringing the ball up court. Smits kept his cool and, in a bit of tough-minded defense that must have surprised himself as much as the officials, managed to wrap his hands around a ball that Shaq assumed was his. The ensuing jump-ball went to the Pacers, and Smits ran the floor for the score.

Through much of the third quarter, neither side could establish a substantial lead. Scoring was low while both teams played with intensity, which made for a strange, sputtering game at this point. An ill-advised drive by Reggie forced him to foul Nick Anderson. But when Antonio retrieved a Miller air ball—a Miller *air ball?*—and went back up at the basket, he managed to draw O'Neal's third foul.

But A.D. only experienced more frustration as he missed both free throws and again, overeager to compensate, committed his fourth foul—followed shortly thereafter by his fifth on a drive to the hoop. An out-of-control drive by Workman looked just as bad.

Yet, somehow, the Pacers never lost their composure. Their mistakes were aggressive ones, which meant they were dictating the game's tempo. They might not have been dancing all that well, but they were still calling the tune.

And the Pacers were doing a bit of everything. Smits was hitting. Fleming stole an inbounds to feed McKey, then drove himself right through the Orlando lane. Reggie was hitting his foul shots, and Smits moved strong to the hoop to draw Shaq's fourth foul.

Still, the Magic were scoring, too. In fact, they were pulling ahead. That persistent six-point lead seemed on the verge of developing into something serious when Dennis Scott hit a floater in the lane to put the Magic up by eight a couple of minutes into the final period. One more blown Pacer possession and the Magic might well step up to a double-digit lead.

Now it was Larry Brown's turn. Calling time-out, he called his team into a huddle and told them in no uncertain terms that *now* was the time to get the job done—that, or they'd find themselves mowing their lawns next week.

It came as no surprise that, when the team came back out on the floor, Byron Scott, ol' Three Rings himself, was in the lineup. He got the ball and immediately buried a jumper, cutting the Magic lead to six and stopping the Pacers' emotional bleeding. On the next possession, Scott took the ball and sliced left to right through the lane, a drive expertly calculated to take him right past O'Neal and daring Shaq to stop him—which Shaq did, with his fifth foul.

O'Neal sat down with nine minutes on the clock, and Scott made the first of two free throws. On the rebound of the second, Smits fought—yes, fought—hard enough to send the ball off Orlando hands and out of bounds. Dale Davis took the Pacers' inbounds and edged it over the rim. The Magic lead was now just three, 78–75.

After a Magic bucket, Smits called for the ball in the post and turned to hit a jumper and draw a slap on the wrist from Tree Rollins, giving him a free throw and—oops, a Rollins technical foul made by Miller—for a four-point play. Suddenly it was Magic up by one...then *down* by one as Reggie buried a jumper for the first Pacer lead in what felt like months. The crowd shook the arena.

Watching his team flap through an 11–2 run in three minutes without Shaq, Magic coach Brian Hill had no choice but to reinsert his mountain. It wouldn't matter.

A bad Magic pass gave the ball right back to the Pacers. Byron, knowing Reggie was feeling it, sent it to him for two more. Pacers by three. Fleming dropped a jumper to push it to five.

The Magic began to crack. Dennis Scott missed both charity shots after a Miller foul, and although the Magic captured the skittering rebound, Smits blocked the attempted put-back. Fleming dove for the ball, flipped it to McKey, who flipped it back to Vern, who took it downcourt where Reggie was waiting, waving wildly just outside the arc. Vern saw him and...

Boom—and broom.

It was electrifying. You can watch the tapes over and over. It still gets you going.

There were some Magic moments after that. In fact, Shaq immediately erased Reggie's three-pointer with a short shot and a foul. After a Pacer miss, Smits was forced to foul to prevent an O'Neal dunk at the other end. But Shaq could only hit one free throw.

And the Davis boys kind of took care of things from then on. Antonio soared up a couple of stories to block what looked to be an easy Hardaway lay-up. Dale Davis dunked an inbounds pass, then pulled down a rebound. Antonio hit a fifteen-foot jumper, and there the Pacers were—up 92–84 with a minute forty-five to play.

Following an Orlando time-out, the Magic tried to climb back into it with a series of desperation three-pointers—clink, clank and clunk.

It all unraveled then. As the last seconds of Round One ticked off, the scoreboard stopped at 99–86. Reggie Miller held the ball just over the time line, waiting for the buzzer to sound. He really couldn't hear it.

By that time, Market Square Arena sounded like the inside of a jet engine.

9
Round Two — FAN-tastic

The Pacers were now going where no NBA Pacer had gone before: Round Two of the playoffs. Their three-game sweep of the Orlando Magic had left them scarcely out of breath.

The rest of the country, however, was still in a huff. Just who did these guys think they were? You'd think the nation's premier sports magazine would know, but *Sports Illustrated* didn't have a clue. If you bothered to read its coverage of Round One—or Rout One, as Hoosiers were calling it—you would have come away knowing that the real story of the series was the Magic's defeat, not the Pacers' victory.

Perhaps it was understandable that *S.I.* should rely on magical metaphors to describe how the Pacers had out-magicked the Magic. Yet the upshot was a downplay, leaving the impression that Pacers had somehow tricked the younger, more deserving and immensely more marketable Magic out of their proper spot in Round Two.

In his May 9 piece "Lack of Shaq," writer John Walters took his time getting to any real discussion of the Pacers and any analysis of their talents and capabilities. First, he was obliged to talk about Shaq, saying that he "did a disappearing act…thanks to the legerdemain of the Indiana Pacers, for years among the league's merest mortals."

Perhaps Walters did not fully consider his categorization. If the Pacers were among the "league's merest mortals," that would make all the teams who hadn't made the playoffs in 1990, '91, '92, '93, and now '94 members of some subhuman species.

Oh, well, perhaps it should come as no surprise that this sports journalism stuff can be as much show–biz and hyperbole as "Entertainment Tonight." Next, he described Byron Scott's winning three-pointer in Game One as "sleight-of-hand." Again, some metaphoric license should be given.

But after that, don't you think a reporter would spend a paragraph or two giving credit where it was due?

But no-o-o-o-o.

We get to read how surprised Hardaway was to lose. "But Hardaway wasn't being done in by any genie," Walters wrote. Aha! Here's where the Pacers get their strokes, right?

Wrong. What followed was a discussion of how the "postseason is a whole new show" and how other teams in other series have gotten rather nasty and violent and how young superstars-to-be such as Hardaway—"whose sublime thirty–one–point effort in Game Two was one point shy of his best as a pro"—would just have to wait a while.

Finally, the article gets to Indiana. It even mentions that the Pacers had the league's second–best record since the end of January—surprise, surprise—suggesting for the first time in several hundred words that the Pacers might have something other than luck and trickiness to explain their victory.

Maybe someone such as, Walters acknowledged, "Reggie Miller, arguably the league's top marksman." Having said that, however, the author felt obliged to immediately counterpunch his own compliment by stating that others consider Reggie the "best pure *bull*-shooter in the NBA." (His italics.)

No respect. None at all.

Although the article does grant notable inches to a discussion of the Pacers' lineup, the final analysis is typically focused on Orlando. It was O'Neal who went scoreless and the Magic who bricked their shots—with no mention of tough Pacer defense. Speaking of Smits, the Davis devils, Sam Mitchell and Derrick McKey, Walters found it all but impossible to believe that "Somehow this motley tag team did its job, especially on Saturday when it harassed the foul-plagued Shaq-Fu into 3-for-8 shooting."

Imagine that. It took five of them to hold O'Neal down, but he was obviously suffering from a case of irksome officiating.

* * *

Game One of Round Two was played on Tuesday, May 10. For everyone who pays attention to such portents, it was also the day of the century's last great solar eclipse. Coincidence? Perhaps.

The Pacers had not played an opponent since May 2. The playoff layoff might or might not work in Indiana's favor. Former Pacers coach Bob "Slick" Leonard revealed a deep secret of his professional fraternity when he told the Indiana television audience before the game that a coach would credit the rest if the Pacers won—and blame the rust if they lost.

Byron Scott told the cameras that, after eight days of hard practice, bumping and pushing his friends, he thought the team was really looking to push around some people they didn't like.

The Atlanta Hawks, on the other hand, were just looking for people—any sort of people—to attend the game.

Slick's and Byron's comments—and, indeed all of that evening's TV coverage—were intended solely for the use of the Indiana viewing audience. Atlanta's hometown TV coverage was nonexistent because, once again, the Hawks had failed to fill the Omni and lift the local blackout. As of Monday afternoon, the game had attracted only about 8,500 ticket buyers out of a possible 16,368. Even though the Hawks had clinched their first-round series against the Miami Heat the day before, total walk-up sales by midafternoon totaled a less-than-lukewarm 535.

Atlanta Journal Constitution columnist Steve Hummer quipped that "disinterest at the Omni apparently has not yet begun to peak.

"When the ticket windows opened Monday," Hummer continued, "...they couldn't have gotten less action at the Omni if the place had been quarantined. Meanwhile in Indianapolis, the first two games there already have been sold out, with some scalpers demanding as much as three tractors for a good ticket."

Guffaw and chortle. Real knee-slapping stuff.

Laugh now, Ha-ha-Hot-lanta.

Hummer summarized the bottom line of local fan apathy: The opposition. "They can't help one drawback—they are the Pacers. The Hawks will have to move on to either the Knicks or the Bulls to rally this public."

No doubt the Atlanta media felt justified—or at least obligated—in picking Atlanta to win the series. After winning the first of five regular-season meetings, the Hawks had dropped two to the Pacers before the All-Star break, including one embarrassing loss in December that broke a fourteen-game home winning streak. They had recovered nicely to win the last two games against Indiana and in doing so returned the favor by snapping the Pacers' eleven-game home winning streak on March 18. "They did it to us so we did it to them," said Hawks' center Andrew Lang.

Overall, the Hawks were 58–38 versus the Pacers, and 35–12 at the Omni. The last time these two teams met in the playoffs, the Hawks won easily. History said the Hawks were bigger and brighter and better. The other sportswriters at the *Journal Constitution* were less haughty, but still predicted a Hawks victory.

They figured the Pacers had the edge when it came to centers and shooting guards. Hawks' two-guard Stacey Augmon may have scored the league's six millionth point on March 23, but that was, of course, just a matter of being in the right place at the right time.

The match-up between Hawks coach Lenny Wilkens, soon to be named Coach of the Year, and Larry Brown they graciously called a draw. They awarded the advantage to the Hawks at point guard, power forward, small forward and, finally the in the category: "Intangibles:

"There is motivation and incentive in abundance," the Atlanta newspaper said. "The Hawks have never reached the Eastern Conference finals and this is the first appearance in the semifinals for the Pacers, who arrive in the midst of an eleven-game win streak. Perhaps it comes down to this: home court. The series should go the distance. If so, a seventh game is in The Omni. Advantage: Hawks."

Reading that in retrospect, it almost sounds as if the Atlanta sportswriters were getting ready to be disappointed. Maybe they were right to this extent: If the series had gone seven, maybe the Hawks would have won. We'll never know.

The Pacers probably didn't have a chance to read either Hummer's column or the more objective pre-game coverage. Perhaps, as Hummer suspected, they were too busy checking the latest pork-bellies quotations, or studying up on no-till herbicides.

If they'd found the time to read Hummer's humor, they might have had their feelings hurt. And that might have thrown them so far off their feed that they would have been unable to beat the Hawks that night 96–85.

More likely, though, they would have laughed—but for other reasons than Hummer had in mind.

The team came into Atlanta feeling very confident. During their mini off-season between rounds, the team had been practicing and preparing. Part of that preparation came in the form of team dinners. These were not secluded evenings in quiet surroundings where the team might enjoy some fine cuisine and a sedate atmosphere best suited to professional concentration and dispassionate analysis.

Nope. The team went to places like Hooters to catch the games on the big screen. LaSalle Thompson remembered that as the Pacers watched Atlanta play in Miami, many of them came to the same conclusion: "Both teams were playing scared. Either Miami was scared to win or Atlanta was scared to lose, but they were scared.

"At that point," Thompson remembered, "it didn't matter who won their series. We all knew that we were the superior team."

* * *

The series began on two empty possessions—a Mookie Blaylock air ball and a powerful but errant Workman drive. Another mistake, a Stacey Augmon offensive foul, was followed by one of Derrick McKey's delightful no-look passes to Dale Davis under the hoop. A Reggie Miller steal, then another Workman effort—there the Pacers were at 6–2.

Blaylock's answering three-pointer was not entirely unexpected. He had made fourteen of the Hawks' seventeen long-range flights in their first-round series, and taken forty-five of their fifty-one attempts. He would have to be defended outside.

For the time being, the game was not intensely played. Whatever pace it had was not to the Pacers' advantage. Eight first-quarter Indiana turnovers led to a 23–

11 Atlanta lead and a Larry Brown time-out. He no doubt wanted to discuss the wisdom of strategies such as letting Rik Smits bring the ball downcourt—an unexpected maneuver, yes, but hardly effective. Stopped in the low post, he turned and flipped the ball to a defender.

Brown's time-out was considerably more effective. The Pacers regrouped with some decent defense—Smits hassled Craig Ehlo into a bad shot—and some good work on the offensive glass—put-backs by Vern Fleming and Dale Davis. By the end of the first period, the Pacers had trimmed the Hawks' twelve-point lead in half, 31–25.

Second-quarter confusion ensued—but with no conclusive shift in momentum. At the start, Brown played this strange lineup: Antonio Davis, Byron Scott, Derrick McKey, Vern Fleming and Sam Mitchell. Scott continued to drive down Atlanta's throat with inelegant-looking moves that managed to get right to the point, or points.

When McKey left with his third foul, the Hawks got their first good look at Kenny Williams, who snatched down the rebound of his own miss to chip it in. And an oh-so-cool Dale Davis dunk on an inbounds from the sideline—more of an NFL than an NBA pass—caught Kevin Willis looking up at the bottom of Dale's shoes.

But Atlanta didn't have the best record in the East for nothing, did they?

Stacey Augmon sparked a mini-run with a three-pointer and suddenly the Hawks had a ten-point lead, 44–34. And just as suddenly, Rik dropped in two buckets.

And just as suddenly, the Hawks were back up ten points. At that point, two-thirds of the way into the second quarter, Brown's game plan still favored Smits in the low post. And it still seemed to work, as Rik hit his next shot, and then Dale reinserted a Smits miss—a scoring method made easy throughout the season by Rik's soft touch on his short shots. His misses tended to hang around the rim waiting for one his Davis friends to complete the deal.

After a Jon Koncak answer—from the outside, not the paint—Dale Davis again rebounded and scored off a Smits miss. As the short swings of momentum subsided at the half, the Hawks led 53–47. The Atlanta margin had leveled off at six points, just where they had left it at the quarter.

The Pacers came strong out of the halftime gate. Smits and Miller, who had only taken eight shots in the first two periods, immediately delivered. Then Dale dunked again.

Hawks coach Lenny Wilkens didn't like what he saw; he called time-out to adjust his team to the Pacers' new-found energy. It didn't help. After the break, Haywoode stole a pass and Antonio took in it with authority. Then Derrick McKey drove the baseline, spun away from the hoop and flipped the ball over his shoulder...and into the basket, just as two defenders were looking toward the free throw line to see where this pass was going.

Clearly shaken, the Hawks botched their next possession; a breakaway pass to Antonio tied the game at fifty-nine with two-thirds of the quarter left to play. The Pacers just kept coming. Willis fouled under the basket. Reggie drove. Haywoode hit just his nineteenth three-point shot of the season. Then he and Reggie set a half-court trap that forced Mookie Blaylock to wobble a weak pass into McKey's hands—for just a half-second before it sailed downcourt for Antonio to flush unopposed. Pacers by five.

But Danny Manning stepped up to demonstrate why the Hawks were willing to trade the franchise for him—and why Larry Brown needed him at Kansas to win the 1988 NCAA title. Two Manning scores brought the Hawks within one at 65–64.

But Manning was an island of offense. No other Hawk could hack it—and the Pacers just kept coming back for more. Taking a Smits feed in the lane, Antonio scored on a short hook. Then he scored again off a Smits miss. Rik atoned with a defensive strip leading to a Fleming slash to the hoop. And yet another fine McKey pass found Dale Davis to put the Pacers ahead 79–72. Indiana cruised into the fourth quarter feeling the power, smelling the win and riding high on Antonio Davis' 6-of-6 gunslinging that quarter.

At the start of the final period, the Pacers continued laying on the baffling defense. Neither team could generate much offensive spark, though; it was two minutes before anyone could score. But it didn't seem to bother Indiana. As the cameras played across the Pacers during a time-out, they looked loose and happy, smiling like a group of guys waiting for some flirtatious waitress to bring them another bucket of wings.

With seven minutes to play, Indiana led 81-74. Empty possessions were handed back and forth, which only worked to Indiana's advantage. It was 83–74 with 5:20 left in the game. The Hawks hadn't scored a basket in nearly five minutes.

This obviously couldn't last—but it only had to last another five minutes. Digging down for some true grit, the Hawks cut it to four with four minutes on the clock, then two at the three-minute mark.

While Larry's brow wrinkled just a tad, Reggie just winked—and took over. He drew a foul and hit both free throws. He flipped a pass to Antonio for another two. Then he drained a three-pointer. The Pacers had withstood Atlanta's challenge and actually increased their lead to nine, 92–83, at the two-minute mark.

The final score, 96–85, was reached with just over a minute to play. Seeing the unenviable grow more and more inevitable, the Hawks just seemed to surrender. As the final sixty seconds ticked away, they let the game just sort of...wander off down the floor.

Neither team had shot well in the fourth quarter. The Hawks were 5-of-21 and the Pacers were 5-of-15. The rebounding trophy went to Indiana, 48–33. No Pacer seemed to care much about the statistics. As back-up point guard Lester Conner said, "We stood there in the locker room and everybody just looked at each other and said, 'Here we go again.' "

And Indianapolis was ready to go again, as well. Here and there around the city, people were letting loose, one way or another. The hometown fans couldn't be there in Atlanta that night, but they were there in spirit—and no doubt in spirits. Driving through the city after the game, you could hear cars honking their horns, and you knew why.

But Wendy Sommers, the Pacers' director of advertising and a member of the staff since 1984, had a slightly different reaction. She remembered sitting at home watching the final seconds with tears in her eyes, "It was all so heartbreaking. It had been so long and so many people had worked so hard to get us to this point. And after all those years of struggling, now we really had a chance to do it. I was just, well…overwhelmed."

* * *

Wherever the Pacers were headed after Game One, they did a disturbing 180-degree turn on Thursday, May 12.

Indiana's Game Two was ugly—stupefyingly so; it was an offensive display so mortifying that the Pacers set an NBA record for fewest points in a playoff game—sixty-nine. The loss ended a twelve-game winning streak that included the last eight games of the regular season, the three-game sweep of Orlando and the home-court theft two days before in Atlanta. Byron Scott said, "Sometimes you forget what losing is like. You think you're invincible, and it takes a loss to bring you down to earth."

The Pacers hadn't just been brought down to earth, they'd been pushed six feet under. Or, with all due respect to the Hawks, perhaps the Pacers just dug themselves deeper and deeper into a hole and couldn't climb out.

It really didn't seem to matter what the Hawks did that night. The Pacers were coming undone all by themselves.

The game began innocently enough with the score tied at 0–0. At the end of the game, Indiana could look back at this time with yearning. The first few possessions also revealed little of the debacle to follow. Baskets were traded politely.

Kevin Willis scored the Hawks' first six points and began to show that angry and/or determined-looking grimace he gets when he does something significant. Then again, he'd often displayed that same look in Game One. If there was any indication of the kind of game it would become, it might have been Mookie

Blaylock's consecutive drives right up the center of the Pacers' defense for uncontested lay-ups.

The Pacers were used to Vern Fleming doing this sort of thing, mostly because no other team could quite believe that Vern's erratic stutter-step indicated anything but indecision. Mookie, on the other hand, just flashed his bright lights and zipped right up on the fast lane.

Perhaps Indiana looked a little lackadaisical, but with two seconds left in the first quarter, the Pacers were only down 21–19. Two seconds can be far too long, though, as the Pacers had found out on several occasions during the season. In this case, Atlanta's last two-second possession of the quarter came after a Pacer turnover. The Hawks inbounded to Duane Ferrell a good five feet behind the three-point arc. Having made but one three-point shot all year, Ferrell figured it was time for his second. He drained it at the buzzer.

Of course, one statistically improbable shot in the first quarter doesn't win a game. But it can set a tone. The Hawks began to feel the rhythm, the same beat that enabled them to win fifty-seven regular-season games.

The second period began with more of the seemingly innocent basketry exchange. Neither team looked exactly like a league champ, but the Hawks slowly crept to a 30–21 lead.

Before anyone on the Pacers stat team could look up, the quarter was nearly half over. The Hawks had taken a mostly unimpressive lead at 32–23. The Pacers' twenty-three-point total in seventeen minutes was a little better than one and a third points per minute. That worked out to about sixty-five Pacer points for the night—barely respectable for a high school team.

Things heated up a bit after that—at least for Atlanta. The Pacers continued to blow easy shots. Reggie missed from about ten inches, but Haywoode got the rebound and took it outside so he could miss from eighteen feet.

A Dale Davis slam to punctuate a Workman lob sent a momentary thrill up the Pacers' spines, but Koncak hit a jumper, then Willis tipped in another and the thrill became a chill: Hawks by thirteen, 42–29.

Then Stacey Augmon was fouled battling three—count 'em, three—Pacers for a rebound that would, in any other game, have been taken off the top by Dale or Antonio or even Haywoode. Hawks by fourteen. A mini-burst from the Pacers threatened to drop the lead below double digits, but the Hawks flapped a bit harder and went into the half leading 47–32.

Atlanta had shot just 40 percent from the field in the first half, but the Pacers were doing worse: 30 percent. Reggie was misfiring at an alarming 1-of-7 rate and his back-up, Byron Scott, was 0-for-5.

But, as every color commentator within earshot was musing, the Pacers had trailed at halftime in each of the previous four playoff wins—if not exactly by so great a margin.

Such words seemed reassuringly prophetic at the beginning of the third quarter as the Pacers skipped into a 6–0 run, looking for a minute or two like the same team that had swept Orlando from Round One. Good ball movement, good defense and shots that fell.

With his lead down to nine, Wilkens pulled the Pacers' plug with a time-out at 10:03. The Hawks came back and reasserted themselves to a twelve-point lead, perhaps somewhat aided by a couple of might-have-been-but-weren't fouls as Rik tried to score inside. Then, as this game had been evolving all night, a couple of quick scores put the Hawks back up—way up.

First Blaylock hit a three. Then Haywoode blew a drive and the ball was re-cycled downcourt for Kevin Willis to leisurely consider before putting the Hawks up 59–42. Time-out, Pacers.

With a not-quite-desperate 2:38 to go in the third, Reggie broke a long personal drought with two free throws, which gave him only eight points total. But the whole team still seemed to be operating on half-power. Kenny Williams provided a moment of electricity late in the quarter, bouncing off the bench to make a mar-velous steal as the Hawks were flying at the basket. He punched the ball out to Byron, who took it downcourt in for a patented Great Scott drive, a foul and two free throws.

With 2:20 to go in the third, the Hawks' lead was down to thirteen at 63–50. The Pacers began to grumble, shift gears and really think about getting back into the game.

They thought pretty darn hard about it.

Byron hit a three.

Dale stole a cross-court pass and lumbered down to the goal where he achingly missed the lay-up, then the tip-in, then another tip-in, then *another* tip-in…then Atlanta finally grabbed the ball and took it back to their basket for two.

But then Reggie hit a three with that familiar two seconds left in the quarter. There it was. The Hawks had a meager eight-point lead at 65–57 going into the final period.

Unfortunately, the Pacers went scoreless for the next two minutes. By the time Vern converted a three-point play, the Hawks had already scored six—and they just kept coming and coming. It was 71–60. Then 72–61. Then 74–61. Then 77–61 with 7:30 left.

Manning was uncanny through the middle of the fourth. A lookless, spinning lay-up revealed an unerring sense of where the basket was, like a Zen archer who only need glance at his target, close his eyes and deliver a score.

The kindest thing that might be said about the game to this point—80–63 with five minutes to play—would be that the Pacers merely looked inept, not dispirited. But then it was 83–63 with 4:52 left. Then 85–63. Then 86–63.

At this point, the Pacers looked like chuckleheads.

Let us spare ourselves the final exchanges. The game ended 92–69.

If there was anything good to come of this, it was the reality check that Larry Brown could now convincingly administer the next day in Indianapolis. His team could only flinch but nod in agreement at his high-decibel blistering of their performance on Thursday. Lester Conner remembered the last time Brown had been so vocal—after a 129–90 deconstruction at Charlotte on April 6—"All we could do was watch the game tapes and say, 'Damn! We were *that* bad.' He made his point well."

The Pacers were now the proud fathers of the worst performance in NBA playoff history. It had been eleven years since any team had been nearly this bad. On April 21, the Golden State Warriors had bumbled through a disaster of near-biblical proportions as the Lakers beat them 126–70. Perhaps the Pacers could take some solace in the fact that they had not lost by fifty-six points.

They would take more solace if they could abandon this painful record on the doorstep of some less worthy successor. Two weeks later, they would do just that.

* * *

Donnie Walsh would remember Saturday, May 14, as "one of the two or three greatest days of my life." There was the day he was named MVP of the New York City high school all-star game. There were the days each of his children was born. (He has five kids, but grand rhetorical statements such as these seem to dictate one all-purpose birthday.)

Then there was May 14, 1994. It's hard to know which part of the day was most special to Walsh. In the morning, he was host for a public ceremony to break ground for a memorial honoring Dr. Martin Luther King Jr. and Senator Robert F. Kennedy. The idea for the memorial had grown out of a Pacers community relations campaign devoted to an anti-violence theme. It was a theme of particular significance at the corner of Seventeenth and Broadway streets in Indianapolis. On that site on April 4, 1968, Kennedy had conveyed the news of King's assassination in Memphis to a campaign rally. His speech that night was credited for helping to defuse a tense situation. Passages from it are carved on Kennedy's grave. The ground-breaking was held on the small hill upon which Kennedy had spoken, fifty yards from the corner.

As Walsh stepped to the podium, a group of dignitaries rose, including Indianapolis Mayor Steve Goldsmith, Indiana Governor Evan Bayh, Senator Richard Lugar, Representative Andy Jacobs Jr., Senator Ted Kennedy, Ethel Kennedy,

Martin Luther King III, Dexter King and—certainly not least—President Bill Clinton.

Two months before, when it was announced that Clinton would probably be coming to Indianapolis for the state Democratic Party's annual Jefferson-Jackson fund-raising banquet, Walsh had simply written him a letter, inviting him to participate in this ground-breaking on the same day. As such things happen, apparently, the president accepted Walsh's invitation only a few days before the event—and then proceeded to move mountains to make the event as significant as it was. The other platform guests were invited, media arrangements were kicked into overdrive, the Secret Service and White House advance teams massaged the site and the schedule until no one in the Pacers office quite knew who was on first, what was on second or if NBA commissioner David Stern was coming, going or even invited.

But it all came together. Coach Brown and the team were too busy preparing for Game Three with the Hawks to attend the ceremony, but reserve players LaSalle Thompson, Malik Sealy, Pooh Richardson and Scott Haskin were introduced to the president. And in his address, President Clinton had thanked the Pacers for making all of this happen.

Then Walsh stepped to the microphone. "Join with us now to honor two great Americans whose names are forever linked in history by this site and whose memories forever hallow this ground," Walsh said. The president, Ted and Ethel Kennedy, and King's two sons walked off the stage, took silver shovels in hand and together turned the first earth.

"There I was," Walsh remembered, "with the president of the United States of America—and I was the one at the podium. Let me tell you, it was something."

And then Game Three. That was something, too.

The last game of the Orlando series had been thrilling, but the Pacers' victory had been a Popeye punch. Even the most ardent Bluto fans—and there were a few that had flown in from Florida, apparently just to get away from the tourists—knew that windmill windup, going faster and faster and faster, was going to knock the Magic into the next season.

To that extent, the crescendo of fan roar at Market Square Arena had been at least partially a matter of relief: After eighteen years in the NBA and half a decade of playoff frustration, the Pacers were in Round Two.

The crowd noise at Game Three against Atlanta was more than a collective scream of relief, though. This time it was fuel-injected frenzy. The crowd was more than just the proverbial "sixth man" on the Pacer team, it was 16,000 men, women and children. And, through the televised miracle of psychic osmosis, it was that entirely unprovable but undoubted effect of millions of instant Pacer fans around the country rooting for Cinderella, cheering for a team that no sports announcer would ever again dismiss as a bunch of hard-working nobodies playing over their heads.

Game Three against Atlanta was not simply a solid, satisfying victory against a tough opponent. It was not just another win. It was the brick that broke the bird's back.

The Pacers and their 16,000 sixth men plucked Atlanta by twenty points. The game was never even close to being close. From the first quarter until the last second, the Pacers dominated and dumbfounded the Hawks. And they did it with confident, coordinated offense and a defense that was more than unflagging: It ran Atlanta up and down the pole until they were in tatters.

It is doubtful that any opponent could have come back from such a shredding to win Game Four on Sunday against the same Pacers and the same 16,000 fanatics. Maybe the NBA champs might have, maybe the Knicks. But then again, the only Knicks victory at MSA came after a humiliating defeat on their home court, so the anger and revenge factor was pumping them hard. If the Hawks had whatever it took to win Game Four, obviously Game Three wouldn't have seemed so decisive in retrospect. But they didn't—and it was.

* * *

Pacer scoring leader Reggie Miller had turned in completely un-Reggie-like performance in Game Two—2-of-13 from the field. Rik Smits had hit only 4-of-15.

The double-whammy on his offense in Game Two must have come as an unpleasant surprise to Larry Brown. How to respond? You can't solve a shooting slump simply by asking your two main scorers to sink more shots.

Reggie, of course, would always be a pillar of Pacers offense. Even if he wasn't hitting, he had to be there trying. As Game Three Began, it quickly became obvious that Larry Brown was unperturbed by Rik's previous performance. Brown's game plan was still to get the ball right into Rik and see what transpired.

Rik didn't just transpire, he transcended. Rik got right into Jon Koncak's face—and over it, over and over again. He would finish the game with twenty-seven points and appeared unstoppable, whether guarded by Koncak or Andrew Lang.

Rik hit his first jumper. Then McKey tied up Stacey Augmon, controlled the tip and the Pacers fed Rik for his second. Manning missed his second shot, Dale peeled it off a low-flying cloud, and the team zipped it downcourt to Rik.

When Haywoode intercepted a pass, the crowd cranked up their engines, and kicked in the early after-burners when Rik hit again over Koncak. The Pacers led 8–2 with three minutes gone.

Reggie missed his first three-point attempt, but promptly sank one after another Atlanta turnover. Then Rik hit again: Pacers up 13–2.

When the lead dropped to 9 at 13–4, Larry called a time-out. Coming out of the break, Reggie immediately hit another three-pointer to reassert the Pacers.

Even in the game's first four minutes, Brown may have felt that a decisive kick in the Hawks' beak might break their spirit early in the game. If the Pacers never gave them a chance to even get within squawking distance, maybe—make that probably—the Hawks would fold like a tent for Game Three and that would probably mean Game Four as well.

But this was only the first quarter. The Hawks still had some squawk left in them. They pulled up to 16–10. Rik hit again, this time over Lang, but Kevin Willis scored on two consecutive drives to make it 18–14.

The action came fast and furiously in the last three minutes of the quarter. For that quarter of a quarter, the Hawks scratched their way back and pulled within two. But an Antonio Davis slam with three-tenths of a second left in the period put the Pacers up 26–22.

A.D. continued to look tough at the beginning of the second quarter. He drew a Kevin Willis foul—and even a brief smile from Larry Brown. He then rebounded a Rik miss. Byron drove to take them up 30–24, then Rik brought it to 33–27.

Even if the score wasn't yet lopsided, the crowd felt the tempo of the game and the team's obvious sense of flow. As the afternoon wore on, the constant, high-decibel assault would begin to wear on the Hawks. It even began to surprise the home team. Any respectable effort from the Pacers—a blocked shot, a stolen pass, a clean jumper as the shot clock wound down—would rouse a long roar. This was the crowd's game. They weren't just rubbing their hands by the Pacers' fire, they were throwing logs, sticks and furniture onto the blaze.

The Pacers were on top by far more than six points. Coming off his triple-double in Game Two, Mookie Blaylock was having a miserable afternoon. He couldn't find his shot and only haphazardly displayed the savvy sense of floor spread and passing skills that had earned him All-Star status that year. Danny Manning was having equal trouble finding the basket but was hustling as hard as any Hawk. Diving after one high-bouncing rebound, Manning dove out of bounds, over the scorer's table and almost succeeded in wiping out the combined sports staff of the local newspapers—but Bill Benner, Dan Dunkin and Conrad Brunner pushed him back onto the floor.

At 38–29, Lenny Wilkens called a time-out, but the Pacers seemed to put it to better use. When the clock restarted, Dale Davis blocked a Willis shot and Smits glued his hands around the ball as Manning swiped at it. The Pacers took the ball downcourt accompanied by yet another sustained standing scream.

A rare Sam Mitchell drive to the hole brought more. Then Rik and Haywoode played an odd little two-man passing drill—back and forth the length of the court. It culminated in one of Rik's long, jolting drives—two strides from the foul line to the cup—to jam. Now *that* was what the crowd wanted to see.

Manning came back with one of his purely instinctive Zen passes down to a sprinting Craig Ehlo—but Ehlo blew the lay-in. Smits, who seemed to be everywhere, drained a short jumper at the other end. The half ended with the Pacers up 53–42. Rik had thrown down eighteen points. Reggie was backing him up with thirteen.

Of course, an eleven-point lead is hardly insurmountable in the NBA. The Pacers knew they would need to come into the third quarter with the same or greater focus.

Not to worry.

Derrick McKey opened the Pacers' second half with a slow, almost casual ramble around the edge of the paint to glide around the baseline for a finger-roll off the glass. For a second, it almost looked as if he was herding everybody together under the basket so they could watch him. It was a moment of strange beauty, a syncopated waltz so deft and unpredictable that it reminded everyone of what Larry Brown had been saying all season—that McKey does so much that can't be calculated from the stat sheets.

Complementing this finesse was the dogged determination of Haywoode Workman. Ever since his evolution to starting point guard, much had been made in the press of Workman's work ethic, his working man's mentality. As convenient as such phrase-making may be, it was undeniably true. He was a worker. Even after the post-season had ended for the team, Workman would stop the coaches in the halls of the Pacers office to ask what he should be working on over the summer.

Today, he was hard at it again—as always. As the Hawks failed to answer McKey's lay-up, Haywoode pulled in the long rebound, turned to sprint up court...and ran smack into an emphatic screen set by seven-foot Jon Koncak. Workman was sent sprawling and lay at the edge of the scorer's table for a long moment with a look on his face that combined dazed disbelief and pain.

Workman, who had been cut from the Hawks roster in 1989, had said before this series that he wanted to show them what a mistake they'd made. So, after his teammates and Pacers' trainer David Craig pulled him to his feet, Workman handled the ball for a while then buried a three-pointer to put the Pacers up 62–48 and, naturally, bring the crowd to its feet.

As the third quarter progressed, Atlanta could find no door to the painted area under the basket and only occasionally could find their perimeter range. Once, Manning managed to penetrate but missed. Willis rebounded but missed. When Lang rebounded another Manning miss, the Pacers triple-teamed him to force a time-out. The Hawks were entirely out their game, and the Pacers were entirely in theirs, leading 65–50.

Vern threw up a delightful little fling almost inadvertently—he had drifted into the lane hoping to dish it off, then realized he might as well shoot. Byron fed Dale for another half-inch shot. Mookie passed the ball to the Pacers' bench and Dale put back a Byron miss to rouse yet another standing O and the Pacers went out of the third leading 76–59.

And they came into the last period just as they'd started the first: Rik hit his patented short shot. Now Byron was really feeling it. His eyes began to glow and he started to talk—chiding the Hawks for their ineptitude. No doubt it was trash talking, mostly directed at Danny Manning, who at this point was probably muttering much the same to himself: He had shot 2-of-11 thus far in the game.

The lead grew—81–59—and hovered around the twenty-point mark for the rest of the game. The Pacers began a mini-clinic of offensive execution—and had a ball doing it. Not even Dale Davis could suppress a laugh when one of his free throws, long a weak spot in his game, hit glass and went in.

The game didn't so much run out of gas as out of road. The two teams traded baskets until the final buzzer and the Pacers cheerfully walked into the locker room with a 101–81 win.

The biggest and most obvious statistical difference between Game Two and Game Three had been the tallest Pacer in history, Rik Smits for twenty-seven points on 12-of-21 shooting. Reggie had shown up well enough with sixteen points, although his 5-of-12 mark was still a little shaky. Overall, the team had hit over half their shots (52 percent) a dramatic improvement over the 32 percent they'd made in Game Two.

But, again, those are only the numbers. In this game, those numbers were merely the digits on the odometer. The Pacers had run away with this almost from the start—slowly, surely, increasing their lead, never letting up on the Hawks or their own driving offensive speed.

The momentum of this series hadn't just swung, it had flown—and left the Hawks choking on their own feathers.

* * *

In what had become their playoff habit, the network commentators opened the pre-game coverage of Game Four on May 15 in Indianapolis with yet more discussion of the Pacers' opponents. In this case, it was what the Hawks had to do to re-assert themselves and win the series that was obviously theirs to lose. Atlanta's task was to "forget and refocus." Coming off a dismal twenty-point loss in Game Three, the Hawks knew they had to get more production out of franchise player Danny

Manning and All-Star point guard Mookie Blaylock. Manning had gone 3-of-12 in Game Three and Blaylock only 2-of-8 from the field. According to Atlanta's Kevin Willis, a players-only meeting after Game Three had indeed refocused the team. No one had pointed any fingers; everyone agreed they just had to go out there and get the job done against a team that was, as the analysts said, "unknown to most of America."

To his credit, NBC's Bill Walton maintained an even-handed approach and even managed to suggest that the Pacers were playing as good as, if not better than, any other playoff team—and that no one should be surprised if their momentum continued.

And, to their credit, the Hawks would show Indiana and the nation a much better ball club early in Game Four. They were shooting better, rebounding with more intensity and generally looking like a team that could reclaim its pride and even the series.

Both teams were hitting the shots they should be hitting. Manning got into his flow early. Koncak hit from the outside. Smits started strong. He hit one then missed one but then sprinted downcourt to rebound a blown fast break led by Stacey Augmon. His quick pass back wound up in Reggie's hands and, a half-second later, at the bottom of the net for three points. The Pacers led 9–8.

If that short sequence weren't enough of a one-two punch to Atlanta's early confidence, the play also saw Kevin Willis limp to the sideline with a knee strain. Although Willis would re-enter the game in fits and starts, this injury would prevent him from playing any substantial role at either end of the court.

The Hawks hardly seemed to notice Willis' absence. Manning was having a rare day, hitting nearly everything he put up: four of his first five shots to give Atlanta a 16–15 lead.

After Manning's last shot, Larry Brown called a time-out to recalibrate his team in an attempt to put the clamps on his former Jayhawk protege and erstwhile Clipper star. But no strategies that Brown devised that day seemed capable of shutting Danny down. The fluid big man continued to have almost unlimited access to the basket and would finish the game with thirty-five points. But, as the Pacers had proven against Orlando, one man can't beat you.

Haywoode Workman came out of the first Pacers time-out and buried a three-pointer. Then Manning drove, drew a foul and hit both free throws. Tied at eighteen.

Then Rik, double-teamed in the low post, found Derrick darting into the lane for quick stuff. Andrew Lang answered with a jumper. 20–20. Then Rik fed Antonio in much the same fashion. Then Manning. All ten cylinders were clicking.

As the quarter came to a close, the Pacers seemed to run into some low-flying turbulence. A flurry of fouls called on both teams—combined with five Pacers turnovers in their last six possessions—produced a 26-22 Atlanta lead going into the second period. Manning finished the quarter with fourteen points.

The Hawks four-point lead melted in the early minutes of the second quarter. The Pacers scrambled back, turning one possession into three with fouls and long rebounds, and tied the game at twenty-six. Veteran two-guard Craig Ehlo hit from behind the arc to lift the Hawks to 29–26, but his counterpart, Reggie Miller, answered with a jumper. Indiana's defense shut the Hawks down, leading to a Pacers break and an Antonio Davis slam to regain the lead at 30–29. The exchanges came fast for the next couple of minutes: Rik found Vern for a 34–31 lead. Mookie hit a three to tie it at 34. Rik took them ahead with two free throws. Mookie answered.

Through the middle of the period, the teams appeared all but even in their energy and accuracy. Both were perfect from the line: the Pacers 10-for-10, the Hawks 8-for-8. The usual smattering of exciting plays at one end of the court seemed to balance the action at the other. Augmon blocked McKey from behind, leading to a Manning jumper. Byron stole an outlet pass and hit a three-pointer. Manning continued to play as well as the rest of his team combined, hitting jumpers, put-backs and short curls to the hoop. He would finish the half with nineteen points on 7-of-12 shooting and provide plenty of highlight footage for the Atlanta media. Miller finished the half with a quiet eighteen—quiet only because, unlike Manning's performance, Reggie's was part of a much more balanced attack.

Despite Manning's performance and the general sense of two tough teams going toe-to-toe, it was the Pacers who were pulling ahead. At times the Hawks looked a little uncertain—five guys passing around the perimeter until one of them, usually Manning, took a shot. If he made it, fine. If he missed, three or four Pacers would be waiting for the rebound. This is not the way to win a ball game.

The Pacers put on few dramatic spurts. They just displayed all-around competence with enough of that extra effort to take the opponents out any hope of controlling the tempo of the game. From an initial four-point deficit, the Pacers built a four-point lead they would maintain almost to the end of the half—when Reggie drained yet another three-pointer with 3.5 seconds remaining to take his team into the locker room leading 55–48. No doubt Atlanta missed Kevin Willis' seven-foot presence under the basket and general scoring agility as the Pacers outscored them 33–22 in this quarter.

If they had any hope of reversing the flow of this game—and with it, the series—the Hawks knew they had to regain control of the tempo and shut off the spigot of Pacers offense. In the second quarter, Indiana had hit 9-of-11 outside shots—6-of-8 from behind the arc. That was almost all the proof Indiana needed to know whose game this was turning out to be—and all the reason Atlanta needed to begin to worry. It's doubtful anyone took an NBA record book into the Hawks' locker room to show them that only four teams had ever come back from a 3–1 deficit in the playoffs. But the Hawks knew a loss that day would likely prove disastrous.

And they began the second half as if they knew disaster was looming—nervous and skittery. They were whistled for four fouls in the first two minutes. The Pacers just continued to play well and play together. Although Reggie and Rik turned in lackluster performances in the third quarter—initially going for a combined 0-for-8 from the field—their teammates kept the Pacers in the game. Derrick McKey tipped a Miller miss to a wide-open Workman, who drove the lane for two. If his jumpers weren't falling, Smits was still attracting enough overeager Atlanta attention to get himself to the line, where he hit consistently. Then Derrick, rummaging around at the back of his bag of tricks, remembered that he could also shoot the three-pointer, which he did, to take Indiana to a 62–50 lead.

Manning responded bravely, scoring his twenty-sixth point on a free throw after a driving basket, but the rhythm of the game—and perhaps the perceptions of the refs—were clearly flowing in the Pacers' direction. Kevin Willis had picked up his fourth foul by the middle of the quarter on calls that were probably closer than they needed to be. The Hawks took a long step into a challenging run, cutting the Pacers' lead to nine. But another offensive foul, called when it might have gone unnoticed, took away an Augmon bucket that would have pulled them within seven. When a short Ehlo jumper was rejected, any hint of a run was squelched.

Nearing the end of the quarter, the Pacers had built what seemed a comfortable ten-point cushion. The two teams traded baskets for a couple of minutes—even Kevin Willis dropped in with a short jumper. It must have enlivened his team. The Hawks flew at the Pacers in the last ninety seconds of the quarter, putting together a 6–0 run to make it 78–72 going into the fourth quarter. At this point, it might have been anyone's game.

Might have been: If the Hawks hadn't played a five-game series against Miami they *might* have been better rested. If Kevin Willis hadn't wrenched his knee in the first quarter, he *might* have been a bigger factor. If the Hawks hadn't gotten three of their starters in foul trouble, they *might* have been more aggressive defending in the final period.

Maybe. Maybe not. Maybe the Pacers were just beginning to play. And play they did. In fact, they romped through the fourth quarter like seniors thrashing the freshmen in a schoolyard mismatch.

It began with a ringer off the bench: Kenny Williams, putting in his first appearance of the game. The fans yelled in unison when he pulled in the first rebound of the quarter, then continued to roar when his quick-release outlet pass ended up with a wide-open Byron behind the arc. Three!

Antonio, not to be outdone, rejected the next Atlanta shot with a fierce swat that sent it into the scorer's table—and again brought the crowd to its feet. Then A.D. did it again. The fans had no time to catch their breath as Haywoode picked up this errant Ennis Whatley shot and flipped it downcourt to a sprinting Kenny Williams. Catching the ball just below the free-throw line on the right wing, Williams cut toward the hoop, leaped—seemingly stopped to check the scoreboard and wave to a friend in the fifth row—and slammed the orange into a bubbling bucket of noise.

Duane Ferrell finally hit a jump shot to end Atlanta's drought. But again, Williams went airborne to scoop a Workman miss off the rim and slam it down. The crowd's crescendo crested even higher. This whole sequence had barely taken three minutes off the clock. And, as roundball wisdom will tell you, a ten- or twelve-point lead with eight or nine minutes to play is anything but a lock. But the emotional force of the Pacers' play—and the overwhelming uplift they were getting from the fans—would prove unstoppable.

The team and the fans conspired to produce a fourth quarter that seemed an uninterrupted torrent of highlights. It was pure joy to watch, the sort of basketball dessert that rewards fans for all the months—heck, the years—of patience.

The Hawks managed to keep the Pacers in sight for another minute or two. But Derrick sank another three-pointer—and an increasingly hapless Ehlo missed an uncontested drive to the basket. Reggie then hit yet another trey. With less than six minutes to play, the Pacers led, 95–81. Kevin Willis came off the bench, but it scarcely mattered.

The crowd went ballistic when Haywoode streaked after a breakaway Mookie Blaylock, caught him from behind, jumped as he jumped and rejected a lay-up that Mookie and the rest of the world must have assumed was automatic. Follow that with an Antonio slam.

With less than a minute to play and one second remaining on the Pacers' shot clock, the fans may have thought they'd enjoyed their last slice of highlight pie. But Antonio took the inbound pass above the arc, spun and launched—and the arena lost it when the thing went in.

NBC's Walton broke out in a laugh. "There's nothing more to say after that." Reggie drained a closing-second jumper to give the Pacers a thrilling 102–86 victory and a 3–1 lead in the series. "Who are these guys?" Walton asked rhetorically. Then he answered, "They're championship contenders."

Back home in Atlanta, the local press were already telling the few remaining Hawks fans that their season was over. Terence Moore of *The Atlanta Journal Constitution* asked his readers another rhetorical question: "Can the Pacers play much better than this? The answer is yes, if only by a slither."

Moore also credited the Pacers with "more talent and depth than the Hawks." Ultimately, Moore said, the Pacers "wanted the game more. When they needed a rebound, they got it, and then they hustled for a couple more…Plus, if the situation called for a three-pointer, you had the feeling that the following was running through the mind of anybody in blue and gold:

"So where do you want it from, Coach, the left wing, the right wing or the middle of Kentucky?"

And finally Moore acknowledged the crowd. "There were cheers, of course. Then more cheers. Then the noise threatened to blow the roof off the place." Market Square Arena, he decided, was the "loudest place on earth Sunday afternoon."

The post-game Hawks locker room may have been the quietest. Danny Manning broke the silence to answer a reporter's question. "I don't know how many teams have done it," Manning said, "but we're going to make history. That's what we've got to do. We're going to go home, take it one game at a time. But we'll be back. This series is far from over."

Manning was right, at least to this extent: The Hawks would come back to Market Square Arena. The series would not be over for another ninety-six minutes of basketball.

* * *

True to Danny Manning's prediction, the Pacers lost Game Five. Fortunately— if any loss can be considered fortunate—it wasn't a record-setting, twenty-point humiliation like the one inflicted on them in Game Two. The Pacers were in Game Five nearly all the way. They just didn't win, basically because they couldn't find the basket with any consistency.

The Hawks continued to have their own problems finding fans. Like the two earlier games in the Omni, Game Five on Tuesday, May 17, failed to sell out— even after nearly a thousand Pacers fans flew down on three chartered jets to watch what they hoped would be the final game of the series.

For the first quarter, at least, their optimism appeared justified. Although Manning scored on a relatively easy drive, Reggie responded with a three-pointer, then Derrick got free inside for an easy lay-in.

If there were any omen of the outcome in the first minutes, it might have been Derrick's technical foul. Normally a player of quiet efficiency, McKey might have been the last Pacer anyone would expect to argue with an official vehemently enough to be whistled for a "T." But that's what happened.

Perhaps this was a symptom of a team too keyed up to relax, playing with too much to lose. Their opponents were trailing 3–1 in the series and almost certainly faced elimination. With next-to-nothing to lose, the Hawks could well afford to play loose. On the other hand, the Pacers had proven their mettle and should have been playing with confidence. If it sounds like a seesaw of speculation and second-guessing, well, that's what the game turned out to be: A seesaw match in which the winning team was the last one to put together a decent run.

While the Pacers connected on their first few exchanges, they came up empty for an equal while thereafter. Compounding their inconsistency, Rik Smits, whose foul troubles appeared to have been clearing up, found himself hit with two personals less than halfway through the first quarter. Still, the Pacers' play was active enough to give them a 13–10 lead on a steal to cap a 6–0 run.

Lenny Wilkens sent Duane Ferrell in early and he promptly hit a jumper. McKey answered. After Augmon scored on a drive, McKey, normally an excellent passer, misfired and gave Augmon another bucket. Back and forth, back and forth.

That changed in the last two minutes of the quarter. First, Willis hit a jump shot, and Antonio missed an awkward, ill-advised answer. Dale tried a short jump hook that missed everything. Then Mookie Blaylock interrupted a telegraphed pass, shot downcourt and buried a twelve-foot jumper. He did it again when Workman clanked a jump shot off the rim and right to Blaylock, who sprinted away just ahead of three defenders. His lay-up made it 22–19 as the Hawks finished the quarter on a 6–0 run.

No big deal. Both teams had produced six-zip spurts in the quarter. Atlanta's had come later, so they were ahead—by a measly three points, just a blink for Reggie. Still, something about the game didn't feel right, and Larry Brown figured lineup changes might improve the Pacers' rhythm. He brought in Vern and Kenny and reinserted Rik to start the second quarter with Byron and Dale.

Kenny immediately fouled Danny Manning, who hit both free throws. A short shot by Byron in the paint was rejected—some would say goal-tended. Kenny then fouled Ehlo. Veteran Vern broke that string of miscues with a drive to the bucket that netted three points after an Andrew Lang foul. Tied at twenty-six.

With four minutes gone in the quarter, the score had barely crept to a 28–26 Hawks advantage. Both teams appeared to be playing with competence but no flair. When the Pacers managed a moment of better basketball—say, a quick feed from Rik to Antonio in the lane—they were just as likely to blow the chance—Antonio bobbled the pass out of bounds. Solid defense by the Hawks obviously had something to do with it, but the fact was clear: Too many Pacers' possessions were ending in bad looks at the basket—or no look at all.

With six minutes left in the half, the Pacers were shooting only 38 percent compared to a respectable 50 percent from the field for Atlanta. As coaches will tell you, good defense creates points—and Atlanta was proving it, scoring repeatedly on defensive rebounds, quick outlets and dashes downcourt for lay-ins.

Still, the Pacers were taking enough shots—34 versus 28 by the Hawks—that they were hanging in the game, down only two, 28–30. And that margin is nothing when Reggie starts to connect. A Miller three-pointer seemed to ignite Derrick for a steal and a long pass to Haywoode for the foul and two automatic free throws. (Workman was a perfect 16-for-16 from the line during the playoffs.) Dale caught the fever, blocking a deft Danny Manning move inside, leading to a McKey drive to draw a two-shot foul: Pacers lead, 35–32. Antonio got to the line next to make it 37–32, and quick as you could say "sluggish offense," the Pacers were disputing the call with a 9-0 run. And the defense was rising as well. When McKey's weak pass ended up in Blaylock's hands, McKey tipped the ball out of bounds before the Hawks could convert the turnover to points.

But this would only last so long. The second quarter would end just as the first quarter had—with a swing to the home-court advantage. Atlanta's defense stiffened and their offense soared as the Mookie-and-Manning show took over. From a 41–40 Pacers lead, the Hawks took off for a 45–41 edge. A Blaylock steal and lay-up took the Hawks into the half with a 47–41 cushion. The Hawks had engineered an eleven-point turnaround.

The usual halftime statistical hindsight showed the Pacers had hit only fifteen of thirty-nine shots, 38 percent. The Hawks, though, were clicking along with 22-of-41 shooting, 54 percent.

But Indiana had plenty of experience coming back from halftime deficits in the half-dozen neighborhood. As the third quarter began, it looked as if this might be another one of those comebacks. First, Reggie hit a three-pointer to make it only 47–44. Then Derrick followed his leader with two, making it 47–46—all in less than a minute. Six-point deficit? Ha.

As if to prove the point, Augmon committed a flagrant foul, throwing a forearm high into Smits' throat, leading to a sudden, here-they-go-again, Pacer lead at 48–47 and potentially a decisive momentum swing.

But veteran Craig Ehlo wasn't going to let that happen. He hit a three-pointer to make it 50–48, Hawks. Reggie answered with two to tie it at 50—but then Ehlo responded even louder, with his second trey. Two empty Pacers possessions and successful Hawks' flights and—wham—Atlanta was back on top 57–50. Again, a 7-0 run had been answered by a 7-0 run. The only thing that seemed to matter was which team got its run later.

As far as the Pacers were concerned, the ups met the downs and the downs came out on top. The Pacers stole the ball, but Reggie missed the twelve-foot jumper. Rik stuffed the rebound but, in the race back downcourt, Reggie came down on Manning's foot, twisting his ankle. He crawled off the court on his hands and knees—a depressing sight that sent chills down many Indiana spines.

Ehlo just kept it coming, hitting a jumper on another break, then led yet another break to give the Hawks a 61–52 lead. That's when another veteran, Byron Scott, demonstrated his resolve. With two determined drives, Scott got the Pacers back in the offensive mood. With less than three minutes left in the third quarter, Indiana had whittled the lead to 63–57. Brown looked down the bench at Reggie; Reggie flexed his ankle, nodded and stood up.

Miller proceeded to hit a monster three, pulling the team to within four at 65–61 as the quarter ended. The swing kept swinging into the fourth quarter, as Vern hit on a drive to make it 65–63. Augmon returned the favor, but Byron found A.D. for a jam at 9:53 to play. But 67–65 was as close as the Pacers would get.

Again the curtain rose on the Mookie-and-Manning show. First, Blaylock hit a driving bank shot that seemed to come off the shot clock to swish through. On the next possession, Manning hit exactly the same shot. In two minutes, the Hawks had built a 9–0 run.

There would be further moments of Pacers momentum, but the team never more than flirted with a lead change. Reggie hit his fifth three-pointer to pull the Pacers within five at 75–70, but the Hawks just reasserted to 78–70. Derrick pulled a sweet move on the baseline to finish with a flush, but then Reggie passed to the fans. Workman found two on a jumper, but Manning scored to put it back up to 80–74.

With one minute left in the game, Augmon dropped in a short hook to make it 83–76. The Hawks would score five quick execution points to make it 88–76 at the buzzer.

Although playing with a broken nose suffered in Game Four, Ehlo had led the way with twenty-two points in twenty-eight minutes. Manning had contributed twenty points and nine rebounds. And Mookie had turned in his second triple-double of the series: fourteen points, thirteen assists and ten rebounds. When Mookie wins, the Hawks win. Moreover, Game Five had been the Atlanta .500—the Hawks hit 36-of-72 shots.

The Pacers, however, hit just a bit better than 35 percent of their field goals. Miller went 8-for-18 and McKey 9-of-18, but Smits could only add six points. He had that many turnovers, as well. And Dale Davis, although a skyhook in sneakers with twelve rebounds, failed to score.

Both Danny Manning and Jon Koncak celebrated their birthdays that night. May 17, 1994, was a happy day for both.

* * *

You gotta love this game—sports reporting that is.

Remember Atlanta columnist Steve Hummer? The guy with the line about scalping tickets for tractors? The fellow who sympathized with the Hawks over their empty Omni, advising them not to expect too much because, after all, Atlantans could hardly get excited about a bunch of games—two, anyway—

against the...uh...now, I know I put the press release somewhere...against the...oh, here it is; yep, that's right, the Indianapolis Pacers.

Remember Hummer?

On Friday, May 20, the morning after sixth and decisive game of the Pacers-Hawks series, he had some more thoughts about this hometown team.

"They got caned....For a team that spent so many months making itself known—building a standing greater than its talent—this series with the Pacers was a sudden cold splash of humility," Hummer wrote of the Hawks. "The three games played in Indiana all followed the course of Thursday: The Hawks barely belonged on the same floor."

Although Hummer couldn't stop himself from one final jab at Hoosierland, labeling Market Square Arena the "biggest and loudest barn for miles around," he admitted in the end that the Hawks had been "spanked."

And the punishment had been administered in front of the usual MSA sellout crowd. Even after the disappointing loss in Game Five in Atlanta, there were few who doubted this would be the clincher. Yes, the local press made as much as it might of the absolute need to seal the series at home. And the Pacers' players and coaches dutifully offered respectful, thoughtful quotations about the meaning of "pressure"—pressure to win, pressure not to lose, pressure to show the world you are who you say you are, etc.

But honestly, folks, didn't you just feel this one coming? Didn't you *know* this would be another waltz?

Because if you didn't, you sure sounded like you did. You started roaring even before that first shot left Reggie's hands, sailed high over the floor and sliced through the bottom of the net. You kept roaring as the Pacers kept coming.

If there was any fear in the pit of your stomach or doubt in the back of your mind, none of it made it to your lungs. And for the last four minutes of the game, you all just stood in place and yelled: 16,565 sore throats soaring with their team.

* * *

The Hawks controlled the opening tip of Game Six. It was downhill from there—well, practically. Kevin Willis did hit the first shot, a short hook over Rik Smits.

Willis, who had been quoted to the effect that Smits was simply a large body who occupied otherwise useful space in the paint, hadn't had a stellar series himself. He had a habit of starting strong, scoring in double digits in the first quarter, then all but disappearing. A hyperextended knee and a torn thumb ligament were at least partially to blame for his less-than-championship post-season.

The Pacers brought their first possession downcourt, passed it crisply around the perimeter and found Miller waiting calmly behind the arc on the left wing. Reggie launched and gave the Pacers their first lead: 3–2.

Manning returned fire to give the Hawks their second lead, 4–3. The lead would skitter back and forth between the teams in a closely played quarter filled with some sparkling moments of offense and equally delightful defensive effort.

Augmon got in a rare stuff, answered in short order by Dale Davis, who was more accustomed to the shot. Rik hit his first jumper to give the Pacers a 9–6 lead, but Augmon answered to pull within one. Derrick dribbled the ball off his own foot, leading to a 10–9 Hawks lead with 6:43 to play in the first. The Hawks weren't going away meekly; they'd hit five of their first eight shots.

Blaylock looked primed and ready. Like Miller, he hit his first three-pointer. Miller, meanwhile had missed four straight treys. Derrick hit, then Rik. Augmon stole a rebound from Smits to feed Manning inside. But Rik bounced back to score on a slam over Koncak, who really looked like a spaceholder in the paint. That got the crowd going, and set the team humming. Reggie zipped away for a break that brought the score even at seventeen, and with new–found energy—as if he really needed any—Antonio ripped down a defensive rebound.

Rik got the ball in the low post on the left side, faked left then skipped right, turned and hit over Lang—his fourth score on five shots—to give the Pacers a 19–17 lead. More cheers, more cheers, more cheers…

…Until Mookie momentarily silenced the crowd with his second three–pointer to push the Hawks up 20–19. But Antonio was having none of that. He recycled Duane Ferrell's next attempt, creating a break for Byron. Fouled going up, Byron hit just one of the free-throws to tie the game at 20–20.

In hindsight, the next two minutes would be seen as Atlanta's last view of a possible victory. A quick series of exchanges ended with Smits hitting his fifth of six shots to put the Pacers up 24–23. The crowd screamed as if it was the game winner. Technically, it was. The first quarter ended on that total, and the Hawks would never again lead or tie.

Another flurry of possessions offered the crowd some exciting long passes, steals and clanked shots. Through it all, the Pacers held serve. Manning missed and the Pacers rebounded. Ehlo missed and Dale snatched it down. The Pacers inched up 28–23.

Both teams moved lethargically into the second quarter. Manning finally broke a 6–0 run to bring the Hawks within three at 28–25. But Haywoode drove to make it 30–25, then Reggie broke his own 2–of–8 slump to make it 32–25. The Hawks clawed back to within two on a spot–up three–pointer from a wide–open Mookie. But Haywoode came right back with a fifteen-foot jumper to make it 34–30. Each time the Hawks made a bid for the lead, the Pacers would score to protect it.

But points were few and hard won. In fact, the second quarter had all the appearances of an arm-wrestling match. The sweat poured down their arms and the veins popped in their heads, but the opponents barely moved. The half ended a mere twenty-six points higher than the quarter—fourteen additional Pacers points and an even dozen for the Hawks—Pacers lead, 38–35. The NBA records go back to 1977 before they hit another quarter of such limited output.

No matter. The Pacers were merely saving it for the second half. The Hawks had nothing more to give.

Rik hit the first shot of the third quarter. Willis was whistled for a moving pick on Workman, then Reggie hit the second Pacers bucket. That three-point lead became seven. Augmon notched Atlanta's first points of the half, but the Pacers hardly seemed to notice.

Rik at the line, McKey to Dale for a lay-in and suddenly it was 46–37. The crowd went wild—not that anyone could tell the difference—and Atlanta needed a time-out. It only postponed a Dale Davis dunk, an offensive foul by Andrew Lang and a Haywoode Workman jumper in the lane for a 50–37 lead. The corn-fed crowd smelled blood and went wilder.

With seven minutes to play in the quarter, the Pacers' fast-forward flight hit a lull—if a furious exchange of buckets could be considered that. The momentum trembled but never really swayed. Down 53–42 with five minutes to play, the Hawks cut the lead to seven—something of a moral momentum swing if not exactly a victory. But then Manning walked and drew a technical foul. The Pacers went back up again by nine, 55–46.

A marvelous effort on the offensive glass, three rebounds of three Pacers' misses, finally produced a McKey three from the wing: 58–46 with 2:50 left in the quarter. This seemed to nudge Derrick to some new level. He stripped Adam Keefe under the basket and shot the outlet to a streaking Byron. Scott made the lay-up, drew the foul and converted the three-point play—61–46. Then *another* McKey three. Smits got into the act, then Reggie, then Smits again, then Haywoode. Tinkers to Evers to the Hawks didn't stand a chance.

The Pacers went into the final quarter of the Hawks' post-season leading 72–51.

Perhaps the team got just a little ahead of itself in the opening minutes of the fourth. Or perhaps the Hawks found some hidden reservoir of resolve. In either case, Atlanta came into the quarter looking crisp and determined. They sprinted to an 8–0 run, holding the Pacers scoreless for nearly three minutes until Reggie hit a short baseline floater. But all that hustle had cost the Hawks—the Pacers were into the bonus with more than eight minutes to play.

From then, the lead hovered around fourteen points. Atlanta continued to display some of the finesse that had given them the best record in the conference.

Duane Ferrell cut the lead to 77–63 on a seemingly impossible spin along the baseline under the basket. But these moments seemed little more than aesthetic gestures at saving face. And the Pacers pulled some aesthetic surprises of their own: Dale Davis getting the ball in low, drawing Manning's fifth foul, then gracefully sinking both free throws.

Some full-court pressure from Atlanta produced little visible effect as the Pacers bounced along 82–68, then 84–70, then 84–72, then 85–72 with four minutes to play. Even though the officials insisted the teams play the final minutes, the crowd needed to see no more. They rose and roared.

Trading baskets would've been fine, but the Pacers decided to throw a few more feathers on the fire. McKey stripped Manning and passed to Scott who found Dale under the basket. Then McKey stripped Manning *again* and Byron raced downcourt to *stuff* the ball—for the first time all season. Some of the Pacers hadn't realized Byron could jump that high.

Rik hit his parting shot of an 12-of-16 night to make it 95–77. Then Reggie demonstrated his own aesthetic flair by draining the last Pacer shot, a three-pointer that hurt more Indiana throats than Atlanta hearts—which by then had already quit beating, anyway.

10
A Date With Destiny —
and the Knicks

For more than twenty years, stretching back to the fabled days of the ABA and the equally storied years of Willis Reed and Walt Frazier, the New York Knickerbockers and the Indiana Pacers have circled each other like two fighters looking for an opening. History was hoping they'd get the chance to go at it someday, when both were healthy and both were feeling their stroke. If it ever were to happen, it would be a match-up peppered and propelled by two decades of basketball tradition in both cities—and maybe a century or so of cultural antipathy between the biggest Big City and the hayseediest NBA city in the league.

But the two had been on—or near—the same page in the history books for some time. In 1973, both teams won the championship of their leagues—the Knicks in the NBA, the Pacers in the ABA. The Pacers made it to the ABA finals again in 1975, but would never equal their former glory in that or the next decade.

Through the 1970s and 1980s, the Knicks experienced their own fall from grace. In the 1973–74 season, the Knicks made it to the second round of the playoffs on the resilient strength of stars such as Walt Frazier, Dave DeBusschere, Bill Bradley, Willis Reed, Jerry Lucas, Earl Monroe—and future Bulls coach Phil Jackson.

The next year, the Knicks slipped yet another notch and were eliminated in the first playoff round by Houston. They reappeared in 1977–78 and again in 1981. The same year, coincidentally, the Indiana Pacers made their first playoff start in the NBA, but couldn't keep pace with the Seventy-Sixers. After that, the Pacers had what might kindly be called a mediocre decade.

When Walsh took over as general manager of the Pacers at the end of the 1985–86 season, his team and the Knicks had the two worst records in the league over that and the previous seasons. The Pacers had four awful seasons in 1983–84–85–86, totaling only 94 wins against 234 losses.

The Knicks, over the three-season span of 1985–86–87 totaled 71 wins and 175 losses.

In short, both the Pacers and Knicks had their work cut out for them. In the mid-1980s, the possibility of the Pacers and the Knicks playing in the 1994 Eastern Conference Finals looked slim to non-existent.

In fact, except for the 1981 season, you'd have to go back to 1953 before you could find a New York team and an Indianapolis team both in the NBA playoffs—

yes, an Indianapolis team. That year, the Minneapolis Lakers knocked the Indianapolis Olympians from the Western Division semifinals on March 22 and 23.
The Lakers, led by George Mikan, the league's first dominant big man, would go
on to beat the Knicks in the championship, 4–1.

But the Knicks and Pacers in the Eastern Conference Finals?

The NBA Draft helped the Knicks take a giant step in that direction. New York
drew the Number One pick, spending it on the future of their franchise: Patrick
Ewing.

Their great fortune came at the expense of the team that drew Number Two:
The Indiana Pacers, who acquired Wayman Tisdale—eventually traded to Sacramento for Randy Wittman and LaSalle Thompson.

But things change. Great players come into the league to sway the balance of
power. Great coaches emerge to help make average players good, good players
great and great players even greater. And then there's always the chance of a general manager putting all of the other factors together.

All of the factors came together in 1993–94. And for the maximum emotional
impact and most profound sense of historical drama, there really was only place to
take the Pacers after that:

New York.

* * *

New York. Bring on New York. We want New York.

Reggie Miller had said it at the end of the semifinal round, when the Pacers
were still awaiting the outcome of the Knicks-Bulls series. Flush with victory, still
soaked in sweat after the final game against Atlanta, Miller was ready to go to it.
He said that either opponent would be just fine, but if push came to shove—as it
most certainly would—he'd be just a tad happier to go up against the Knicks.

Why?

Well, to put it bluntly, Chicago—despite its status as "three-peat" NBA champion and its admirable performance this season—just wasn't the Chicago of
storybook or record book fame. Without Michael Jordan, the Bulls had managed
to bull their way through the season and the playoffs on sheer momentum, like a
great beast that continued its charge even though shot through the heart. Soon,
very soon, its legs would fold and its head would bow. There would be glory, perhaps, but little joy if the Pacers were asked to put that last bullet through its head.

But New York?

Now here was an opponent. Yes, a match-up against the Knicks would give the
Pacers a chance to avenge last year's first-round elimination. And, yes, it would
give Reggie an opportunity for another stimulating tête-à-tête with his old head-

butting buddy, John Starks. But most of all, it was because of what the Knicks represented. They were a symbol of tradition.

They were the embodiment of tough. Black-topped schoolyards and chain nets, big-money hustle games and kids from the projects fighting their way to daylight. They were the friendly elbow to the throat, just to remind you: "Hey, we play for keeps around here."

If New York was the heartless Big City, Indiana was basketball's heartland. The hoop nailed to the side of the barn. Skinny kids earnestly practicing in the late-summer sun after the chores were done. The hick from French Lick who went out East to show those folks a move or two.

OK, OK, the stereotypes fall short of the facts. Miller was a middle-class kid from L.A. with a reputation as the worst trash talker in the league. Smits grew up polishing wooden shoes in Eindhoven, Holland, not speaking a word of English. Someone would have to teach him to say, "Oh yeah? So's your mother." Pacer stalwart Vern Fleming *grew up* on Long Island.

But the emotional appeal of the match-up somehow transcended the merely true—it went right to the heart of every doubt and every moment of pride that Pacers fans had ever felt. It was the Hicks vs. the Knicks.

Miller, though, wanted to play New York for one overriding reason: They were the best. To be the best, you have to beat the best. Miller's command was a challenge, yes. But more than that, it was a compliment.

In New York, however, it was taken as an insult, an upstart's taunt. The New York press—which is also to say, the national media—viewed the Pacers as a bunch of "overachievers," or "pesky" at best, some sort of insect to be dispatched before the NBA Finals. Miller, never exactly softspoken on-court or on-camera, was suddenly spending more time and emotion than he'd ever anticipated just trying to explain himself for apparently "dis-sing" the Knicks.

Larry Brown would later recall that "Reggie was misunderstood. He meant it as a compliment, but it backfired on us. The media brought that out. If people had just taken it the way it was intended, we wouldn't have worried about all that."

All season long, Brown had stressed "just playing our game." And so far—which was, indeed, pretty darned far—that had meant coming in and getting the job done, doing whatever it took to win. "Our game" did not include a truckload of media hype. It was simply a distraction.

It wasn't by any means a fatal distraction. It didn't cost Miller or the Pacers Game One at Madison Square Garden. It didn't take them so far out of their game that they might as well have been back home in Indiana. The Knicks did that.

Perhaps in retrospect you could say the Pacers came into Madison Square Garden ready and maybe even a little willing to be impressed by all the hype, all the banners in the rafters, all the movie stars in the seats. Even Larry Brown couldn't help but admit to a certain sense of awe. When he was a kid, he told reporters, he had always dreamed of playing for the Knicks.

But it is important to remember that awe is not simply the unavoidable mood of David before Goliath. It is inseparable from the sense of tradition and respect that fuels the game. Tradition and respect were the reason people like Brown were still in this sport. They were the reason Brown started Vern Fleming at point guard—because New York was Vern's hometown and he had family in the crowd. Earlier in the playoffs, Vern had been in agony—not because of any physical pain, but because his late-season injuries had kept him from playing. This start was just one way Brown could make it up to him.

Further, you could say that the Pacers had every right to feel impressed. It was part of the thrill. After all, the Pacers weren't simply here for yet another in a seemingly endless series of regular-season spankings. This time the Pacers were here as equals—weren't they?

* * *

They weren't—at least in Game One.

True, there was a fairly delightful surge out of the gate. The Pacers zipped to an 8–0 lead, like some giddy kid who can't wait for his big brother to pay for the tickets and races ahead into the movie theater.

A running bank shot by Reggie gave the Pacers a 2–0 lead. Five seconds later, Charles Oakley reminded the Pacers who the Knicks were by oh-so-subtly slamming into Reggie as he deposited the ball on the baseline and started downcourt. However, Oakley did so right in front of an official who promptly whistled up the technical foul.

Vern drew two free throws on the next Pacers ball. Then Smits hit. Pacers eight, Knicks nowhere—yet. Patrick Ewing was a little perturbed by this first minute and a half, so he told the officials about it. Another "T."

Hey, the Pacers' TV audience was thinking, this ain't so hard. Heck, at this rate the game will be over by halftime. All too true.

The Knicks' early drought was broken by Derek Harper's three-point shot. Smits answered. Another Harper three, an offensive foul on Dale Davis. Rik hit again, but then hit Ewing. Antonio missed, but so did Starks. McKey hit one free throw, but then Antonio missed again, then Reggie missed a three, and so on.

If the Pacers were having a heck of time finding the bottom of the net, the Knicks were no better. A couple of minutes of running back and forth may have been good exercise, but it was more likely an exercise in frustration for both teams. Finally Oakley tied the game at thirteen halfway through the quarter.

Dale Davis showed double effort in diving for his own rebound from the second of two missed free throws, but it was just a valiant effort. And that frustration must have been sufficiently painful, because on his next trip to the line he made both shots to tie the game again at 17–17.

When it was 17–17, it was a very good game. Then it wasn't anymore.

The Knicks' bench guard Greg Anthony hit a trey to make it 20–17. The Pacers were still looking for the energy they'd had in the first two minutes. These nice guys hadn't made a field goal in nine tries—and missed again after a steal.

Anthony Mason, the man with the playoffs' most creative coiffures since the departure of Dennis Rodman, hit two more free throws. Brown was getting perplexed. He brought in Byron Scott and Kenny Williams in an attempt to generate more offense. Kenny promptly fouled Mason again. Then Anthony, who actually shot better from behind the arc than in front of it during the season, hit another three. The was Knicks led 26–20 at the end of the first.

Coming out into the second quarter, the Pacers may not have know precisely how poorly they were shooting—it was 1-for-11 since their initial eight-point run—but Brown was willing to try most anything to break the cold spell. Sam Mitchell, not normally a part of the first-half rotation, came in and gave the team a lift by hitting a jumper, then breaking away for another bucket.

That was more like it, but only for a moment. The Knicks went on an 11–0 run over the next 2:50. Rik Smits finally broke through with a short jumper to make it Knicks 37–26. Ewing got the same idea, and answered his opposite number with twice the points at twice the distance: Two long-range jumpers to make it 41–26, then put back an increasingly rare Knicks miss to make it 43–26.

The Pacers looked uncertain, out of sync, almost stunned—as if they'd come out of the hotel to see someone driving away in their car. Even old reliable, Vern Fleming, missed a drive at the bucket. And the Knicks just kept punching them. If it was painful to watch, it must have been worse to play. How many Pacers shots were boggled by tough defense even before they left the shooter's hands? How many were just a quarter-inch off and rattled around and out?

At times like that, it's almost comforting to look through the coolly abstract lens of statistical analysis—as if to say, "Oh, isn't that something? We're shooting 27 percent this quarter while our opponents are doing much better, 57 percent." Can pain be abstracted?

Rik finally got one to roll the right way and interrupted the Knicks' run at 43–28. But Ewing just did his number again. Reggie connected with 3:45 left in the half. Although the shot seemed to have come a year after his last field goal in first quarter, it did appear to give his teammates a bit of confidence. Dale got free inside for two more, then even took the ball in on a fast break—not the most elegant display of athleticism, perhaps, but somehow always in control and certainly effective. For a long, encouraging minute or so, the Pacers had rediscovered their flow to pull within 13—hey, that looked pretty close—at 47–34.

The Knicks seemed a bit unsettled by this resurgence. For most of the half, the Pacers had looked far worse—severely shaken. The Knicks were accustomed to winning as much by psychological pressure as by physical defense. When the underdog bit back, the Knicks weren't always sure how to handle it. John Starks stepped up with his idea: Comedy. Starks provided the half's one moment of goofball entertainment when he dashed downcourt with a stolen pass, took a giant stride toward the rim, spun in midair with boyish joy—and missed the dunk. Knicks Coach Pat Riley couldn't wait to share his laugh with John and promptly called a time-out.

The break woke the Pacers from their brief dream. Rik hit an eighteen-foot jumper immediately after the time-out. But Reggie missed one of two free throws as the ever-inventive New York crowd reprised its regular-season chant of "Cheryl, Cheryl."

For their part, the Knicks just kept doing what they do, scoring six more points and challenging every pass, every dribble. They even hassled the Pacers' last full-court inbounds with four seconds in the half, almost causing a turnover. The Pacers, to their credit, did not run out of the arena, even though the locker room must have been beckoning like a fallout shelter after their 53–37 first-half shelling.

The Pacers brought new energy into the second half. Smits, the team's high scorer with fourteen in the first two periods, continued to play well, grabbing rebounds and shooting over Ewing almost as if he weren't there. Regardless of how much or how little his teammates were intimidated by Knickerbocker history, Dutch-born Smits seemed immune. Maybe he just didn't know enough to be awed, living proof of the cliche: If you can keep your head while everyone around you is losing theirs, you probably just don't understand how serious the situation is.

One way or the other, Smits kept his head. He ended the with twenty-seven points and ten rebounds, team highs in both categories. And he must be credited with playing a major part in holding Ewing to essentially the same numbers. The Knicks' superstar center had twenty-eight points and eleven rebounds. But to this extent, Smits actually outplayed Ewing: Smits did what he did twenty-seven minutes; Ewing had forty.

In any case, Rik came out of the half ready. In the first few minutes of the third quarter, he hit the first jumper, drew Ewing's third foul, converted from the free throw line after attracting a flagrant foul from Oakley and hit another short jumper. He wasn't the only player in the game, of course. Reggie sank another shot, and Ewing and Starks added points to their side. With seven minutes to play in the third, the Pacers were climbing slowly back into the game, 59–48.

The last half of the quarter witnessed an intensely and fairly cleanly played series of possessions. Kenny Williams scored on a put-back. Byron hit a jumper. Ewing was hammered on an inside move, and even that display of disrespect seemed to rev the Pacers' engines.

Vern slipped inside to pull the Pacers within eight—66–58. Then Byron made it 66–60. Oakley grunted and put it back to 68–60 and the Knicks knuckled down to prevent two successive possessions, and were able to rely on the Pacers relative inaccuracy from the line. Still, Indiana inched it up to 68–62. It was 70–63 at the end of the third quarter.

Thirty-year-old Sam Mitchell, again showing the veteran resolve that had earned him praise all year, hit the first Pacers score of the fourth, making it a five-point game.

Ewing, showing the stuff that had made him Ewing, answered with a great, high-arching shot over tough defense. The Pacers squinted, but didn't blink. Smits made it 74–67, then 69. Hubert Davis, who had been stabbing the Pacers all year at crucial points, hit a three. But Antonio got loose inside for two, and Smits hit again over Ewing's outstretched arms; it was a three-point game, 77–74.

The Knicks found some reserve strength in Hubert Davis and Greg Anthony, who combined for a jumper and a drive on a steal to push the Knicks back to 81–74. Indiana found its own reserve in Antonio, who pushed back to 81–76. The Pacers were looking good, executing crisply even this late in a physically draining game.

Then the veterans took charge. Ewing hit, but Vern Fleming penetrated and drew the foul to make it 85–81. Then Vern did it again and there the Pacers could almost reach out and touch it: 85–83.

That's when Hubert Davis sank another three. Fleming remembered it as a "heartbreaker."

And then Starks, held to only three points so far, got free for two more. With 2:30 to play in a game that had seemed a hard climb up a tall tree, this new seven-point Knick lead suddenly looked like a sequoia to the Pacers—especially after rookie Antonio had a spasm of indecision. A bad pass ended up in Derek Harper's hands. Antonio then took a defensive chance by coming out in front of Ewing to prevent a pass.

And then a New York whistle put an offensive foul on Reggie—for inadvertently decking Ewing on a drive-and-dish move in the lane.

The last few possessions only confirmed the inevitable Knick victory 100–89. There was nothing remarkable about these final plays except to say that even with victory obviously in sight, the Knicks hustled on every play with the same intensity they had applied all night.

If there was need to point any fingers in the Pacers locker room, no one was really in the mood. Workman and McKey had combined to produce 0–15 shooting. But Reggie Miller, who had gone 5-of-11 for fourteen points, stepped up and told the press, "I'm the man. I take responsibility for this loss."

The loss wasn't just a deficit in statistics. It had been a war of hearts, minds and muscle; and the Knicks had shown more of all three. When push had come to shove, the Pacers hadn't been able to shove back hard enough.

* * *

Game Two was played on Thursday, May 26, again on New York's home court. The mood of the game was different from Game One. The ebbs and flows between the teams were different. But the result was the same: Knicks, 89; Pacers, 78.

It is hard to read the game stats and say, Aha! There's the problem. Having publicly accepted responsibility for Tuesday's loss, Reggie Miller played with greater determination. He took nearly twice as many shots in Game Two, twenty-one as opposed to eleven, but only made eight—three more than he'd made in Game One. Smits scored twenty-two points, down only five from his twenty-seven-point performance in Game One, but his rebounds dropped from ten to four. Well, maybe something can be made of the Knicks' edge in rebounding: 47–35, versus only a 39–37 advantage on Tuesday. But to compensate, the two starting no-shows from Game One, Workman and McKey, both improved their scoring. Workman went from zero to eight points. McKey improved, albeit slightly, from three points to four. But both teams scored eleven points fewer than they had in Game One.

Of course, stats do not win or lose games; players do. After the game, the Pacers' players agreed they'd been out-hustled. Some cynics would tell you that's just another way of saying the Knicks are a better team. Sam Mitchell disagreed. "I don't see that they're better," he told the press. "But they're playing like they want it more."

LaSalle Thompson offered this post-season reflection. "In the first two Knicks games, we played scared. And maybe we started thinking that the media might be right: We *had* accomplished a lot just getting there. Maybe that was enough for some of the guys. I think there were some guys who deep down inside didn't think we could beat the Knicks."

Brown concurred, "In New York," he said, "I think there were a bunch of guys who doubted if we could beat them. At the time, I thought Reggie was one of them."

That would change, but it would take some time. Perhaps the longest forty-eight minutes of that time came during Game Two.

The game started less than propitiously. After back-to-back touch fouls on Smits and Ewing, the Knicks returned the Pacers' Game One favor, sprinting to a 10–2 lead in the first three minutes. Brown called his first time-out to break that rhythm, and the Pacers came out with a tailored play from Rik into Dale for a jam.

Derek Harper hit his first jumper, Reggie got a tip-in. Dale made another successful cut through the lane, answered by Ewing's tip in at the other end. The two teams traded even through 16–8, then to 18–10. Reggie was visibly more active, drawing fouls and finally hitting his free throws with consistency. Haywoode looked more aggressive too, driving into the lane for a spinning lay-up that, though unsuccessful, certainly looked as if he meant business.

As the teams exchanged hoops, the Pacers seemed to be taking just a bit more and giving a bit less. If Reggie looked more confident in his shot, Rik looked just a bit more tentative; he soon picked up his second foul and was forced to sit down. Somehow the Pacers edged closer, to 23–16 on an Antonio slam, then 23–19 on Vern's three-point play on a drive and a foul. The quarter ended with the Knicks up 25–21.

The Pacers came into the second period with an extra edge of energy. Byron Scott hit a jumper to pull them within two at 25–23. Ex-Pacer pivotman Herb Williams was forced to foul Smits, but Rik could only hit one charity shot. The spurt almost bogged down when Rik missed an easy one in the lane and Byron missed two jumpers, but the defense held until Sam Mitchell could restart the engine with a tough fall-away on the baseline.

And there they were, tied at twenty-seven all with just under eight minutes to play in the half. Then Smits hit another—and another—over Ewing. By this time, Ewing realized that even with his arms straight up, he could not halt Rik's shots; Smits might not make it, but at least it was going up. Pat Riley realized that his team was behind 31–27 and needed to talk things over.

Perhaps he talked about this: In the middle of the first half of Game One, the Pacers had gone 1-for-11 from the field. Now the Knicks had gone Indiana one better—or two worse—hitting 1-for-13 in the first six minutes of the second quarter.

After the time-out, the Pacers came right back at the Knicks, Byron driving into the lane and drawing two free throws. Harper came back, but so did Rik with a fifteen-foot bank shot after a McKey steal. All through their struggle up from the 10–2 deficit and now into this building lead, the Pacers looked as if they'd begun to solve the puzzle of New York's style. If they could just get a few more numbers in the combination, they'd break through and the Knicks would be forced to play to *their* style. It looked for a moment as if the Pacers had done just that. Suddenly they were leading 37–29, then 39–31 with under four minutes left in the half. Wow!— for a while, anyway.

Something had to break, but it wasn't the Knicks' will. Rik sat down with his third foul, and the Pacers' lead went south. The Knicks forced the Pacers into two shot clock violations, a three-second call and a couple of awful shots. Not that the Knicks were burning the net, but Greg Anthony's three-pointer and a bunch of free throws gave them a 9–1 run to take the game into the half tied at forty.

Offensively, it had been a tepid performance for both teams. The Knicks were shooting 36 percent, the Pacers were hitting only one percent better. But nobody had figured this series for an explosion of points. Defense was to be the name of the game, as it obviously had been in the closing minutes of the first half.

Zealous defense tore the ball out of Dale's hands in the game's first second-half possession—but the Knicks couldn't score. Zealous defense took Reggie's first basket away from him, but the televised replay clearly showed Ewing knocking the bouncing ball out of the cylinder over the basket. Zealous defense enabled the Knicks to steal an inbounds pass and score, and it gave Rik a free throw after his quick turn to the hoop for a bucket. All that defense and so little scoring—tied at forty-three. It wasn't a slugfest, it was more of a slapfest, with balls slapped away on drives, slapped out of dribblers' hands, slapped in the air. There were even some good-old-fashioned slaps on arms and wrists to stop shots. Even Ewing got into the act, coming high above the key to double-team Haywoode and slap the ball out of his hands. Now that was defense.

There were a few moments of offensive display: A Smits hook, a long jumper from wing that McKey seemed to take reluctantly, a fast break finished by a Starks stuff, although even that was ignited by Oakely's rebound of a Smits air ball as the shot clock was dwindling. It was nip-and-tuck, grind-it-out basketball. Five minutes into the half, the Pacers had ground ahead, 49–48.

Reggie's jumper took it to a three-point lead, but any hope of padding it was delayed when Harper hit a trey to tie. So Reggie shot back with a three of his own—Pacers, 54–51. Smits looked very tough grabbing a rebound away from any and all, leading to a 56–53 lead. Starks tried a three that missed, but Ewing was there with the tip to bring the Knicks back within one. The New York fans, 19,000-plus, took up the chant of "De-fense, de-fense"—as if any such encouragement was necessary for the Number One defensive team in the league.

Haywoode couldn't hear them. He drove the lane to give the Pacers a 58–53 lead. The Knicks responded. Then Smits rose on the right wing as if to shoot, and shot the ball into Derrick stepping into the paint—60–57. Then Reggie, then Ewing, then back and forth until Rik's jumper bounced once, then twice around the rim and down into Knicks' hands. It went downcourt to Harper who *banked* in a three-pointer and turned to his teammates with a shrug and a grin as if to say: "Gee, I didn't call that but, hey, it counts."

Luck, maybe. But that shot off the glass seemed to act as a shot in the Knicks' arms. They picked up their effort a notch, stealing an inbounds pass and turning it into a four-on-nobody break that ended with a Ewing stuff. Then they hustled the ball away from Smits in the paint and the quarter ended. Knicks, 66; Pacers, 62.

The fourth quarter began with a spark in Smits' eye as he and Anthony Mason almost went at it—Smits bent down to give Mason an earful, perhaps advising Anthony to consider a new hairdresser. Smits fire wasn't catching, though.

Byron went blank, then Ewing hit. Rik bobbled a ball in the lane, and the Knicks capitalized again. Two minutes into the fourth, it was 69–62, then Oakley made it 71–62. Haywoode finally hit a twenty-foot jumper, but the Knicks just kept pounding the ball into Ewing, who kept pumping it up at the basket.

The Knicks seemed poised to blow the game open, but the Pacers' defense caught its breath and kept the lid on.

Unfortunately, Indiana could only hold its own for the next few minutes—and they began to sense that. With just over half the final period to play, the Pacers crept within seven points on two Workman free throws. But Rik's fourth foul put Mason on the line for a 77–68 lead. Ewing was stopped inside, but fouled. Smits drained a jump hook, but Ewing hit an eighteen-foot jumper that was followed by a muscular move inside by Oakley. The lead grew to a deadly dozen.

With four minutes to play, the Pacers had reached a point where it would've been easy to say: "There it goes again." They'd been here in Game One, and it looked familiar. But Larry Brown changed the scenery. He started telling the refs what he thought of the whole operation and quickly got slapped with a "T."

It almost worked. Dale stole an inbounds pass and turned to stuff it. Rik hit from the line. Reggie almost stole another long pass, but couldn't quite hold on as it flew out of bounds. In his frustration, he slapped a courtside computer printer hard enough to terminate its stat-scribing functions with 2:44 to play. Maybe it was Reggie's revenge on a night of bad stats. He was 8-of-21 from the field, prompting one wag to later remark, "The way he was shooting, we were surprised he hit the printer." After the game, Miller was unrepentant. "That thing shouldn't have been in my way."

With the printer down, the stat crew would have to rely on pencil work. It didn't prove difficult. Rik again got too close for the Knicks' comfort and drew a two-shot foul to get the Pacers within seven at 83–76—but that was pretty much it.

Two Oakley free throws and a McKey miss sealed the deal. A mop-up minute took the final tally to 89–78. The Pacers were now down 2–0 in the series. It wasn't a pretty picture for the Indiana faithful.

* * *

PACER POWER

Indeed, after Game Two, there were more than a few folks in the country who thought the whole affair reeked. In print and on television, the recurring adjective for the basketball being played was "ugly."

"Winning Ugly" was the title of *Sports Illustrated*'s coverage of the series.

It was ugly for Pacers fans, mostly because Indiana had lost. Knicks fans, on the other hand, thought their 2–0 had a certain golden charm to it. They couldn't lose now, of course.

Others were puzzled by the characterization. Ugly? No, not really. Intense, yes. Overwhelmingly defensive, yes. But ugly?

No—just hard. One observer offered this insight—a particularly insightful insight considering the source.

"Sure, offense is important to the popular appeal of the game," admits Donnie Walsh. "But we—the players and the league—would be better served if television wouldn't focus so much on the phenomenal scorers.

"All that does is create the impression that everybody in the country should just sit around all season waiting for Jordan or Bird to do their thing in the finals. And when the guys on TV sit around talking about all this 'ugly basketball,' I should say, 'You're killing yourself.' If those guys want mass appeal they should just stick Charles Oakley in a WWF outfit. He'd do just fine.

"Magic and Jordan and Bird just made it too easy on the media. All they had to do was say, 'Roll the tape,' and people applauded. If everyone doesn't begin to see the beauty in *this* kind of basketball, the networks are in for a tough time. And that's because we're coming into an era of parity in the league, when no one or two players can dominate the sport. It's only going to get more and more a matter of being able to play like *this*.

"And that's why this series was so meaningful for guys who love the game. It's so much closer to the real meaning of the game: Defense is harder than offense.

"And it speaks directly to the heart of the game because it's so hard. To play great defense, a player has to do the things nobody wants to do, dive for the loose balls, take a charge, fight for a rebound. That's really hard especially if you know you're going to have to expend a lot energy and there's a lot left to play. But it means so much to your teammates because it means you're willing to sacrifice yourself to win.

"We all have our money—win or lose. But after we get the paycheck, there's still this. And boy, it's hard; but it can be beautiful if you know what it means."

* * *

De-fense! De-fense!

The Knicks had taken a 2–0 lead in the Eastern Conference Finals by sitting on de-fense. Their fans paraded giant cardboard pickets around Madison Square Garden.

Much had been made in the media and the barrooms of how these two intensely defensive teams had produced two games that were offensive to the best aesthetics of basketball. Witness the ugly percentage of Reggie's shooting—13-of-32. Ugly? Maybe.

Larry Brown told the TV that it was time for the Pacers to get down and get even. "If the Knicks are going to grab and push, so will we. We gotta play the same way, do the same things they do."

As far as NBC commentator and basketball legend Julius Erving was concerned, that would only mean the Pacers would be sitting by the pool that much sooner. Indiana was "overrated and overmatched" against the Knicks, Erving said. "The problem with playing the Knicks' game is that they're always going to be better at it. This series will be over in...five," he said in a mild attempt to avoid sounding patronizing.

Patrick Ewing had already said what he thought of the Pacers' attempt to play the same tough-minded and roughneck style of Knicks basketball: No soap. "They're a carbon copy of us, only we're a little better. They're the copy. We're the real thing."

Only Bill Walton, sitting next to Erving on the network's pre-game show, had a different perspective. "I disagree wholeheartedly," Walton said. "The Pacers are fine, and this series is going the distance."

Donnie Walsh remembered that and laughed. "Oh yeah. I can just see the network guys saying, 'Jesus, Bill, what are you talking about? We gotta get this guy off the air with stuff like that coming out of his mouth.'"

Yes, indeed. Get that stuff out of here.

* * *

Game Three will be remembered for many things and for one thing in particular: One point. Patrick Ewing's one point.

It was a record for Ewing, and it was a huge contribution to the record established by the Knicks that Saturday afternoon in Indianapolis. The fewest number of points ever scored in an NBA playoff game: sixty-eight.

De-fense. De-fense.

Before the game the record was held by the Indiana Pacers, who had scored just sixty-nine points in Game Two of their semifinal playoff series against the Atlanta Hawks. It had been a sobering experience for the Pacers, who would have preferred to remain intoxicated by their heady run through the last weeks of the season, their Round One sweep of Orlando and their theft of Game One in Atlanta.

Now the Pacers were more sober than they ever wanted to be. New York had beaten them twice in Madison Square Garden. These hadn't been embarrassing, record-breaking defeats. Perhaps worse, they had been slow, twisting-the-broken-bottle-in-your-face defeats. New York had never gone for the jugular in those games. They didn't appear to know where it was—or care. It was sufficient to pound opponents steadily into submission with unrelenting defensive pressure.

So the Pacers fought back—and they definitely appeared to know how.

As befitting a low-scoring contest, the Pacers' first possession ended in a three-second violation—too much waiting around for some offense. As befitting a defensive battle, the next possession lasted about half-a-second—before Haywoode intercepted the Knicks' inbounds pass.

The tone had been set, and the rest of the team just harmonized all afternoon. The Pacers' great defensive forward Derrick McKey, missing in offensive action from Games One and Two, provided the game's first score after Workman's pilfer. Their greatest offensive player missed his first three-point attempt—but then Reggie stole a pass and broke away for a deuce.

And then, as if the crowd needed any encouragement to vent some of its well-deserved anxiety, Rik Smits blocked Ewing's shot. But the fire would prove short-lived; there seemed to be so little to feed it.

The score mounted—oh so slowly. After three and a half minutes, it was a whopping 8–3. Conventional wisdom said that a low-scoring game favored the Knicks. But these were the new Pacers, back from the maddening pit of despair—or Madison Square Garden—and grimly determined after an emotional team meeting on Friday. They were ready to do whatever was necessary. If low was the way to go, they would out-limbo the Knicks until New York fell flat on its back.

The Knicks could feel it. They started to slip a little here and there—a sloppy pass bounced out of bounds. McKey then posted low and scored. Charles Smith finally hit a jump shot, but Riley wanted to huddle. After the time-out, Smits answered Smith.

Ewing tried to enter the conversation, but missed his second shot.

Another Pacer three-second violation brought the teams back, and Reggie picked up his second foul—an elbow suddenly stuck into a Knick—with half the first period to play. This was not good news, but it sent a message. The score crept up—12–9, 14–9, 14–10. Smith fouled Derrick, then Smits tied up Smith. Never a great jumper, Smits lost the tip, but Starks' ensuing three-pointer clanked away. Byron drove down the lane, but Ewing took the charge.

Ewing then returned Smits' block, and Rik, who shot well for the game (7-of-10) but not enough, promptly missed a fifteen-footer. Neither team seemed to feel any rhythm. It wasn't so much an ugly game as an existential comedy—*Waiting for Godot*, for instance, in which the characters sit around discussing the arrival of a fellow who never appears. The fans, schooled as they were on the thrill of action, may have found it hard to appreciate this new Pacers pace. They might have cheered harder if they had known Patrick Ewing had been cast as Godot.

The score was 16–11 with under three minutes to play in the quarter. The Pacers had hit a shooting slump—if anyone noticed—going 0-for-6 in the latest attempts. But the score kept sliding forward as Byron hit one of two free throws to make it 17–11. The crowd wasn't really into it at this point and, fortunately, it seemed the referees were paying about as much attention. Smits fouled Ewing, but no one with a whistle seemed to notice.

The action picked up slightly as the quarter ticked away. Hubert Davis stole another ball. Dale Davis got free inside with a good feed from Vern. Greg Anthony was fouled—and got the whistle—but only hit one free throw. Byron drove again and this time converted. The quarter would have gone out with a whimper if Hubert hadn't fired a desperate but well-aimed heave for three with three seconds left in the first. With twenty-one points, the Pacers were well on track to score in the mid-eighties—as they would.

With nineteen points to this point, however, the Knicks were overachieving.

Something exciting was bound to happen sooner or later. The second quarter began with Greg Anthony's jumper and Vern's foul. Naturally, Anthony missed the penalty shot but managed to end up with the rebound and scored again to suddenly give the Knicks a 23–21 lead—their first of the game. Byron responded to tie, but Herb Williams sank a jumper to reassert the Knicks 25–23.

Antonio was stripped on the return possession, but Anthony, perhaps overcome with all the recent excitement, traveled coming up court with the ball. With veteran savvy, Byron faked to pull Hubert Davis into the air and down again on Byron. Scott tied the score with two free throws.

Enter Mason, who drained a fifteen-footer. Mason was fouled by Kenny Williams and made both free throws. That was four in a row, something of a rampage in this game. The turnovers were piling up in two even mountains: ten for the Pacers, nine for the Knicks. Perhaps both coaches were getting restive as well; both brought their top scorers off the bench for the last two-thirds of the quarter. Shortly after Reggie and Ewing re-entered the game, Smits was reinserted as well. After a quick series of whip-around passes, Rik scored to pull the Pacers within two at 29–27. But counterpart Ewing couldn't counterpunch. Hauling down the rebound, Mason was fouled by Reggie and hit both free throws for another four-point Knick advantage with seven minutes in the half.

Byron missed another lay-up, but Greg Anthony made his immediately thereafter. The game still showed no discernible rhythm, but it continued to be played with intensity. Though slow, the half had been punctuated by occasional breaks down the floor. Increasingly, though, the dashes seemed only a counterpoint to the game's slogging mood. It became clear that this was not some temporary lethargy that the teams were going to shake off. And as it did, the game also became almost perversely satisfying to watch, as if it were a great fight between two heavyweights, but being fought underwater.

Ewing was fouled by Smits—it was obvious this time—but he missed both free throws. By now, Ewing was beginning to get the idea that something was really missing. Still, the score crept on: 34–32, then 36–32, then 36–33. As the first quarter had, the second ended with a minor flurry. McKey hit a turnaround and Starks hit from behind the arc. Antonio got inside Ewing's defense and drew the big man's third foul, bringing the Pacers within two, 39–37 at the half. Ewing ended the half having gone 0-for-7. Some of that was due to early foul trouble. Reggie, also playing limited minutes because of foul trouble, was not much better, contributing only four points.

Scoring in the second half began with Oakley's jumper, but it was the Pacers who got the jump-start. Reggie fired back but missed. Haywoode found the rebound for a lay-in. Ewing promptly picked up his fourth foul, going over McKey's back for a rebound.

And coming downcourt, Haywoode caught the Knicks with their knickers down and drove to the hoop while everyone else was waiting for Rik to post up. A Dale Davis steal led to a Smits jumper. At the other end, Derek Harper couldn't hit. It took an Oakley goaltend to put the Pacers back up, then Smits reclaimed another missed Pacer shot and put it back in to put them ahead 44–41. If there was any ugliness to all of this, it was not in the defense, but in the too-casual passing and missed free throws.

As was true of the first half, neither team could pull ahead decisively. From 44–43, Smits took a pass off Derrick's rebound and extended the lead to 46–43. Dale was called twice for pushing Oakley away from rebounds, lending some credence to Dr. J's televised analysis that the Knicks were simply better at this kind of work than the Pacers—in as much as the Knicks tended to get away with it.

With the game stuck at 46–43 with 6:45 left in the third, Smits all but tackled Harper on a drive and tried to look sheepishly ashamed. Apparently, he was sufficiently successful; no flagrant foul was called. Harper did his part in this glacial epic by hitting just one free throw to make it 46–44. Reggie hit from the baseline to make it 48–44, but then foolishly hit Starks going up for a jumper. Starks could only connect on one free throw.

Then Starks fouled Byron, then Oakley fouled Antonio—maybe the Knicks weren't quite as good as some might think. The Pacers pulled ahead 50–45 and Dale Davis decisively fouled Starks on a drive—and Starks missed both penalty shots. On the next possession, Byron drove and had his legs taken out from under him by Oakley, a longtime believer in no lay-ups and no prisoners. This time someone got hurt. Byron landed hard on the floor, bruising his back severely. After missing both free throws, he walked slowly off the court and back to the locker room to assess the damage.

Instead of being disheartened by the potential loss of their inspirational veteran, the Pacers responded with more defense. On the next Knicks possession, Greg Anthony was forced to lob up an air ball as the shot clock expired. Haywoode connected on the Pacers' return to take a 52–45 lead. Mason came back for two. Antonio tipped in a Dale miss. Starks was fouled and made both free throws, pulling the Knicks within five. But Haywoode, showing the fight he'd brought to the floor all season, drove again up the gut of the Knicks' defense and laid it in. LaSalle tipped in Antonio's bouncer, but then Vern drew his fifth foul when Starks kicked his foot out coming down from a jumper and caught Vern blowing by—a move he may have found on some old page of Reggie's playbook.

The quarter finished on a series of plays that put the Pacers up by ten—their largest margin of the game. The last bucket came with a flourish, on an A.D. dunk. But the real story of the quarter had been the Pacers' defense. It had held the Knicks underwater, allowing only thirteen points to bubble to the surface, the Knicks' lowest quarter total of the series. Pacers led, 62–52.

Reggie missed the first shot of the fourth quarter, but Antonio drew the foul on the attempted put-back. He hit one. Then Reggie was whistled for his fifth foul on what looked to be minimal contact. Some consolation was found in Ewing's next shot—clank and out. Lester Conner, taking a rare shot in his limited duties as backup to the backup point guard, sank an eighteen-footer.

The teams jockeyed back and forth, up and down the court. Mason hit one of two free throws. Byron returned to action but missed a three-point attempt, looking a little stiff and perhaps pained. A couple of empty possessions ended when McKey hit a jumper to make it 67–53. Ewing was stripped by Antonio, but that came to naught. Starks hit a jumper, and Harper broke away for a lay-in.

To deflate this mini-burst, Derrick McKey pulled a smooth move on Starks, holding his wrist and dragging him through the lane and somehow making it look to the officials that Starks was clutching him. Pleading the whistle with the referee, Starks genuinely looked heartsick, like a young boy about to cry, "But Dad, *he* started it." When Oakley attempted to calm him, Starks knocked his hand away in anger.

This was a sign. The Knicks would get not much more than frustration for the rest of the game. Derrick reached down and slapped the ball out of Starks' hands. Rik hit a jumper to make it 71–57 with half the final period left to play.

The big news came when Ewing was fouled on a baseline move and got to the free throw line to make one of two. By this time, Ewing's no-show on the scoreboard was the talk of the arena. Half of the MSA crowd was upset he'd made one; the other half found some aesthetic pleasure in the thought that he might be limited to just one point. The fans started to salute Ewing with their first fingers raised: You're Number One, heh-heh.

Harper was not going to quit. He fouled Reggie, who hit both free throws, then buried a three-pointer of his own to make it 73–61. But McKey found Dale under the hoop for a jam, then Rik hit again, then Dale did his up-and-flush act again and the confidence just kept building. Reggie made a balletic move through the lane to finger-roll the ball just over the rim, making it 79–61.

Starks and Oakley made three free throws to bring them up to sixty-four. But with 3:30 to play, the Knicks would be able to muster only four more points. The Pacers, meanwhile, just played a nice normal offensive game for the last minutes. Coupled with their extraordinary defensive display, it was more than sufficient to bury the Knicks, 88–68.

There were two tense moments before the buzzer. Hubert Davis drove to the hole for a lay-in and a foul, taking the Knicks to sixty-eight points with a chance to make it sixty-nine, thus saving New York from the humiliation of breaking the Pacers' record for fewest points scored in a playoff game. He couldn't. Then, as the last seconds of the game ticked away, bottom-rung Knicks reserve Rolando Blackman was pitched into the game on the prayer that his fresh eyes might see the rim at last. He couldn't either. The record was broken. Tag, New York—you're it.

* * *

The Pacers strode confidently into Game Four on Monday, May 30. They'd crushed New York two days earlier, and neither of their top two scorers had turned in much of a performance. Miller and Smits had contributed only fourteen points apiece; McKey had led with only fifteen. It was, in short, a complete team victory, and that was true of their defensive effort as well. One shooter may pull a game out of the mud and onto a silver platter—as would be seen in Game Five—but an entire team must play defense to produce that kind of lopsided score.

And if the team needed an extra dash of support, they got it at Sunday's running of the Indianapolis 500, when the benediction included a kind word for "our Pacers"—and 400,000-plus race fans said "Amen."

The opening tip went to the Pacers, but Rik missed a short hook off the glass. Ewing missed his first shot as well, and a shiver of anticipation ran through the crowd: Would Patrick be pointless again? No such luck; Ewing had only packed one debacle in his luggage. The crowd would be forced to watch him perform at his usual team-leading levels, finishing the game with twenty-five points and thirteen rebounds.

Pacer leader Reggie Miller also improved his performance from Saturday's C-minus game. Maybe it was numerology: Reggie, wearing jersey Number Thirty-one, found some ineffable inspiration from Al Unser Jr.'s Indy 500 success in car Number Thirty-one and went out on Monday to score thirty-one points. That was six more than Ewing—and the ultimate margin of the Pacers' victory, 83–77.

After Rik and Ewing exchanged clunkers, Reggie hit two free throws. But the offensive pace of the game had been established. As the quarter wore on, both teams would hit more metal than twine, grinding through the opening minutes with abortive bursts of offensive energy met head-on by defensive intensity. With a couple minutes left in the quarter, the shooting figures for both teams were hovering around 30 percent. In medical terms, it was a stress test, a test of the heart: Who had enough to get through this?

The Knicks came out on top—in points, anyway. But the Pacers found more than enough reason to smile at plays such as Dale Davis' gravity-defying rejection of Ewing's jumper. It was a thing of beautiful surprise: Just when you thought there wasn't any more of Dale's arm attached to those fingers, up slide another couple inches.

But other than that, the quarter was another example of what was becoming standard operating procedure for this series: intercepted passes, forced shots to nowhere, off-balance jumpers taken when the defensive doorway popped open for half a second. The Knicks led at the end, 20–17. Showtime it wasn't.

The second quarter started with Byron's jumper and Antonio rejecting an Oakley lay-in. Vern was shut down on a drive through the lane, but earned a trip to the charity stripe to put the Pacers up 21–20. The Knicks pushed it back to 22–21, sinking their first field goal in nearly six minutes going back to the first quarter. Vern answered with a steal, a drive and a finish. Derrick committed an offensive foul on the Pacers' next possession. But when the Knicks came back downcourt, Antonio harassed Ewing's shot enough to throw it off the rim, into Pacer hands and down the floor to Dale for a lay-in.

Starks replied to all of that by draining a jumper to put the Knicks back up 26–25 with about seven minutes to play in the half. Dale got loose again for two, then Haywoode stole another pass and drove for a bucket, taking the Pacers up 29–26. Starks replied again, draining a three-pointer to tie.

Back and forth, up and down. Reggie hit. Then Ewing. Then Rik for a three-point play—the world is still waiting for Smits' first long-range three— then Oakley. Back and forth, up and down. Reggie acted his way into a Ewing foul, but as the game wore on—indeed, as the series wore on—the close calls were traded fairly evenly.

The exchanges came and went and came back again. Reggie was beginning to hit from the field and get to the line. Ewing had obviously forgotten all about his dismal performance on Saturday. By halftime, Reggie had dropped in fourteen points and Ewing had twelve. The Pacers led 42–39. NBC's Julius Erving remarked on the halftime show, "It's about time we gave this team some credit."

The second half sputtered to a start. The first Knicks possession ended in Charles Smith's technical foul—which Reggie promptly missed—and then Rik picked up his third foul. It was beginning to look like a very long quarter.

And then Derrick McKey, seemingly surprised but trying to act nonchalant, found himself alone with the ball just above the three-point arc. Deciding he really didn't feel like going through another well-rehearsed play, he simply cocked and flipped the ball in the net without so much as a glance toward a more likely shooter.

This seemed to send the Pacers a message. Haywoode got it first. Bending down as if to pick up a quarter, he stole a bounce pass and threw it down to McKey. McKey, unfortunately embarrassed by his last self-centered play, flipped the ball to a driving Smits. Never the team's most agile open-court player, Rik committed a charge, his fourth foul. He sat down with nearly ten minutes to play in the quarter.

Without their big man, the Pacers stiffened their resolve, just as they had when Byron was injured in Game Three—tightening their defense and cranking up the offense. Admittedly, against the Knicks it's hard to tell when anyone's offense is cranking, but the Pacers managed to creep forward to take a 47–39 lead.

Then, to no one's surprise, the Knicks crept back. Harper hit to make it 47–41. Dale was fouled but could only make one from the line. Starks put down a jumper to bring the Knicks within five. And then Reggie hit a very long two—he wanted that third point, but the ref just smiled and pointed to the line and Reggie's sneaker.

Still, it was close enough for rock and roll, as the saying goes. The emotional effect of that size thirty-one extra-long pair of points was much the same as a trey. It pushed the Pacers through a decisive spurt. But almost before it began, the Knicks, sensing the shift, responded with their usual aplomb. Charles Smith promptly set an overly forceful pick on Reggie, as if to say, "Try this on for size, Skinny."

As LaSalle said later, "Reggie gets beat up all the time. But he never complains." He didn't have to this time. Smith was whistled for the offensive foul, giving the ball back to the Pacers and giving McKey the opportunity to hook in another two points, then hustle back to swat the ball out of Smith's hands as he pivoted through the lane.

McKey threw the ball downcourt to a streaking Haywoode who pulled and fired a jumper from the free throw line. It looked good for a split-second then rimmed out. The rebound found its way out to Reggie for a three-pointer, but the shot bounced back long into the lane; Reggie dashed to grab it, went up and…ssswisshh. In twenty seconds of instant replay material, the Pacers had scored, stolen and scored to take a 54–43 lead. With 7:30 left in the quarter, Pat Riley called time to recalibrate.

The time-out took some of the steam out of the Pacers, but the Knicks weren't exactly boiling, either. Both sides came up empty the next few possessions. Antonio broke the stalemate with a lay-in. Ewing answered, but Antonio came right back at the towering New Yorker, driving around him, through the paint and finishing with a high hook that came down to punctuate the net like a giant aerial question mark: "So, how tall are you? Huh?"

Ewing decided to show him. He backed into the corner almost to the three-point line and lofted a jump shot that rimmed out. He then grabbed his own rebound and hustled inside to draw two foul shots that cut the Pacers' lead to single digits, 58–49.

Things got a little gray for the blue-and-gold when McKey traveled and Starks converted the turnover with a jumper. LaSalle was forced to foul Oakley—although one suspects he enjoyed it—to disrupt a fast break. The Knicks were punching back, but the Pacers weren't reeling. McKey hit another long shot to put the Pacers back up 60–51 with about three minutes left in the quarter. On the return possession, Anthony Mason traveled as he attempted to post up against LaSalle. Mason, surprisingly agile for a man of his bulk, looked to be backing into the larger Thompson. But LaSalle cannily stepped back a half-step as he saw Mason make his move. Meeting no resistance, Mason had to take steps to keep his balance.

It was a small thing, really, but indicative of the kind of craft and determination the Pacers were applying to the game. They had seen Reggie limited by fouls, then Rik forced to sit, and had responded splendidly. The third-quarter test became a testament to their heart. The quarter closed as Byron, still somewhat in pain, borrowed a play from Reggie, curled off a screen and hit the jumper.

Again showing his youthful enthusiasm, Hubert Davis drained a three to give the Knicks some hope at the end of the quarter. He gave them even more when he stole the ball and drove downcourt. He was fouled, but only made one as the period ended with the Pacers up 62–55. Still, his energy fueled the Knickerbockers as they came into the final period.

After all, they were the Knicks. And these other guys? They weren't even the Bulls, they were the Pacers. They would have to be shown that the fourth quarter belonged to New York.

So the Knicks came out tough. When Smits tipped back Vern's skittering lay-up, Oakley answered with a bucket. The Pacers may have stopped to think a second too long—and drew a three-second violation. Then, maybe, the Knicks got just a little too eager—and threw the ball out of bounds.

It looked even, but the psychology was different. The Knicks pulled within six points, then exchanged scores to keep it there. Ewing's free throw made it 67–62, and then his third foul put Rik on the line. But Rik, a little out of sync after sitting nearly all of the last quarter, missed both free throws. The Knicks rebounded and hustled downcourt to score. Suddenly it was a three-point game, 67–64. And that lead, as everyone knew, could vanish in a blink—or a prayer, as when Greg Anthony lofted a desperation shot as the twenty-four-second clock wound down. Tie game.

The Pacers had seen a thirteen-point lead cut to zilch with well over half the final period to play. It was a new game, a seven-minute game with this on the line:

Either the Pacers would pull it out and pull even in the series….

Or the Knicks would head home to New York with a comfortable 3–1 lead in their suitcase. The Pacers knew their chances of coming back from that deficit. They had found out a couple weeks before. Sure they were good, but were they *that* good? Better not to find out.

Reggie hit a technical shot on an illegal-defense call, giving the Pacers the first point of this seven-minute test. But that Hubert Davis kid popped back up with another trey. Knicks 70–68. Haywoode lost a pass inside, but that increasingly famous Pacers defense ("It's about time we gave this team some credit...") tightened up to force a shot clock violation.

With five and a half minutes in the game, Reggie shot through that same curling move, got the ball and lofted it for two to tie. Then Reggie drew the defense out of the paint and fed the ball back to Rik at the line for another two. Then Haywoode stole the ball and got it to Reggie and—bingo! That seven-minute game was off to a sizzling Pacers start thanks to two Miller buckets and an assist.

The Knicks wiped their foreheads and looked around for an idea. You want to shoot? Do you? No one seemed ready, and the shot clock went off.

Reggie continued his domination of the quarter with two free throws after a Derek Harper foul. Starks whined to the officials that Reggie had said something nasty to Derek that had prompted his unfortunate response. Reggie, Starks said, should receive an official reprimand for taunting, a technical foul. "But, Dad, *he* started it."

Ewing got to the line for two and made it 76–72, but Harper just couldn't keep his hands to himself. He sent Reggie to the line again to give the Pacers a 78–72 edge with 2:30 to go.

And then Harper fouled Reggie *again*—80–72. Starks got real then, hitting a three-pointer at the two-minute mark to make it 80–75. Both teams were jazzed now. Reggie missed a potential coffin-nail three with 1:35 to play, but a free-lance defensive trap by the Pacers at halfcourt turned into a held ball—and the tip ended up in Reggie's hands.

The Knicks got tougher still—and maybe the Pacers figured a whole shot clock was a good thing to waste, taking the game clock down to a minute. It appeared to be a decent gamble—if such it was—when Harper missed a three and the Knicks kicked the rebound around and around and finally out of bounds for their twenty-fourth turnover of the game.

But the never-count-'em-out Knicks stole the inbounds pass and Starks laid it in to pull within three at 80–77. With half a minute to play, Derrick missed both free throws and the Knicks saw the door opening—if only they could take that step.

They spun the ball around the perimeter until Ewing turned to his right and saw Hubert Davis, the guy who had the spark all night long, spotting up behind the arc on the right wing, right in front of the Pacers bench. Ewing whipped the pass right at him, and a whole line of standing players and coaches and trainers sucked in their breath simultaneously—and sucked that pass right through Davis' hands and out of bounds to the Pacers.

It was over.

With 6.8 seconds to play, Haywoode hit one free throw, then Reggie put the cherry on top with two more to make the final 83–77. The series was now even—and headed back to Madison Square Garden.

The Pacers hadn't won there since...well, no one quite remembered when. It may have been that high school game of Donnie's.

* * *

It was a game for all seasons—pre-, regular, and post-. It was a game to savor even in the off-season. It was *the* game of the playoffs, and certainly the biggest game in Reggie Miller's career.

It was Game Five of the Eastern Conference Finals, played Wednesday, June 1 in New York City—a specific event at a specific place at a specific time. But in a sense, this game was the whole season condensed in forty-eight minutes.

Like the season, Game Five started poorly for the Pacers, very poorly, in fact. Their opponents jumped out to a crippling 15–2 lead. John Starks hit a three-pointer to start the game—a quick shot in the gut to stagger the Pacers.

Derrick McKey came right back with two points, but his teammates couldn't find the trigger. The Pacers should have had their confidence up. They had just taken two at Market Square Arena, but for some reason they couldn't focus. An offensive foul turned another Pacers possession into another Knicks score.

Then a shot clock violation turned it over again. Ewing hit, then it seemed everybody in a Knicks uniform was hitting. Rik finally hit back with a bucket to cut the Knicks' lead to lucky thirteen at 17–4.

The Pacers were used to slow starts. Not only had the 1993–94 season started like molasses in November, several of their games in the post-season had seen the Pacers crank and crank and crank just to hear the engine whinny and die.

But they'd learned something in the process. They had played through the first month of the season at a humble 4–8 pace and come out stronger. And they would play through this first quarter, too.

Staring up at the Knicks from that thirteen-point hole, the Pacers started to fight back. They ran off two baskets. But the Knicks counterpunched to make it 20–8, then 22–8. Rik hit a short one to push the Pacers into double digits. The Knicks shrugged and hit some more: 24–12, then 26–12. Vern got into the paint but couldn't connect. Reggie missed a three—John Starks was glued to his side and constantly in his face.

There was little to cheer about as the Knicks took a 28–16 lead at the end of the first—and they only kept at it in the second, scoring the first two baskets to double the Pacers' output, 32–16.

Vern finally found the bucket to make it 32–18. A glimmer of hope went out when Antonio missed two free throws from a Mason foul, but the Pacers weren't going to live on glimmers. There had to be something brighter down the road. They were beating the Knicks on the boards 15–8, but their work wasn't translating into points.

Dale tipped an Antonio miss back and through for the team's twentieth point with nine minutes to play in the half. The Pacers' second unit was scrapping hard under the basket, still getting the rebounds but, again, they just couldn't get them to go. Byron, still feeling some lingering effect from that bruised back from Game Three, wasn't quite the same Byron. And the whole team felt disjointed on offense.

With the starters back in the game, their rhythm improved tangibly. Reggie hit a baseline floater, then Haywoode broke through the Knicks defense on a tough drive. This would simply take some time, and the team seemed to know it. There was no sense of desperation in their play. If anything, they looked measured and calm, pushing a little here, a little over there and, with four minutes to play in the half, they'd pushed the score to a respectable 35–28. With a quiet but persistent 12–3 run, the Pacers had cut the Knicks' sixteen-point lead to seven.

But there was a down side. The Pacers were 0–7 from the foul line. Even if their tenacity could keep them in the game, their foul shooting might well lose it for them. Or John Starks might beat them all by himself. In quick order, Starks hit a three-pointer, answered by Reggie's two, then another three-pointer to put the Knicks up 41–30.

Just like the first plays of the game, those treys seemed to suffocate Indiana's spirit. The Pacers mistimed an alley-oop, then threw a pass to the sidelines. And their free-throw woes continued: 1-of-9, then 1-of-10. It was almost a moral vic-tory that they managed to gather their wits and push back again to within eight, cutting the Knicks' lead to 43–35 at the half.

Reggie had only nine points so far, and the team was managing only 37 percent shooting, 16-of-43. The Knicks weren't a whole lot better, 17-of-39, but they didn't have to be if the Pacers continued to play this way.

If the Pacers thought to come out of the half blazing, they were quickly dis-abused of that notion by the Knicks. Charles Smith went hard to the hoop to make it 45–35. Rik came back with a stuff, but Ewing responded easily.

A sharp series of perimeter passes found Haywoode open for two, but on the next possession Smits committed his fourth foul. So Haywoode bore down to hit again—and again Ewing drew a foul, this time a real gift that Antonio paid for. Starks was relatively inactive at this point in the game, but Charles Smith took up his slack, driving to draw two shots, then spinning free in the lane for an easy lay-in.

Derrick finally answered, but by then the Knicks' lead had climbed back to 55–43. At least Reggie was getting some looks, and he didn't appear shy about shoot-ing; but he'd hit only 4-of-14 by the middle of the third quarter. At 57–43, with no sign of any significant swing in the tempo of the game, there was a nagging appre-hension in some minds that this evening might turn into the sort of embarrass-ment the Pacers had inflicted on the Knicks in Game Three at Market Square.

Then Reggie hit a three.

Maybe he was just due. After the game he said he hadn't really felt out of sync all night. If he was missing, well, sometimes that's just out of the shooter's control. If the stroke feels right, you just shoot through it and the shots will fall.

Workman hit another jumper to make it 57–48. Harper, with veteran resolve, promptly buried a three-pointer. Then Starks got the message, too, and hit a trey of his own—his third of the evening.

Just like that, the Knicks' lead was 64–52, then 66–52 after LaSalle fouled Ewing in the low post.

But the Pacers' veterans stepped up. Vern drove the lane for two. And LaSalle, who had played only briefly since breaking a bone in his hand during the Orlando series, settled down and spotted Antonio free in the paint, then rebounded yet an-other missed free throw.

With the Pacers almost blind from the line, the Knicks were content to let the game become a charity ball. And if they could keep the action slowed to that pace, they could also be reasonably sure of winning the war of the whistles. Larry Brown thought so, too—and earned a whistle of his own after letting the officials know what he was thinking.

The quarter ended with the game grinding along in second gear and New York ahead 70–58. Like a big truck lumbering up a steep hill, the Knicks had no intention of hurrying to the top. If you were behind them, you'd just have to stay there.

Unless, of course, you had the RPMs—and the guts—to whip across the double-yellow line and shoot on by.

Unless you had the Reginald Wayne Miller to do the whipping.

There really was no warning.

Reggie didn't even know it was coming. The players who have been there say it just happens. One minute you're playing your game—and then, suddenly, you're playing The Game. Certainly the Knicks had no sense of anything unusual happening, and the Pacers didn't give them any hints as the quarter began.

Smits missed his first shot. But Kenny rebounded and managed to zip the ball out to Reggie.

So, OK, this time he hit the three. He'd been firing all night with little effect. He couldn't miss 'em all, right?

And, yeah, he just hit another. Go figure. The guy had been cruising along at 33 percent up until then. He couldn't miss 'em all, now could he?

The question should have been, could he make 'em all? The answer was yes. When Reggie stepped behind that three-point line, he had crossed over into the Zone. In the first six minutes of the quarter, Miller scored nineteen points. Five of his fourth-quarter shots were three-pointers, an NBA record for single-quarter performances. And one of those would come from too far away to be taken seriously…until it just went in.

His fourth-quarter total of twenty-five points would take second place in the record books behind a twenty-nine-point quarter by Eric "Sleepy" Floyd. The Knicks may have wished they were asleep, so they could wake up from this nightmare.

With a twelve-point lead and their opponents seemingly on the ropes, the Knicks had seen their game—and maybe their season—pulled out of their hands and dropped into Reggie Miller's gym bag.

His teammates would add four more points in that six-minute war. And when it was over, the Pacers had taken an 81–73 lead.

The game wasn't quite over, though. Harper drove for two, then Ewing hit for two more, then two more free throws—six unanswered points to pull the Knicks within a bucket at 81–79. Then Reggie, perhaps a little tired from lifting all those weights, stepped in front of the arc for a two-point shot. Dale dunked for another two, then Reggie stepped to the line for two freebies after Ewing pushed him out of bounds in frustration. The brief threat was over; the Pacers tidied up before they turned off the lights and went home with a 93–86 win. By that time the fans were booing—the Knicks. Nice city, New York.

Even in video retrospect, the game is almost too much to comprehend. You can see what happened. The facts and the stats are there in the newspaper stories. But that doesn't really explain how it happened—or why.

Perhaps the why is obvious: Reggie wanted to win the game.

But that, too, explains nothing. Maybe there's another reason, something that has to do with some cosmic sort of symmetry. Reggie's unearthly burst occurred just when it was needed most—just as had the Pacers uninterrupted run through the last eight games of the regular season and into the playoffs. Then the team—and now Reggie—could not miss. Their eleventh-hour success had earned them all sorts of karma—and Reggie had cashed much of it in.

* * *

Miller's performance was more than extraordinary, it was practically extra-human. To that extent, it transcended anyone's admiration. It no more needed applause than does a lightning storm.

LaSalle's effort, though, was more human, and certainly deserves admiration. Once, twice, then three times, the veteran stepped around Ewing and stole his entry passes—to send back to Miller for his pleasure.

Here you go, Reg. I figure you could use this better than Patrick. Throw in a couple of grizzly-bear rebounds and a handful of granite picks to clear Miller's path, and what you had was one heck of a defensive stand from a guy with knees kept together only by a surgeon's skill.

Miller earned more national ink that evening than the team had garnered all season—and that was great.

But an editorial—an editorial, mind you, not a sports story or even a sports column—in *The Indianapolis News* gave LaSalle the kind of appreciation he hadn't seen in quite some time, and might not see again as his career winds down. "It was Thompson…who when the Pacers were down by a dozen going into the fourth quarter, stepped up and made the steals, blocked the shots and lit the team's fuse, setting the stage for Miller's pyrotechnics."

The greatest media fuss, though, resulted from the war of words between Reggie and short-stuff movie director Spike Lee sitting on the sidelines. Their exchanges were pretty much non-stop. Reggie put his hands to his throat (Choke? You want to see choke?) and even, some said, put a hand to his shorts.

It goes without saying that Lee's banter could not keep Reggie from his appointed rounds. But that didn't stop the New York media from saying all sorts of nasty things about the hapless Lee, who was, after all, only trying to distract a Knicks opponent.

"Thanks a lot, Spike," read one huge headline. This was pretty much a quote from Pacers President Donnie Walsh, who had walked by Lee as the team went to the locker room and said the same thing loud enough for any interested bystanders to hear.

In his own defense, Lee responded that *he* hadn't missed any shots; *he* hadn't failed to get a pass to Patrick Ewing. When he arrived in Indianapolis to see Game Six, Lee also told the press that he would be staying at the Governor's Mansion—"in the slave quarters." And he didn't want any of the Indiana fans to use the newsprint masks of his face that had appeared that day in the local papers because the Hoosiers "might lose their membership in the KKK."

NBA Commissioner David Stern would also take some exception to the reports of Miller's lower gesture. He called to express his concern that such actions—although failing to appear on national television, where the camera angle made verification of these reports impossible—might cast the NBA in the wrong light. Reggie, who had a hard time remembering every detail of his time in basketball heaven, gladly apologized to Stern's answering machine. He couldn't specifically recall the incident, but he could assure the commissioner that, if it had happened, it was only in the heat of verbal battle—and it certainly wouldn't happen again. Have a nice day.

* * *

The team had seen it when they swept Orlando. They had seen it when they beat Atlanta. They had heard the fans get louder and louder and louder until they didn't think Market Square Arena could withstand the decibels—and then the fans got louder still.

Still the team wasn't really prepared for the thousands of people waiting for them at the airport when they flew back from their victory in Game Five in New York. Kathy Jordan, the Pacers' director of community affairs, had been there to welcome the team and remembered the scene inside the private terminal. "The guys just stood there for a minute. They really weren't prepared for all those people waiting outside. They really hadn't expected it. Someone said, 'Gee, look at all those people.'"

Gee, look at those Pacers.

The town was in heaven. The team had taken them to the gates, and Reggie had unlocked the door. It was all that anyone could talk about, all that anyone could think about. It was, maybe, more than anyone could dream.

Pep rallies, special TV shows, Pacers signs in every store window, in every bar in the city.

It was a lot to live up to—maybe too much.

So far in the playoffs, the Pacers' home court had been impregnable. The team could not lose when the fans at MSA opened their throats. The outcome of Game Six was practically a foregone conclusion. You could almost see the headlines: "HICKS NIX KNICKS IN SIX."

Time to start making those reservations for Houston.

The Pacers and more than a few longtime NBA watchers were a bit more circumspect. It's not over yet, said the Pacers' leaders. Sure, we can't really say that we haven't done anything yet, because we have. We're this far—and, yes, that is cause for some celebration.

But we haven't gone all the way. We haven't done it yet.

But the fans knew they were just being modest. That was just what the guys were supposed to say to the press. What time zone is Houston in, anyway?

Well, maybe the fans were right.

But maybe the Knicks were too tough to fold just because a few hundred thousand Hoosiers thought they should.

* * *

The opening minutes of Game Six did not go according to Indiana's plan. The Knicks hit their first shot. Then again. Then again. Derek Harper stripped Workman for a quick two. The Knicks had a 10–2 lead before the Pacers could quite get their warm-up jackets off.

Brown took a time-out. Come on, guys. Settle down.

Then Ewing hit. A stolen pass led to Oakley's lay-in. Smits' outlet pass was intercepted. Starks hits a three. Rik hit one, but Oakley answered. Halfway through the first quarter, the Pacers had caught their breath, but they hadn't caught the Knicks. New York led 22–11.

But, hey, we'd seen first-quarter scores like that, hadn't we? Remember last Wednesday. The Pacers had been down 32–16—and look what happened.

A hum of confidence started to come back. It wasn't exactly a song in the Pacers' hearts, but it would do for starters. Haywoode hit a three-pointer to make it 22–14, and that felt pretty good.

But Starks immediately replied in kind. Antonio made a twelve-foot baseline jumper. Oakley couldn't answer, but on the next Knicks possession, Harper practically drove a truck up the lane without anyone so much as raising a hand in protest.

Derrick McKey came back with a truly delightful head fake this way and bullet pass that way—right to Dale under the basket. And that, finally, seemed to ignite and unite the team. The Pacers shot to within six, 27–21, then to five on an Antonio free throw. Then to three when Derrick again whipped a precision pass to Reggie on a back-door cut to the hoop.

Then Vern stripped Mason and careened downcourt for a lay-up, 27–26. Now that was more like it. But Starks grabbed a chance off a steal and buried a three-pointer. Mason continued to have his troubles—not that he was getting much sympathy—when Antonio blocked his shot, but Greg Anthony showed up, as he had all series and all season, to sink another three-pointer. A Fleming three-point play helped bolster hopes, but the Knicks got out of the quarter leading 33–31.

Smits and Ewing had each been slapped with two fouls, keeping them both benched for much of the quarter. As the second period began, Rik was back in and immediately banked one in after a strong pivot move. Tied at thirty-three.

Oakley came back for two, and Rik missed his next shot. It produced no disadvantage, though, as Ewing lost the ball out of bounds. Greg Anthony then hit Workman and Workman hit two free throws—he alone of the Pacers consistently making his charity shots. But Ewing was hitting from the line as well, and put the Knicks back on top 37–35 after Kenny Williams fouled him.

Kenny, perhaps too eager to make amends, missed a jumper. The rebound went to Anthony and Anthony went to the air and sank an eighteen-footer. Another Smits miss and another Anthony score, a Byron miss and an Oakley tip—and there were the Knicks atop a 43–35 lead. It had been a 10–2 New York run, hardly a marathon, but perhaps enough to show the Pacers that this was going to be a longer game than they might have guessed from all the brouhaha outside the arena.

Meanwhile, there was a game to play. Rik got into the lane and connected. But on his next trip down, he missed. Ewing continued to play his usual All-Star game, finding his teammates inside the paint. Mason scored, then knocked the orange out of Dale's normally iron grasp, sending it downcourt for two and a 45–37 lead.

The Pacers stuck to their game plan and continued to feed Rik in low, but Rik was having a tough time of it. He was getting the looks, but his shot just wasn't falling.

To both teams' credit, it was an exciting, well-played game. The whistles were fewer, but the intensity hadn't flagged a bit. The miscues were evenly distributed and usually forced by pressure from the other side. The sparkling moves were hard to create—but that much more thrilling when they occurred.

Although Reggie would come away with a game-high twenty-seven points, he dropped a few en route. One errant Miller shot—an air ball—came down in Knick hands, then back to Vern's hands when he stripped it from Mason, then back to Reggie who launched from the corner, only to have Mason hustle back and swat it out of bounds.

It was a wild sequence, and it didn't end the way Pacers' fans would have preferred. But it was tough-minded basketball, gutsy and brilliant and evenly matched.

Another back-door cut by Reggie made it 48–40, then Dale grabbed a Knicks lob pass—probably just a bad shot—and zipped the ball ahead to Antonio who got in close to bring the score closer: 48–42.

Just as he'd done all series, Riley moved quickly to protect the lead. He called time-out and made an adjustment—or broke the Pacers' concentration. The result: Ewing got the ball in low, drew the foul from Antonio on a close call, and sank both free throws. The Knicks took heart at that, and again snatched the ball from Dale's grasp.

Another series of exchanges—a three-second violation on the Knicks, a McKey hook in close, Charles Smith's put-back of a Ewing miss, a McKey rocket pass to Reggie at the rim—failed to change the margin: 52–46 with three minutes to play.

Some more back-and-forth, mixed and matched blunder and splendor brought the score to 56–48 with a 1:30 to play in the half. Two Miller free throws and a Mason lay-up and freebie made it 58–51 at the buzzer.

It had been a half of alternating strength and weakness. There had been plenty of moments of hard-nosed defense and finely tuned offense and often combinations of the two within the same possession. It had been, as so many other stretches of this series had been, a rigorous, vigorous battle that proved difficult even for the network experts to decipher. The Pacers look too nonchalant, said Dr. J. The Pacers look too tight, said Walton. Whoever was right, at least it was the Pacers they were talking about.

The second half continued in essentially the same rhythm as the first. If Rik's shots still weren't dropping, he was at least diving to the floor for loose balls—and that's quite a distance for him. The Knicks, though, padded their lead, first by a couple, then a couple more until it hung around the double-digit mark.

Even the empty possessions were at times thrilling. And again, it was hard to point to this obvious advantage or that glaring deficiency. Yes, Rik gave up three bad passes in succession, but Ewing was shooting 2-of-8 in the quarter. The period ended with the Knicks still definitely—if never decisively—in the lead at 80–69.

If there was any change as the fourth quarter unfolded, it came from the MSA crowd. They decided they weren't going to let their team down—and they wouldn't let the team let them down. The fans began to holler—right after a twenty-four-second violation on the Knicks' first possession. They hollered louder when Reggie promptly buried a three-pointer. Now they were going, and they weren't going to stop.

It made a difference. The Pacers fought just a little harder. The Knicks' lead was down to 82–76 with just under nine minutes to play. With 7:30 to play, it was 86–82. When Reggie scored to make it 88–86, the crowd went berserk.

Ewing hit a fall-away, but Rik hustled hard to score and pull the Pacers back at 90–88. It was punch and counterpunch, score and counter, foul and rebound, back at you and back at you. It looked at times like two, scrapping, biting, kicking animals rolling across the floor. But somehow it was also an elegant dance, or maybe a karate match—or somehow it was all of that.

It was gripping to watch. It could have gone on and on and it would have been beautiful. The cheering would never have to end. There might never be a winner, but the game—the game was the thing.

With two minutes to play, it was tied at ninety-one. Reggie had just made one of two free throws. Harper brought the ball downcourt and for a long, long moment, no one came out to challenge him. He took it to the foul line and hit a jumper. He was far too open. And he took the shot with such casual ease—like a kid shooting alone in his driveway—that the intensity seemed to drain from the game.

On the return possession, Derrick found Reggie curling through the lane, but the ball slipped through Reggie's fingers, off his hip and away to Starks. McKey fouled him, and he only made one free throw, but the air had gone out of the Pacers' game. With less than a minute to play, Harper expertly stripped Vern on a break, and the last few points really had no effect on what was a done deal.

Yes, the Pacers tried to the last second. And maybe another opponent would have given them a chance by making a mistake or two. But these were the Knicks.

If box scores can explain it, point to Starks' stats. Reggie had hit five threes in Game Five. Starks hit five in Game Six, just not all in one quarter. Starks ended the game with twenty-six points, one fewer than Miller. It wasn't rebounds—the Pacers outboarded the Knicks 36–33. Maybe it was shooting percentage: The Knicks shot 52 percent; the Pacers, 42 percent. Maybe it was steals: The Knicks had 17, the Pacers only 11.

But it wouldn't be fair to say the Knicks had stolen Game Six. No, they had knocked on the door and the Pacers had let them in—and once they had made themselves comfortable, they just wouldn't leave. When the visit was over, and they had won it 98–91, the Knicks stood up and walked out the way they came in—tough.

If you want to be the best, you have to beat the best. That night the Knicks were the best.

* * *

The seven-game series of the 1994 NBA Eastern Conference Finals had come down to this: The Best of One. Game Seven on Sunday, June 5, at Madison Square Garden.

All the hoopla and hype that had preceded this series and every game leading here were forgotten. The New York press and the national network had gotten over their patronizing notions of the Pacers as "overachievers" lucky to be mentioned in the same paragraph with the soon-to-be-champion Knicks. The Pacers had disabused them of that.

The Indiana fans, likewise, had awakened to the reality of playoff basketball—throat-grabbing, teeth-rattling, protractedly defensive. A test of will, a test of skill, a test of muscle, a test of heart. The New York Knicks had shown them that.

.Now it was down to this: Forty-eight minutes, four quarters, two halves, one winner.

* * *

The game did not start aesthetically, nor did it end that way. But for most of the time in between it was a wild, exciting ride. Despite all the jive surrounding this series, all the holier-than-Naismith talk about awkward, ugly and impure play, this one was a good, good game. At times a circus, at times a ballet with brass knuckles.

Some might even say it was a great game—but the good guys didn't win.

The opening tip was ruled illegal. How's that for omens? Except no one knew what it portended. Instead of jumping against Dale Davis, Ewing stepped to the side to catch the ball when Davis swatted it. Nice try, Patrick. Where'd ya learn that?

Pacer ball.

The Knicks were immediately whistled for illegal defense. Then another jump ball as Ewing tied up Haywoode. Nice try, Haywoode.

In this initial test of inertia, the scoreboard finally blinked when Ewing hit a jump shot from the left side. An errant McKey pass turned over the Pacers' return possession, and the Knicks pushed the ball up quickly to Ewing posting low. Ewing turned to the hole and Smits stood straight up to avoid an early foul. Dale Davis had no such trepidation. He flew over Ewing to prevent an easy score and on his way down grabbed Ewing's shoulder with one hand, pulling the big man over. It was ruled a flagrant foul. Free throws and Knicks' ball again.

Flagrant? OK, Dale decided to show a tad more restraint on the next play, sending John Starks sprawling with an elbow to the chest as Starks cut through the lane.

Reggie scored the first Pacer points on that patented dash underneath the hoop and out on the left wing to curl in, get the pass, elevate and shoot. this time, Smits set the crucial pick on Starks under the hoop. This poor guy was getting knocked all over.

Ewing answered at the other end, hitting a jumper over Smits' outstretched arm. Smits and Haywoode came back with a nicely executed two-man game: in to Rik, back to Haywoode, in to Rik, back to Haywoode, in again and two. Oakley needed only himself to sink his first jumper—and then foul Antonio on the next exchange. Antonio had been complaining to the officials all through Game Six that Oakley and crew had been going out of their way to hit him on his sore right hand. Intentional or not, Oakley did it again.

No pain, no gain, apparently. Harper got the ball to Ewing in the lane and as Patrick went up for the short hook, the ball slipped from his fingers—Ewing's one obvious physical shortcoming is his relatively small hands—and Antonio swatted it right into Reggie's hands. And off he ran.

Starks stopped the lay-in, but Reggie sank both free throws. These first possessions had set a fairly energetic pace. It would not let up. With 8:30 to play in the first, the Knicks led 8–7.

A Starks travel. Another of Derrick McKey's look-away passes to one of the Davis dunkers in the lane. The next possession turned into a wild-eyed, hand-slapping, floor-rolling scramble for the ball—which ended up squirting out of bounds. It was just one of several such scurrying pinball runs—all caused by defensive intensity. Surprisingly, no one seemed to ever be called for a foul, even when the ball changed ownership four or five times in the space of that many seconds.

In plays such as this—not to mention Dale Davis' aggressive display—the Pacers looked as if they might push their way to the top with defense. It was an encouraging sign this early in Game Seven.

Better yet, the ball ended up with Rik posted up against Ewing. Smits took the quick step around him and emerged on the opposite side of the basket for a reverse lay-down—not quite a stuff, but more than a lay-in.

Harper promptly threw the ball out of bounds, leaving Ewing wondering if the pass had been intended for him. Three quick Knick turnovers had fueled a 7–0 Pacers run. Ewing, showing him how it was supposed to happen, passed to Harper in the lane for two. The Pacers led 11–10 with just over six minutes to play in the quarter.

The game crawled forward, neither team gaining an appreciable advantage. Considering the near-glacial starts the Pacers had produced in the last two games, though, this was a considerable improvement. And no one was seriously suggesting that another slow start like Game Five would lead to another sublime fourth-quarter shooting performance by Reggie. Lightning could hardly strike a second time so soon after the first—and everyone knew it.

Through most of the quarter, the Pacers' offense sparkled. Antonio blew by Oakley for a stuff. Derrick stole the ball and made a terrific bounce pass to Haywoode streaking toward the bucket. There were some highlight-worthy replays.

Although hardly telegenic, the Knicks' defense was doing an equal job. There were times when Mason and Oakley seemed to be chunks of mobile rock rolling into place—and rolling anything else out of the way—to grab a rebound. The Knicks also had an offense, of course. Still cranked from Game Six, Starks continued to hit from deep—two treys in the first quarter, both times to tie the game.

Even Oakley got into the act, hitting a jumper with his back foot on the arc. No one in New York really believed he could do it. Sam Mitchell, also not known for his long-range skill, answered with practically the same shot—but taken off balance with a defender in his face—as the quarter ended. It was a close one, but the Knicks were there at the buzzer, 24–23.

The energy was still crackling at the start of the second quarter. Vern stole the first Knick ball but was whistled for charging on the break downcourt. It was a dubious call, but the Pacers got the long bounce off the Knick miss—only to see Starks steal a slow pass, and again fail to convert. It took a minute-and-a-half before either team scored: Mason hit for a 26–23 lead.

The Pacers' hero of the second quarter would turn out to be Byron Scott. His hard fall to the hardwood earlier in the series had limited his minutes in the previous two games. But he came out strong in Game Seven, hitting five straight shots from the field and a couple of free throws for thirteen points before halftime.

The Pacers fed off the veteran's energy throughout the period. He was always there to defeat the Knicks defense—and they generated no sustained offense to counter him, perhaps because Ewing was resting on the bench.

The shots rained more freely now. McKey hit to pull the Pacers within two at 30–28. Oakley came up empty, and Dale stuffed in Oakley's face to tie. Hubert Davis answered, but Byron answered him. Then Byron reiterated with a three-pointer. Ewing rose from the bench.

McKey hit a jumper with five minutes left in the half to give the Pacers a 39–34 lead, but the Knicks came back. A Ewing tip, another Byron jumper and it was 43–38. In a game that tight, five points looked large—but Starks cut three off with a deep shot. Then Reggie answered with a three of his own.

On it went, harder and harder. Ewing got away with an obvious elbow up high on Antonio while both leaped for a rebound, and the ensuing stuff by Charles Smith tied the game at 46. Reggie hit a long three to make it 49–46, but LaSalle's shoulder-shiver on a pick put Starks at the line to make one free throw. Just before the half ended, Reggie stepped around Starks, who was otherwise stuck to him like flypaper, and banked in a twenty-five-footer to give the Pacers a 51–47 lead.

It had been a very solid half for the Pacers offensively. Their fifty-one-point total equaled their highest halftime output of the series—but, perhaps ominously, that had come in the Game Six loss. Their shooting this half had been exceptional, but the Knicks certainly seemed able to hang around until the end of the party, thanks largely to their 21–13 rebounding edge. Ewing had eleven, along with eleven points.

Even though the Pacers looked good—and certainly capable of winning—the Knicks also appeared comfortable with the game's quicker tempo. After Larry Brown had adjusted his defense, cranking it up a couple of notches, Pat Riley seemed to have had an appropriate response: put the offensive pedal to the metal—more fast breaks, more run and gun.

Maybe that would work, maybe not. For the first few minutes of the third quarter, however, all the action was in close. Shortly into the third quarter, another of those hot-potato exchanges popped the ball out to Reggie, who ended up with two free throws to give the Pacers their biggest lead at 55–48. Then same thing happened again—Reggie couldn't hit the three but Rik got the rebound at the top of the key and made it 57–48. Then McKey hit to make it 59–48—an eleven-point lead. Could it be?

It was starting to look like another Pacers quarter. The lead shrank and stretched through most of the third. A Harper three-pointer made it 59–53. But then Rik would muscle up against Ewing, back him away and turn to drain a jumper. It was hard to tell from many of these exchanges that Rik wasn't one of the five or six best centers in the league.

As it would turn out, however, Rik was playing this game against the league's second-best center—this year, anyway. It was hard to tell for a while, especially when Ewing picked up his fourth foul with the Pacers leading 65–53. Riley gambled and kept him in. It was a good bet.

With Ewing's rejection of Antonio, his feed to Oakley underneath the basket, his willingness to stand tough and take Antonio's charge and, finally two late-quarter moves inside, the Knicks pulled within two, 69–67. A last-second stuff by Dale as the quarter ended pushed the Pacers lead back up to four, but the Knicks could feel it now—and the Pacers could almost feel it slipping away.

The fourth quarter was nothing but high-octane drama. It was simply more of the same, all the offensive accelerations and the same defensive brick walls. The first of what would become two much-discussed plays occurred when Derrick McKey hit a three-pointer from the left wing as the shot clock was just about expired—actually *was* expired as the unofficial replay would demonstrate—to give the Pacers a 74–71 lead at the ten-minute mark. Harper answered with his own. A great court-length pass from Ewing found Harper streaking for two, but Rik answered again to tie.

The Knicks pulled ahead 81–76, but Rik and Byron pulled the Pacers back to 81–80 with 5:30 to play. The blows and counterblows came in rapid succession. Knicks by four, Knicks by one. Knicks by three at the two-minute horn, Knicks by one after Reggie's jumper, 89–88.

Oakley travels—Pacers' ball. Rik misses. Knicks blow the shot clock. Pacers' ball with forty-six seconds to play. With 34.5 seconds left in someone's season...DALE DUNKS!

AND IT SHOULD HAVE BEEN EWING'S SIXTH FOUL...but it wasn't.

And Starks, playing as if there might be no tomorrow, drives along the baseline and almost lays it in...and Ewing leaps, catches the ball and slams it back down.

More than a few folks thought at the time and after subsequent replays that Ewing's reinsertion was goaltending. Look at it from one angle and, yes, it sure was. From another angle, hard to say.

The Pacers still had plenty of time, though, to get a shot up and down—and even snag the rebound if necessary, or foul to stop the Knicks if absolutely necessary. But they didn't. The dribbled and passed around looking for a better shot until Reggie was forced to heave up an air ball.

And then, in the last of the game's controversies, Reggie fouled Starks to stop the clock—and referee Mike Mathis called it flagrant. The Pacers had a foul to give—a regular foul call would have simply meant an inbounds pass. But with a flagrant foul, Starks got two shots and the Knicks got the ball back. It was a hell of a way for a season to end.

Maybe it would have been over anyway, even if the Pacers had gotten one more possession with 3.2 seconds in the game.

Maybe.

Larry Brown was nothing but gracious after the game. "I'm not going to criticize my player, and I'm not going to criticize an official. It was a great basketball game and they won it with a great player making a tremendous play," Brown told the press.

Later, he would still remember it painfully. "We had our chances," he said. He would remember the final thirty-four seconds in retrospect and only blame himself. "If I had it to do over again, I probably would have called time—but I was afraid they might pressure the inbounds.

"I had no idea we'd wait so long to come out and take that shot. It did come too late. But I know we talked about what to do and just didn't do it. It's too bad. We were playing at such a high level. I was confident we could beat Houston."

And so it ended.

The team filed into the locker room. The press wanted some quotes, and Brown and a few others complied. But when the pens and the microphones all turned toward Reggie, he sat there, looking down, trying to speak...but only tears would come.

11
Savoring the Memory

Monday, June 6, was the fiftieth anniversary of the Allied invasion of Normandy. A lot of media attention was focused on that historic event, and maybe it was good that the Pacers' loss wasn't the only thing to occupy the spotlight.

Mike Mathis, the official who had made that last, hope-crushing foul call at the end of the Eastern Conference Finals, made another call to Indianapolis that day. He'd been scheduled to play in the Youth Links Golf Tournament here, a charity affair in late June that attracts race drivers and other sports figures from around the country. Mathis canceled his appearance.

Donnie Walsh got a call from Indianapolis Mayor Stephen Goldsmith. The mayor wanted to hold a parade through downtown Indianapolis to celebrate the Pacers' season. It would be a bang-up event, Goldsmith said. The city is grateful for everything you folks have done. We want a chance to show you. Walsh thought about it for a moment, but then said he didn't think that was such a good idea.

"Parades are for champions," Donnie said. "We aren't champions of anything yet."

* * *

Around the country, though, there were more than a few sportswriters who knew the Pacers had won something. They had won the attention and respect of basketball fans everywhere who revered the finesse and elegance at the heart of the game. They had won the affection of every sports fan who loves the underdog—and who doesn't?

"To the disgust of hoops purists and those who prefer form over function, the Knicks will be in the NBA Finals," wrote Bill Lyons of the Knight-Ridder news service. Bernie Lincicome of *The Chicago Tribune* wrote, "The Pacers deserved a better ending. They were the best story of all these playoffs."

And Donnie had been fielding phone calls all morning. Old friends from around the league were calling, offering that brand of condolence that was also a kind of congratulations. The NBA is a close-knit fraternity—and most of the guys who run it are genuinely happy when an old friend does well. And, maybe in a way, some of these folks just wanted to get near success. It might rub off.

Donnie was flattered by the calls, certainly by the mayor's suggestion. But at the moment, he had work to do. For most of the afternoon, Donnie and Larry, along with assistant coaches Bill Blair, Gar Heard, Billy King and the rest of the basketball staff, got together in Donnie's office and closed the door.

Donnie's door was almost always open. You could walk by and wave. He'd almost always wave back. But people understood that when that door was closed it stayed closed until Donnie opened it. Don't knock. Even if you think it's very important, it'll wait.

For three hours or more, Donnie and the basketball staff stayed in that room. When the door finally opened, a small cloud of smoke rolled out. Everyone in the room was smoking a big fat cigar and laughing.

The emotion hung in the room as thick as the smoke as, one by one, the men got up and made their way out. They were laughing, but they looked a little sad. It looked a little like a wake. Or maybe like a bunch of guys sitting around after graduation—one last bull session before they split for the summer. Maybe in a sense it was that. But it also was business.

They had been reviewing the season. Talking about the team's strong points and weak spots. Figuring how they could improve and where changes had to be made. The season wasn't really over—just the basketball games. Now, with the draft coming up in less than a month, there were other games to be played—deals and ploys to be made with other teams in hopes of finding just the right piece of the endlessly evolving puzzle.

They almost had it, that championship team. Maybe if we could trade this player for that one. Maybe if that kid is as good as we think he might be. Maybe if he really worked on his game over the summer. Maybe if he comes back healthy after the operation....

It never really ends.

For that reason, it was hard for Walsh to think about a parade. As far as he was concerned, the whole thing was an endless parade. He didn't need a sense of closure—and maybe he was a little leery of giving anyone else in the organization any sense of finality. Nothing was over. We haven't done anything—yet.

But he also understood why the mayor wanted something special to occur. It wasn't for the team, really. It was for Indianapolis. The team and all the people in the organization didn't need some confetti-strewn grand finale. The office staff was calmly going about their business. Maybe a few of them were sucking on cough drops—from yelling through most of the past month and probably at the television the day before—but they still had tickets to sell, advertisements to approve, press releases to write, marketing strategies to analyze. And besides, it was just another game and another season, wasn't it?

Well, no one really believed *that*, but these folks had seen a lot of big victories, and a lot of defeats. Even a loss like this had to be taken with some kind of professional restraint. They'd do their crying in private, thank you. And more than a few of them did.

But the city needed something, and it was the mayor asking, so Donnie said sure. On Tuesday, June 7, in front of the City Market just across the street from Market Square Arena, several thousand people came to stand in the hellish heat to cheer the team that had almost taken them to basketball heaven. The rally was broadcast live on television.

The mayor spoke, team co-owner Mel Simon spoke, Donnie spoke, the players spoke—but most of all, the fans cheered. It had been *their* team that had won those games and lost those games. It had been *their* year to go farther than any of them had gone before. It had been *their* ecstasy in *their* city in *their* state. And for one long minute, it had been the center of the world.

Maybe that minute had begun when Byron hit the game-winning three-pointer in Orlando. Maybe when Reggie sank his fifth long-range dagger in that final quarter of Game Five in New York. Maybe even back in late January, when the Pacers beat Houston in the Summit. It didn't matter, it was theirs forever.

Donnie understood what that meant. And finally he knew the mayor was right. It really wasn't just about a championship—although that was the only way to talk about it.

It was about the city. It was about the lives of every man, woman and child who ever went to a Pacers game or just sat there screaming for them in front of the TV.

"The mayor said there needed to be a sense of closure," Donnie recalled. "And my first reaction was, well, how very touching. But when I got there to the rally, all I could say was, 'Wow! I had no idea it could still be like this.' Sure, I understood the cheering in the arena, at a game. But I had no idea.

"When I first took this job and Herb Simon asked me what I wanted, I told him straight out, 'I want to win a championship.' It seems so obvious to say that, and it's simply because you want to win. But why?

"This is just a bunch of men putting on short pants, going out there and playing a game. The guys who get the most points win, the other guys lose. People cheer, people boo. Nobody's getting killed. But it isn't like you've discovered the cure for AIDS. It's fun. That's what it's supposed to be: Fun. It is a purer thing when it's fun.

"And winning a championship will give that fun the kind of longevity it should have. When we win a championship, people will never forget. And every time they think of the Pacers from then on, it will be with that deep memory of how great it was to be at the games—how great it was to take your date or take your kids to see the Pacers play. It won't matter if we win or lose that game because people will always be thinking, 'Yeah, but we were the champs…and it could happen again.' "

Until it does happen, this season—and the memories it created—will do just fine.

Donnie Walsh and Larry Brown, high school rivals in New York City as teens, were teammates at the University of North Carolina from 1960–62. This team photo, taken in Walsh's senior year and Brown's junior year, shows the two side by side (front row, fourth and fifth from left).

They were reunited before the 1993–94 Pacers' season began when Walsh, Brown's former assistant at Denver, announced that his old friend had been hired as the Pacers' head coach, succeeding Bob "Bo" Hill.

With assistant coaches (from left) Gar Heard, Bill Blair and Billy King looking on, Coach Brown makes his point to the team during a time-out.

...And proves he's just as adept at making his point with a referee during a game.

Top scorer Reggie Miller eludes a Boston defender and heads for the hoop.

Miller goes up and under to score against the Knicks' Patrick Ewing.

(left) Center Rik Smits, who emerged this season as a consistent scoring threat, holds his position in the paint and calls for the ball. (right) At a mobile seven-foot-four, Smits also makes his presence felt as a shot blocker.

(left) Power forward Dale Davis shows no mercy to Calbert Cheaney, slamming one over the former Indiana University standout in one of the Pacers' two home wins over Cheaney's Washington Bullets in 1993-94. (center) Davis skies to reject an Alonzo Mourning jump shot. (right) ... And delivers on the offensive end as well, flushing two points on a breakaway.

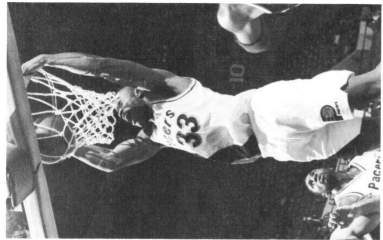

(left) The other member of the Davis duo, forward Antonio Davis, is a physical presence inside, a fact borne out in his 302 free throws during the regular season, second on the team despite averaging only 21.4 minutes a game. (center) A.D.'s rebounding was vital to the Pacers' effort. He averaged more than six per game, second-best on the team behind Dale Davis. (right) ... And rebounding leads to scoring — sometimes crowd-pleasing scoring like this put-back jam.

(left) Point guard Haywoode Workman, thrust into a starting role after Pooh Richardson's injury, responded well, hitting his shots at an eight-points-per-game clip. (right) More important perhaps than his scoring punch, Workman ran the Pacers' offense skillfully, threading passes like this one around Utah's John Stockton for an average of nearly seven assists per game.

(left) Fluid forward Derrick McKey, who came to the Pacers in the pre-season trade that sent Detlef Schrempf to Seattle, brought a lot to the table. At six-ten, he's a strong rebounder. (center) But he also has the ball-handling skill to draw bigger players such as Charlotte's Larry Johnson away from the basket, where he can hit the jump shot, look for the open man, or... (right) ... take the ball to the hole, as he did against Schrempf on February 20, Seattle's only visit to Market Square Arena this season. McKey poured in twenty-seven points and grabbed nine rebounds against his former team in a 101-95 win for the Pacers.

Veteran guard Vern Fleming, a Pacer his entire ten-year NBA career, epitomizes point-guard savvy.

Fleming also displays an almost-uncanny knack for finding a path to the bucket—and no fear about taking the path once he's found it.

Forward/center LaSalle Thompson, the Pacers' "elder statesman" at thirty-three, remains a force under the basket with his strong defense and rebounding.

At six-eleven, 250 pounds, 1993 first-round draft pick Scott Haskin looks to be a force for the Pacers' future in the paint.

Forward Malik Sealy, a first-round pick by the Pacers in 1992, got off to a quick start this season, scoring twenty-seven points and hauling down ten rebounds in the season-opening loss at Atlanta. By the time Indiana was making its playoff run, however, Sealy was in street clothes, as the coaching staff opted for more guard strength on the playoff roster.

Forward Kenny Williams shows off his forty-inch vertical leap, going airborne to swat away a shot.

Forward Sam Mitchell, who came to Indiana along with Pooh Richardson and Micheal Williams in the 1992 trade that sent Chuck Person to Minnesota, helped strengthen the Pacers' bench. He saw action in ninety of the ninety-eight games in 1993–94, averaging two-plus rebounds and nearly five points while playing about fourteen minutes a game.

Richardson, for his part, seemed to be the point guard the Pacers had long sought. And he got off to a respectable start, scoring at a ten-points-per-game clip while doling out 6.4 assists. But his season was shortened to only thirty-seven games because of injuries.

Early in the season, the Pacers front office knew the team needed more depth and scoring punch from their guards—and they found it in Byron Scott, a three-time NBA champion with the Lakers. Scott, released by L.A. after ten years with the Lakers, was signed by Indiana in early December.

Besides his court awareness and a soft shooting touch, Scott also brought with him something the still-young Pacers needed: confidence that this team could achieve at the highest level—and the championship experience that helped make that confidence infectious among the other players.

Fueled by that confidence, the Pacers roared into the playoffs against Orlando riding an eight-game winning streak. Reggie Miller was a force in that series, averaging twenty-nine points per game as the Pacers dispatched Shaquille O'Neal and the Magic in three straight games.

In the Eastern Conference semifinals against the Atlanta Hawks, Reggie cooled off a bit, scoring 18.5 points per game. But the Pacers found another way to win in that six-game series. Byron Scott found his way to the basket for nearly eleven points per game, one of four Pacers who averaged double-digit scoring against the Hawks. More important, the Pacers did it with defense, limiting the potent Atlanta team to eighty-five points per game on just .311 shooting.

Indiana's stingy 98–79 win over Atlanta in Game Six was the kind of performance that couldn't help but bring smiles to the faces of Head Coach Larry Brown and assistant Billy King—both staunch advocates of tough defense.

The Pacers' win over highly favored Atlanta—and the near-rabid enthusiasm of the Market Square Arena crowds—seemed to make the nation begin to take notice of this team from Hoosierland. A postgame interview of Reggie by Ahmad Rashad of NBC was all but drowned out by the noise of the Pacer faithful.

The Indiana fans—long hungry for the type of playoff success the Pacers had earned against Orlando and Atlanta, packed Market Square Arena for every home playoff game.

And when the Knicks came to town for the Eastern Conference finals, bringing with them their unofficial Number One fan, filmmaker Spike Lee, the Pacer fans were more than ready.

Reggie Miller reassumed the pre-eminent scoring role in the seven-game series against John Starks and the Knicks, averaging nearly twenty-five points per game. His heroics included a thirty-nine-point performance in Game Five that featured a stunning twenty-five-point fourth quarter to seal an important win on the Knicks' home court.

Center Rik Smits also was a stalwart in the Knicks series, battling Pat Ewing every step of the way to average sixteen points and just under six rebounds per game in a rough-and-tumble match-up.

The Pacers lost that hard-fought series against New York—and their chance to meet eventual champion Houston in the NBA Finals. But their playoff prowess had earned them a lot: self-confidence, well-deserved national recognition and a healthy dose of local adulation. When they returned to Indianapolis from New York City, a huge downtown rally was held June 7 in their honor, and Reggie needed only

INDIANA PACERS 1993–94 REGULAR SEASON STATISTICS

Player	G	GS	Min	FG-FGA	Pct	3FG-3FGA	Pct	FT-FTA	Pct	Reb	OR	DR	Ast	PF	St	TO	Blk	Pts	Avg
Miller	79	79	2638	524-1042	.503	123-292	.421	403-444	.908	212	30	182	248	193	119	175	24	1574	19.9
Smits	78	75	2113	493-923	.534	0-1	.000	238-300	.793	483	135	348	156	281	49	151	82	1224	15.7
McKey	76	76	2613	355-710	.500	9-31	.290	192-254	.756	402	129	273	327	248	111	228	49	911	12.0
D.Davis	66	64	2292	308-582	.529	0-1	.000	155-294	.527	718	280	438	100	214	48	102	106	771	11.7
Scott	67	2	1197	256-548	.467	27-74	.365	157-195	.805	110	19	91	133	80	62	103	9	696	10.4
Richardson	37	25	1022	160-354	.452	3-12	.250	47-77	.610	110	28	82	237	78	32	88	3	370	10.0
A.Davis	81	4	1732	216-425	.508	0-1	.000	194-302	.642	505	190	315	55	189	45	107	84	626	7.7
Workman	65	52	1714	195-460	.424	18-56	.321	93-116	.802	204	32	172	404	152	85	151	4	501	7.7
Sealy	43	5	623	111-274	.405	4-16	.250	59-87	.678	118	43	75	48	84	31	51	8	285	6.6
Fleming	55	5	1053	147-318	.462	0-4	.000	64-87	.736	123	27	96	173	98	40	87	6	358	6.5
Williams	68	1	982	191-391	.488	0-4	.000	45-64	.703	205	93	112	52	99	24	45	49	427	6.3
Mitchell	75	18	1084	140-306	.458	0-5	.000	82-110	.745	190	71	119	65	152	33	50	9	362	4.8
Conner	11	0	169	14-38	.368	0-3	.000	3-6	.500	24	10	14	31	12	14	9	1	31	2.8
Paddio	7	1	55	9-23	.391	0-0	—	1-2	.500	5	0	5	4	2	1	4	0	19	2.7
Thompson	30	1	282	27-77	.351	0-0	—	16-30	.533	75	26	49	16	59	10	23	8	70	2.3
Haskin	27	2	186	21-45	.467	0-0	—	13-19	.684	55	17	38	6	33	2	13	15	55	2.0
PACERS	82	—	19755	3167-6516	.486	184-500	.368	1762-2387	.738	3539	1130	2409	2055	1974	706	1440	457	8280	101.0
OPPONENT	82	—	19755	2978-6614	.450	273-815	.335	1768-2422	.730	3285	1132	2153	1902	1986	826	1340	389	7997	97.5

INDIANA PACERS 1994 PLAYOFF STATISTICS

Player	G	FG-FGA	Pct	3FG-3FGA	Pct	FT-FTA	Pct	Reb	OR	DR	Ast	PF	St	TO	Blk	Pts	Avg
Miller	16	121–270	.448	35–83	.422	94–112	.839	48	11	37	46	34	21	32	4	371	23.2
Smits	16	103–218	.472	0–0	—	50–62	.806	84	23	61	31	64	10	43	9	256	16.0
McKey	16	58–142	.408	8–24	.333	31–47	.660	98	32	66	67	59	26	40	9	155	9.7
A.Davis	16	48–89	.539	1–1	1.000	37–66	.561	106	37	69	7	47	11	22	18	134	8.4
Workman	16	45–131	.344	6–21	.286	32–38	.842	51	11	40	112	40	28	38	1	128	8.0
Scott	16	38–96	.396	9–19	.474	40–51	.784	33	10	23	20	22	12	25	2	125	7.8
D.Davis	16	56–106	.528	0–1	.000	11–36	.306	159	63	96	11	52	18	30	17	123	7.7
Fleming	16	39–76	.513	0–5	.000	17–20	.850	21	12	9	38	27	10	22	1	95	5.9
Williams	12	9–25	.360	0–0	—	2–2	1.000	17	6	11	5	18	5	5	3	20	1.7
Thompson	7	4–11	.364	0–0	—	2–3	.667	10	3	7	5	9	3	4	1	10	1.4
Mitchell	15	9–26	.346	0–1	.000	3–4	.750	17	5	12	5	22	2	4	2	21	1.4
Conner	6	2–5	.400	0–0	—	2–2	1.000	4	1	3	0	2	1	0	0	6	1.0
PACERS	16	532–1195	.445	59–155	.381	321–443	.725	648	214	434	347	396	147	285	67	1444	90.3
OPPONENT	16	510–1199	.425	69–201	.343	309–437	.707	623	227	396	337	398	143	280	92	1398	87.4

Larry Brown's Coaching Career

Season	Team	Record
1972–73	Carolina (ABA)	57–27
1973–74	Carolina (ABA)	47–37
1974–75	Denver (ABA)	65–19
1975–76	Denver (ABA)	60–24
1976–77	Denver	50–32
1977–78	Denver	48–34
1978–79	Denver	28–25
1979–80	UCLA	22–10
1980–81	UCLA	20–7
1981–82	New Jersey	44–38
1982–83	New Jersey	47–29
1983–84	Kansas	22–10
1984–85	Kansas	26–8
1985–86	Kansas	35–4
1986–87	Kansas	25–11
1987–88	Kansas	27–11
1988–89	San Antonio	21–61
1989–90	San Antonio	56–26
1990–91	San Antonio	55–27
1991–92	San Antonio	21–17
1991–92	L.A. Clippers	23–12
1992–93	L.A. Clippers	41–41
1993–94	Indiana	57–41

TOTALS

ABA ------------------------- 229–107
NCAA ----------------------- 177–61
NBA ------------------------- 491–383
Career ---------------------- 897–551
Pct. ------------------------- .618

1993–94 PACERS' RESULTS

Date	Opponent	Result
11/ 5	at Atlanta	L—110–116
11/ 6	Detroit	L—107–113
11/ 9	at Orlando	L—98–104
11/11	at New Jersey	W—108–105 (OT)
11/12	New York	L—84–103
11/16	Charlotte	L—93–102
11/18	Houston	L—83–99
11/20	Boston	W—100–94
11/22	at Boston (Hartford)	W—102–71
11/24	Philadelphia	L—97–108
11/26	L.A. Lakers	L—100–102
11/29	at Sacramento	W—105–103
12/1	at L.A. Clippers	W—120–100
12/2	at Utah	L—87–103
12/4	at Golden State	L—92–99
12/7	Sacramento	W—105–87
12/9	Orlando	W—111–105
12/11	at New York	L—91–98
12/14	Washington	W—106–87
12/16	at Atlanta	W—99–81
12/18	New Jersey	W—108–98
12/20	at Phoenix	L—94–102
12/21	at Seattle	L—88–91
12/23	at Portland	L—96–108
12/26	at Cleveland	L—103–107 (OT)
12/30	San Antonio	L—82–107
1/4	Cleveland	W—104–99
1/5	at Washington	L—95–97
1/8	at Detroit	W—101–92
1/11	at Milwaukee	W—82–76
1/12	Denver	W—107–96
1/14	at Philadelphia	L—102–104 (OT)
1/15	Atlanta	W—94–91
1/19	Miami	W—109–92
1/21	at Chicago	L—95–96
1/22	Chicago	L—81–90

(Continued next page)

Date	Opponent	Result
1/24	Milwaukee	L—88–96
1/26	at L.A. Lakers	L—99–100
1/27	at Denver	L—106–113
1/29	at Houston	W—119–108
2/1	Washington	W—116–96
2/2	at Charlotte	W—124–112
2/4	Minnesota	W—114–93
2/5	Charlotte	W—111–102
2/7	Golden State	W—104–99
2/9	at Miami	W—102–98
2/15	at San Antonio	L—100–109
2/17	at Dallas	W—84–73
2/20	Seattle	W—101–95
2/22	Dallas	W—107–101
2/23	at Orlando	L—99–103
2/25	Detroit	W—110–90
2/26	at Chicago	W—96–86
3/1	Portland	W—106–94
3/4	New Jersey	W—126–110
3/5	at Atlanta	L—88–90
3/9	at Milwaukee	W—105–94
3/11	at New Jersey	L—73–87
3/12	Milwaukee	W—104–97
3/15	at New York	L—82–88
3/16	Phoenix	W—109–98
3/18	Atlanta	L—78–81
3/19	Utah	W—107–103
3/22	at Cleveland	L—61–93
3/23	Cleveland	W—78–77
3/25	New York	L—82–85
3/26	at Chicago	L—88–90
3/28	L.A. Clippers	W—126–93
3/30	at Boston	W—103–99
4/1	at Miami	L—91–101
4/2	Orlando	W—128–113
4/5	Detroit	W—105–89
4/6	at Charlotte	L—90–129

(Continued next page)

Date	Opponent	Result
4/8	Chicago	L—94–100
4/11	Boston	W—121–108
4/13	at Philadelphia	W—115–87
4/15	at Minnesota	W—130–112
4/17	at Detroit	W—104–99
4/19	at Washington	W—111–110
4/20	Cleveland	W—109–98
4/22	Philadelphia	W—133–88
4/23	Miami	W—114–81

Playoffs:

Date	Opponent	Result
4/28	at Orlando	W—89–88
4/30	at Orlando	W—103–101
5/2	Orlando	W—99–86
5/10	at Atlanta	W—96–85
5/12	at Atlanta	L—69–92
5/14	Atlanta	W—101–81
5/15	Atlanta	W—102–86
5/17	at Atlanta	L—76–88
5/19	Atlanta	W—98–79
5/24	at New York	L—89–100
5/26	at New York	L—78–89
5/28	New York	W—88–68
5/30	New York	W—83–77
6/1	at New York	W—93–86
6/3	New York	L—91–98
6/5	at New York	L—90–94

Signposts of the Season

• April 21, 1986: Donnie Walsh, then an assistant coach under Pacers Head Coach George Irvine, is named general manager of the club.

• June 7, 1993: Larry Brown—Walsh's high school rival, his teammate at the University of North Carolina and the head coach at Denver while Walsh was an assistant coach there—signs as head coach of the Pacers, replacing Bob "Bo" Hill.

• November 1, 1993: All-Star Pacer forward Detlef Schrempf is traded to Seattle for Derrick McKey and Gerald Paddio.

• December 6, 1993: The Pacers sign guard Byron Scott, a three-time NBA champion in his ten-year career with the L.A. Lakers.

• December 7, 1993: Scott's first game as a Pacer. Indiana wins over the Sacramento Kings, 105–87.

• December 30, 1993: The Pacers fall with a thud in San Antonio, losing by twenty-five to the Spurs to notch their fifth straight loss.

• January 27, 1994: Losing 113–106 in Denver, Indiana buried itself under yet another five-game losing streak. But the Pacers dug out. They'd lose no more than two consecutive games the rest of the year.

• January 29, 1994: Indiana knocks off the Houston Rockets 119–108 in a pivotal game at the Summit that sparks a sixteen-game stretch in which the Pacers will notch fourteen wins.

• February 26, 1994: The Pacers beat the defending NBA champion Bulls in Chicago Stadium. Their 96–86 win caps off a fabulous February in which Indiana won eleven of its thirteen games.

• March 22, 1994: Indiana's up-and-down regular season—particularly maddening in March—goes way down in a 93–61 loss at Cleveland. It was the Pacers' lowest-scoring game ever.

• April 11, 1994: Indiana hammers Boston at Market Square Arena, 121–108, the first win in a season-ending, eight-game win streak that propels them into the playoffs.

(Continued next page)

• April 28, 1994: Byron Scott's late-game three-pointer gives the Pacers its first-ever win in an initial NBA playoff game as Indiana beats Shaquille O'Neal and the Magic at Orlando.

• May 2, 1994: To the deafening delight of the Market Square Arena crowd, Reggie Miller's thirty-one points lead the way to a 3–0 sweep of the Magic, sending the Pacers where they'd never been before: Round Two of the NBA playoffs.

• May 10, 1994: A balanced effort gives the Pacers a 96–85 win in Game One of the semifinal series on Atlanta's home court.

• May 12, 1994: The Pacers score a playoff-record-low sixty-nine points in losing Game Two at Atlanta, ending what had been a twelve-game winning streak.

• May 14 and 15, 1994: The Indianapolis fans go back-to-back ballistic as they watch their Pacers handily beat the Hawks twice in Market Square Arena—101–81 and 102–86—to take a commanding 3–1 lead in the series.

• May 19, 1994: Again in MSA, the Pacers wrap up the series against Atlanta behind a twenty-seven-point performance by Rik Smits.

• May 24, 1994: The Eastern Conference finals begin in New York's Madison Square Garden. Despite another twenty-seven-point game from Smits, the Knicks prevail 100–89.

• June 1, 1994: Reggie Miller's thirty-nine-point performance—including a highlight-film twenty-five-point fourth quarter that Spike Lee probably won't include in his personal videotape library—gives Indiana a 93–86 win on the Knicks' court. The win puts the Pacers up 3–2 in the series, just one win away from a berth in the NBA Finals.

• June 3, 1994: The series moves back to Indianapolis and, in a classic, hard-fought game, the Knicks prevail, 98–91, forcing a decisive Game Seven.

• June 5, 1994: The Knicks' 94–90 win in Madison Square Garden—another classic battle of evenly matched teams—ends the Pacers' Cinderella season and sends New York into the NBA Finals against eventual champion Houston.

• June 7, 1994: Thousands of appreciative fans gather in sweltering heat at a rally in downtown Indianapolis to pay tribute to the Pacers' best-ever NBA season.